DATE DUE

NORTH VIETNAM: A DOCUMENTARY

NORTH VIETNAM:

A DOCUMENTARY

BY

JOHN GERASSI

WITH AN INTRODUCTION BY
CONOR CRUISE O'BRIEN

THE BOBBS-MERRILL COMPANY, INC.
Indianapolis and New York

The Bobbs-Merrill Company, Inc.
A Subsidiary of Howard W. Sams & Co., Inc., Publishers
Indianapolis · Kansas City · New York

To those very few newsmen, all over the
world, who really report what they see

CONTENTS

LIST OF NORTH VIETNAMESE (DRV) DOCUMENTS

ILLUSTRATIONS

INTRODUCTION

THE CALCULUS OF PAIN, OF PEACE AND OF PRESTIGE

'They tell you, Sir, that your dignity is tied to it [coercion of the American colonists]. I know not how it happens, but this dignity of yours is a terrible encumbrance to you; for it has of late been ever at war with your interests, your equity and every idea of your policy. Show the thing you contend for to be reason; show it to be common sense; show it to be the means of attaining some useful end; and then I am content to allow it what dignity you please. But what dignity is derived from the perseverance in absurdity, is more than I could ever discern.'

(Edmund Burke, Speech on American Taxation, 1774.)

* * *

On October 11, 1967, the *New York Times* reported that Secretary of Defence McNamara had informed the Senate Preparedness Investigation Sub-Committee that he did not think that the bombing of North Vietnam 'has in any significant way affected their war-making capability'.

He also said that bombing had not seriously deterred the flow of men and materials from North to South and he added that 'all of the evidence so far is that we have not been able to destroy a sufficient quantity of war material in North Vietnam to limit the activity in the South below the present level and I do not know that we can in the future' and that there was no 'direct relationship' between the level of bombing in the North and the United States forces required in the South.

The Secretary of Defence—whatever he may have said in private—gave the public no intelligible reason for persisting in a policy, that of bombing the North, which he admitted to be militarily unrewarding. 'On balance', he said, 'we believe it helps us.' As the 'best evidence' for this proposition he adduced 'Hanoi's strenuous and vigorous propaganda campaign to force us to stop it'.

His basic argument in favour of the bombing policy, according to the *New York Times*, was that the bombing was having the political effect 'of increasing the price' North Vietnam 'was paying for its aggression in South Vietnam'.

The American public should know exactly what this price is and how and by whom it is being paid. Mr Gerassi's book contains some first-hand information as well as some documents about this. A part of 'the price' was paid, for example, by the child whom Mr Gerassi saw in Hanoi's General Surgical Hospital who 'had been struck by a pellet in one temple, exiting through the other, blowing out both eyeballs in the process; the child was technically alive, although of course blind and incurably deranged'.

From the type of weapons which are being used against the North Vietnamese and the conditions in which they are being used, as reported by observers like Mr Harrison Salisbury and Mr Gerassi, and from Mr McNamara's statement, it becomes evident that the fate of this child is not a by-product of military necessity but is an intended result, satisfactory to those who make policy in Washington. It is one among many thousands of similar items in the price which the North Vietnamese are to be made to pay for, in the language of Washington, their aggression in South Vietnam, or, in their own language, for resisting American aggression.

The man who holds principal responsibility, under the President, for this policy, has now indicated that it does not serve any military purpose. What purpose then does it serve?

The most respectable-looking answer which has been attempted to this question—though it is one in which Mr McNamara himself does not seem to have much faith—is that the continuation of the bombing will bring Hanoi to the conference table—that is to say, will bring it in sight of accepting United States terms. The policy-makers in Washington and their specialist advisers—who are paid to consider all possibilities and evaluate them in the light of the known preferences of their superiors—have certainly considered the possibility that the bombing will have no effect at all on Hanoi's policy, and also the possibility that it will stiffen the determination of Hanoi and the North Vietnamese people to continue their struggle against a foe whose arrogance and cruelty they are given daily additional reasons to hate.

There is not the slightest evidence that the bombing policy which has been in operation since February, 1965, has produced, or is likely to produce, any weakening in Hanoi's determination to carry on the struggle and it is now admitted that it has not significantly weakened Hanoi's capacity to carry on this struggle. Yet the terror-bombing continues. Why?

If a reason which was both avowable and plausible could be produced, the policy-makers in Washington have both the motive and the opportunity to bring this reason home to the public. As they have not done so, we must conclude that the motive is either not avowable or not plausible or neither avowable nor plausible.

We are necessarily driven to speculation as to what the motives covered by these descriptions may be.

We know the general outlines of the situation in which the decision to continue the bombing is being maintained. President Johnson cannot find a way of bringing the war to a successful conclusion and he will not accept responsibility for an unsuccessful conclusion. Withdrawal from Vietnam would therefore be intolerable. It would supposedly mean a loss of prestige to the United States; it would certainly mean admitting that Johnson has been the most unsuccessful President in the history of the United States. The argument from prestige has similarly weighed with many governments in the past, including that of George III in relation to the rebellious American colonies. On that occasion the argument from prestige was definitively refuted by Edmund Burke in the passage quoted at the beginning of this introduction. President Johnson and his advisers have not shown the thing they contend for to be reason, or common sense, or the means of attaining any useful end and they continue to derive such dignity as they can from perseverance in absurdity.

Men in power who feel that their dignity is menaced are dangerous men. In the absence of avowable and plausible explanations for the bombing policy, we cannot overlook the possibility that 'the price' which the children of North Vietnam are being made to pay is a price for the wounds which their rulers have inflicted on the self-esteem of President Johnson, Secretary McNamara and the Joint Chiefs of Staff. To judge by Mr McNamara's language, the principle behind the bombing is primarily one of punishment, that is to say, of revenge; the primitive idea of exacting a price for an offence.

Presumably there are also some calculations involved. Some members of the military establishment are known to favour more extreme and ruthless forms of offensive, possibly rising to the use of nuclear weapons and war with China. President Johnson and his civilian advisers are still apparently sane enough not to want to be carried all the way in that direction. At the same time, as Mr Roger Hilsman made clear in his recent book *To Move a Nation*, the Joint Chiefs of Staff can command enough domestic political power to make it difficult for even such a President as Kennedy to risk a confrontation with them. In trying to avoid such a confrontation, Mr McNamara accordingly agrees to continue the bombing of North Vietnam, while rejecting the military arguments on which that policy was supposed to be based. As he made clear, it is a political decision, but not perhaps political in quite the sense in which he meant to be understood. It is a policy both agreeable to the feelings of those in power and convenient for them in political terms in the domestic context.

15

It can even be plausibly defended, in the domestic context, *in terms of the preservation of peace*. After all, if Mr McNamara's consent to the bombing of North Vietnam, while serving no military purpose, yet enables him to withstand military pressures for even greater escalations of the war, is Mr McNamara not really serving the cause of peace by continuing the bombing—and even by escalating it, at a pace slower than the military chiefs, without Mr McNamara, would exact? And are not those who support the Administration—conscious of its brave, subterranean struggle against the Generals—wiser in their service to peace, ultimately more compassionate, and more intelligent in their compassion, than those who adopt the easy way out of calling for peace, through withdrawal from Vietnam? Nay more, even if peace were attainable, it might prove to be a trap. A recent writer in *The New Republic* who describes himself as 'bitterly critical of the war', and even as preferring NLF victory in Vietnam to continuance of the war, nonetheless dreads the consequences of peace. On certain assumptions about the future of the New Left—assumptions which he seems to regard as probably valid—he thinks it likely that 'power will go by default to conservatives and reactionaries', and adds:

'This seems especially likely if the US fails to suppress the South Vietnamese revolution and withdraws. Any such about-face in Vietnam could produce a right-wing reaction even stronger than the one produced by the collapse of Nationalist China and the stalemate in Korea. . . . America may be headed for an era of repression which will make McCarthyism seem relatively innocuous.' (Christopher Jencks, 'Limits of the New Left' in *The New Republic*, October 21, 1967.)

In America, then, both peace-minded people and liberals may be shown arguments to persuade them that McNamara's 'price'—payable by people in Vietnam—is worth paying. New questions enter the calculations. How many Vietnamese children and others is it necessary to kill now, and in the future, to strengthen McNamara's hand against the Chiefs of Staff, and prevent more rapid escalation? How many Vietnamese children and others is it necessary to kill in order to preserve a relatively liberal climate of opinion in America?

Again precise answers would be hard to attain, but it is obvious that the relevant calculations are going on, in more acceptably formulated ways:

> *Behind each liberal, peace-loving eye*
> *The private massacres are taking place**

It does not much matter that the evidential base for such reasoning

* After Mr Auden.

is dubious. We have not been given serious reason to believe that if the President and Mr McNamara decided to stop the bombing, members of the military establishment could nonetheless force a more serious escalation. Nor has it been proved that going to war for Nationalist China would have produced a more amiable domestic climate than 'losing China' actually did. As regards Korea, the conclusion of peace—under a Republican President—seems to have led to an abatement, rather than an intensification, of the fury of domestic reaction. Nonetheless, arguments tending to support the view that the Administration's policy on Vietnam is preferable to some terrifying if vague alternative carry some weight with a public which is already frightened and which has much to lose. The child whom Mr Gerassi saw in the Hanoi General Surgical Hospital may after all be helping to keep an American Professor in his job.

Admittedly the policy, while convenient in Washington, and capable of being suitably presented to many sections of the American public, looks unrewarding in Vietnam. Yet there is, after all, the possibility, however faint, that the bombing, if persevered in, and appropriately, though cautiously, intensified, may, in time, produce some desirable result from Washington's point of view. And even if it should produce no significant and desirable local results—as is admitted to be probable—at least the price which the North Vietnamese will have been made to pay may serve to deter those who in other parts of the world may be tempted to engage in courses liable to be classified by the United States Government as 'aggression', or in other ways running counter to United States policy and interests, or those of a President and his military advisers.

These gains are remote and doubtful. Yet since they are gains for United States policy, and in United States prestige, in the terms in which the government may itself derive reflected prestige from them, they far outweigh the actual physical sufferings of living and dying men, women and children in Vietnam. The Vietnamese, who are being sacrified, are external to the American political process and can only be indirectly apprehended within it, through the effects on sections of the American public of the cost of inflicting on the Vietnamese the required degree of suffering.

The calculations required here are necessarily of a complex character, and even then inconclusive. If one could establish that the killing of x thousand Vietnamese children would result in raising or lowering President Johnson's popularity on the polls by one per cent, then the problem would be simple indeed. But in practice the position is much more complex. The reduction of the terror-bombing would swing the political influence of the Joint Chiefs of Staff against the President and thereby reduce his popularity rating; on the other hand, the reports of the bombings, the American casualties in carrying them out and the general cost in American lives and welfare in sustaining the whole policy and in amplifying it, rule out any easy assumption that there can be a predictable positive or negative co-relation between the number of deaths of Vietnamese and the President's popularity rating.

Towards this calculus of pain, of peace and of prestige, elaborate equipment is available in Washington for the collection and analysis of data. But the data are of such a nature that, however elaborate the equipment, their evaluation will still largely depend on the pressures of the situation and on the subjectivity of the evaluators.

Among the pressures of the situation is the fact that the President is known to be set on a certain course and only wants to hear such evaluations as suggest that this course, modified only within certain narrow limits, would, or at least could, lead to success. In this situation the most sophisticated position papers can be of little more scientific value than, say, the predictions of Hitler's astrologers. This is not, however, to say that the existence of such calculations—even if, as may well be the case, they are never really understood or even considered by those who make the decisions at the top—are without meaning or without importance. They are important in convincing the men in power themselves—and others—that their activity has, or could be found to have, a rational base and that it could be proved to be capable of being pressed to a successful conclusion or at least to the avoidance of a disastrous one. They seem to be important— in Mr McNamara's case if not President Johnson's—in spreading a veil of abstract cerebration between the men responsible and the concrete reality of what they are perpetrating. They are important finally, and perhaps mainly, for theocratic validation, for conveying to the American public the impression that their rulers are possessed, through mysterious channels, of ineffable certitudes which can be contested only by those who are ignorant of vital facts, which the government, for reasons of security, cannot release. For the public, those banks of computers take the place of the numinous equipment of ancient shrines in providing unutterable, and therefore unanswerable, confirmation of the otherwise obscure and often silly statements of the custodians of the equipment.

As regards the subjective aspects, the character of the remaining advisers whose advice is to any extent heard must have been to a great extent conditioned, through a sort of natural selection, by the pressures of the situation. It is known that many of the Kennedy advisers have dropped away and at least one of them—Mr Roger Hilsman—has subsequently indicated that the reason for this dropping away was his knowledge that President Johnson was determined to win military victory in Vietnam. Granted the nature and history of the war, the adviser who remains, or who emerges, to be heard advising in such conditions must be of a rather special kind. I suspect, perhaps wrongly, that the type of mentality, or psychology, which is likely to be drawn to nuclear games theory may be liable also to find it congenial to think about the exact price which it will be most profitable to make Vietnamese people pay for their government's persistence on a course which United States policy has decided to present as aggression. A man who enjoys thinking about himself, thinking about the unthinkable, has already cast himself in a particular role which may inflect his advice.* If you are accustomed to thinking in terms of how many tens of millions of deaths and maimings among *American* civilians constitute an acceptable price for some political action, then the vicarious and hypothetical stoicism thus acquired will be helpful—in terms of such reasoning—to you in the practical business of calculating the amount of terror which can most profitably be applied to the Vietnamese population. When men come to regard the making of such calculations as proof that the calculator is on a superior intellectual plane to the mushy-minded sentimentalists who complain about specific forms of casualty—such as the loss by children of eyes and reason—which are statistically predictable, and assimilable to known patterns of policy, then certain consequences follow. The characters of some of these advisers and their images of themselves become such that they will tend to advocate terrorism, *whether in reality it is likely to be profitable or not*, in order to demonstrate their own cold intellectuality. This is the type of adviser who can most easily find a living at present. And of course this kind of mind, perpetually confirming its lack of squeamishness, will have an even higher propensity to accumulate around the heads of the armed services than around the Presidency, thus giving rise to competition in cerebration about terrorism: a cerebration which is, however, in reality subordinate to the results of calculations about domestic politics.

* I do not here refer specifically to the author of the well-known book, *Thinking About the Unthinkable*: my comment is on a class of men whom I conceive to be touched by the intellectual *hubris* reflected in his title. My friend and colleague, Mr Peter Nettl, with whom I have discussed this, considers, on the other hand, that the influence of the games theorists is most likely to be exerted *against* the present Vietnam involvement. This may well be true of them as a class. My point here, however, is that the type of calculator whose calculations are likely to ascend to a relatively high level in the *present* decision-making process—granted the President's known predilections—is likely to be covered by the description in the text. And any calculations which show—for example—the bombing to be militarily futile turn out—as Mr McNamara has demonstrated—to be politically irrelevant.

Into the horrible calculus of these sick men, there necessarily enters, however, one limiting factor on which relatively normal human beings have some slight purchase. This is the growing disgust which the accumulated results of these calculations have caused in widening sections of the American public. While Johnson remains in the White House, this cannot be expected to do more than exercise a certain restraint—through the flickerings of that popularity rating—on the President and his entourage. If however—as seems to be happening—rejection of the war becomes more wide-spread, more determined and more open, then the next occupant of the White House is likely to be led to end the war in the only way, short of genocide, in which it can be ended: by the withdrawal of the American troops. (If this leads to a revival of McCarthyism, liberals will have a chance of showing their mettle.)

It is to be hoped that the documentary parts of Mr Gerassi's book, as well as his eye-witness accounts, will play a part in widening and intensifying the rejection of the war. His quotations from American sources—notably the Air Force's definition of 'psycho-social targets', schools, hospitals, etc.—are even more horrifying in their implications than is the direct impact of what he reports. His book also contains a number of documents from North Vietnam sources. The style of these documents, and a number of the historical and other assumptions on which they are based, are not likely to be acceptable to Americans. The public has been so conditioned as to combine a marked dread of contamination of Communist propaganda, with an equally marked willingness—now somewhat eroded—to accept Washington-manufactured propaganda as constituting news. The North Vietnam documents cited by Mr Gerassi are of course propaganda, as are the statements of Messrs McNamara, Rusk and others. American readers have had unlimited exposure to the propaganda of their own side. They should also study these presentations of the views of the North Vietnamese and the Front of National Liberation. Those should be considered in the light of the long war, bearing in mind that in this war, so far, the Americans—like the French before them—have been fighting only Vietnamese. Dean Rusk likes to talk about Chinese aggression, but the hundreds of thousands of foreign troops now laying waste in Vietnam are neither Chinese nor Russian. They are the troops of the United States and her allies. The task they are attempting is the subjugation of national resistance of a peasant country, through the fullest possible application of the intellectual, scientific, industrial and military resources of the wealthiest country in the world. The idea that perseverance in this enterprise of terrorism is conducive to the prestige of the United States is no longer plausible even in Washington. But in the meantime, the population of Vietnam must continue to pay the price here described for the high ambitions they have thwarted and the high reputations they have injured.

CONOR CRUISE O'BRIEN

PREFACE

'I have never talked or corresponded with a person knowledgeable in Indo-Chinese affairs who did not agree that had elections been held [in 1956] . . . possibly 80 per cent of the people would have voted for the communist Ho Chi Minh.'

Dwight D. Eisenhower in *Mandate for Change*

'Even Premier Ky told this reporter that the Communists were closer to the people's yearnings for social justice and an independent life than his own government.'

James Reston, *New York Times*, September 1, 1966

'I have only one [hero]: Hitler.'

Premier Nguyen Cao Ky of South Vietnam,
London Daily Mirror, July 4, 1965

'Premier Ky, who has announced he is running for president of South Vietnam, said today if a civilian whose policies he disagreed with won the post he might oppose him militarily.

' "If he is a Communist or if he is a neutralist I am going to fight him, militarily," Ky said. "In any democratic country you have the right to disagree with the views of others," Ky added.

'Ky also told reporters that press censorship would continue during the election.'

AP (Lai Thieu, Vietnam, May 13, 1967)
as printed in the *New York Post*, May 13, 1967

'I would like to see American students develop as much fanaticism about the US political system as young Nazis did about their political system during the war.'

Lyndon B. Johnson in a speech given to a group of
students, February 5, 1965; *New York Times*, February 6, 1965

'Many of the "enemy" dead reported by the government to have been shot were ordinary peasants shot down because they fled from villages as troops entered.'

New York Times, July 25, 1965

'The CIA has employed some South Vietnamese and they have been instructed to claim they are Viet Cong and to work accordingly. . . . Several of these executed two village leaders and raped some women.'

Senator Stephen Young of Ohio in the
New York Herald Tribune, November 21, 1965

23

'Indochina is a prize worth a large gamble. . . . Even before World War II, Indochina brought an annual dividend estimated at 300 million dollars.'

—*New York Times*, February 12, 1950

'Let us assume we lose Indochina. . . . The tin and tungsten that we so greatly value from that area would cease coming. . . . So when the United States votes 400 million dollars to help that war, we are not voting a give-away program. We are voting for the cheapest way that we can prevent the occurrence of something that would be of a most terrible significance to the United States of America, our security, our power and ability to get certain things we need from the riches of the Indochinese territory and from Southeast Asia.'

—Statement by President Dwight D. Eisenhower
at a conference of State governors held on
August 4, 1953, in Seattle

'One American helicopter crewman returned to his base in the central highlands last week without a fierce young prisoner entrusted to him. He told friends that he had become infuriated by the youth and had pushed him out of the helicopter at about 1,000 feet.'

—Jack Langguth in the *New York Times*, July 7, 1965

'Anyone who has spent much time with Government units in the field has seen the heads of prisoners held under water and bayonet blades pressed against their throats. Photographs of such incidents were common until the Government decided the publicity was not improving Saigon's public relations. In more extreme cases, victims have had bamboo slivers run under their fingernails or wires from a field telephone connected to arms, nipples, or testicles. Another rumoured technique is known as "the long step". The idea is to take several prisoners up in a helicopter and toss one out in order to loosen the tongues of the others.

'Some Viet Cong suspects do not survive long enough for the third degree. Earlier this year, in an operation along the central coast, a Government detachment failed to flush v c troops suspected of lurking in the area. However, several villagers were rounded up and one man was brought before the company commander. The Vietnamese officer briefly questioned the suspect, then turned to his adviser, an Australian warrant officer, and said: "I think I shoot this man . . . Okay?"

' "Go ahead," said the adviser.

'The officer fired a carbine round point-blank, striking the villager

below the chest. The man slumped and died. The patrol moved on.'
—William Tuohy, *New York Times Magazine*,
November 28, 1965

'In one known case, two Viet Cong prisoners were interrogated on an airplane flying towards Saigon. The first refused to answer questions and was thrown out of the airplane at 3,000 feet. The second immediately answered all the questions. But he, too, was thrown out.

'One of the most infamous methods of torture used by the government forces is partial electrocution—or "frying", as one US adviser called it.

'This correspondent was present on one occasion when the torture was employed. Two wires were attached to the thumbs of a Viet Cong prisoner. At the other end of the strings was a field generator, cranked by a Vietnamese private. The mechanism produced an electrical current that burned and shocked the prisoner.

'Vietnamese officers report that sometimes the wires are attached to the male genital organs, or to the breasts of a Viet Cong woman prisoner.

'The water torture, also used by government forces, is painful but seldom fatal. One person forces the prisoner to gulp water, while another applies pressure on his stomach. This forces the water out and creates a feeling similar to drowning.

'Other techniques, usually designed to force onlooking prisoners to talk, involve cutting off the fingers, ears, fingernails or sexual organs of another prisoner.

'Sometimes a string of ears decorate the wall of a government military installation. One American installation has a Viet Cong ear preserved in alcohol.'
—Beverly Deepe, *New York Herald Tribune*,
April 25, 1965

'When I moved up on the last one, he raised up, his arms extended, eyes wide. He had no weapon. I said "Good, we got a pris——"

'Cowboy stitched him up the middle with his AR-15. He didn't even twitch.

' "Goddamn it," I said, "we could have got some good information from that guy."

' "Sorry," said Cowboy, "I get, you know, excited." '
—Captain James Morris, *Esquire*, August 1965

'I was greeted by an officer with one of the helicopter units. He was a jovial man, almost ready to return to the US after a year in Vietnam.

'When he had talked with gathering gloom about problems in his province, I asked the question that usually ended a discussion.

' "What's the answer?" I asked.

' "Terror," he said pleasantly.'

—Jack Langguth, *New York Times*, September 19, 1965

'In one place nearby, the Americans found three North Vietnamese wounded. One lay huddled under a tree, a smile on his face. "You won't smile anymore," said one of the American soldiers, pumping bullets into his body. The other two met the same fate.'

—*Reuters*, November 18, 1965

'Suddenly a few yards away a wounded enemy soldier lifted one arm weakly and an American sergeant poured a long burst of M-16 rifle bullets into him. "Was he trying to give up, Sarge?" a man asked. "I'd like to find more of those bastards trying to give up," the sergeant said bitterly. No one disagreed with him.'

—Raymond R. Coffey, *Chicago Daily News*, November 19, 1965

'One of the world's richest areas is open to the winner in Indochina. That's behind the growing US concern. . . . Tin, rubber, rice, key strategic raw materials are what the war is really about. The United States sees it as a place to hold—at any cost.'

—Excerpt from the article 'It's the key to control all of Asia', US *News and World Report*, April 4, 1954

'The Vietnamese woman ignored the crying baby in her arms. She stared in hatred as the American infantrymen with shotguns blasted away at chickens and ducks. Others shot a water buffalo and the family dog.

'While her husband, father and young son were led away, the torch was put to the hut that still contained the family belongings. The flames consumed everything—including the shrine to the family ancestors.'

—AP (Giongh Dinh, Vietnam), as printed in *The (New York) World-Journal-Tribune*, April 22, 1967

Akron (Ohio) Beacon Journal, Monday, March 27, 1967
Editorial:
'*Americans At War*
'More compelling, more graphic than any editorial we have written about the war in Vietnam is the letter printed on this page today.

'Here are the reactions of an Akron district boy—he could be that lad from across the street—who willingly donned the uniform to serve his country.

'He is sickened and conscience-stricken at the murderous devastation he is ordered to commit.

'Here is a father who is torn between loyalty to his country and frustrated anger that his son should be plunged into such a mess.

'And the 16-year-old sister who just can't believe that her big brother could be killing defenseless people.

'This is the way the United States is "protecting" the rest of the world.

'Read the letter—and weep.'

'*To The Editor:*

'Here are portions of a letter I have just received from my son, who is now stationed in Vietnam.

'My son enlisted in the Army, asked to be sent to Vietnam and backed the government's strong policy toward the war in Vietnam— at least he did when he left this country last November. I believe what he has to say will be of interest to you and to your readers:

' "Dear Mom and Dad:

' "Today we went on a mission and I'm not very proud of myself, my friends, or my country. We burned every hut in sight!

' "It was a small rural network of villages and the people were *incredibly* poor. My unit burned and plundered their meagre possessions. Let me try to explain the situation to you.

' "The huts here are thatched palm leaves. Each one has a dried mud bunker inside. These bunkers are to *protect* the families. Kind of like air raid shelters.

' "My unit commanders, however, chose to think that these bunkers are offensive. So every hut we find that has a bunker, we are ordered to burn to the ground!

' "When the ten helicopters landed this morning, in the midst of these huts, and six men jumped out of each 'chopper', we were firing the moment we hit the ground. We fired into all the huts we could. Then we got 'on line' and swept the area.

' "It is then that we burn these huts and take all men old enough to carry a weapon and the 'choppers' come and get them (they take them to a collection point a few miles away for interrogation). The Viet Cong fill their minds with tales saying the GIs kill all their men.

' "So, everyone is crying, begging and praying that we don't separate them and take their husbands and fathers, sons and grandfathers. The women wail and moan.

' "Then they watch in terror as we burn their homes, personal possessions and food. Yes, we burn all rice and shoot all livestock.

' "Some of the guys are so careless! Today a buddy of mine called 'La Dai' ('Come here') into a hut and an old man came out of the bomb shelter. My buddy told the old man to get away from the hut

27

and since we have to move quickly on a sweep, just threw a hand grenade into the shelter.

' "As he pulled the pin the old man got excited and started jabbering and running toward my buddy and the hut. A GI, not understanding, stopped the old man with a football tackle just as my buddy threw the grenade into the shelter. (There is a four-second delay on a hand grenade.)

' "After he threw it, and was running for cover (during this four-second delay), we all heard a *baby* crying from inside the shelter!

' "There was nothing we could do. . . .

' "After the explosion we found the mother, two children (ages about six and twelve, boy and girl) and an almost newborn baby. That is what the old man was trying to tell us!

' "The shelter was small and narrow. They were all huddled together. The three of us dragged out the bodies onto the floor of the hut.

' "IT WAS HORRIBLE! !

' "The children's fragile bodies were torn apart, literally mutilated. We looked at each other and burned the hut.

' "The old man was just whimpering in disbelief outside the burning hut. We walked away and left him there.

' "My last look was: an old, old man in ragged, torn, dirty clothes on his knees outside the burning hut, praying to Buddha. His white hair was blowing in the wind and tears were rolling down. . . .

' "We kept on walking, then the three of us separated. There was a hut at a distance and my squad leader told me to go over and destroy it. An oldish man came out of the hut.

' "I checked and made sure *no one* was in it, then got out my matches. The man came up to me then, and bowed with his hands in a praying motion over and over.

' "He looked so sad! He didn't say anything, just kept bowing, begging me not to burn his home.

' "We were both there, alone, and he was about your age, Dad. With a heavy heart, I hesitatingly put the match to the straw and started to walk away.

' "Dad, it was so hard for me to turn and look at him in the eyes but I did.

' "I wish I could have cried but I just can't anymore.

' "I threw down my rifle and ran into the now blazing hut and took out everything I could save—food, clothes, etc.

' "Afterwards, he took my hand, still saying nothing and bowed down touching the back of my hand to his forehead.

' "Machine gun fire is coming into our village (Base Camp). We are being attacked, NOW as I am writing I must go.

' "Next day: Everything's OK. It was just harassing fire. I was up for the better part of the night, though.

' "Well, Dad, you wanted to know what it's like here. Does this give you an idea?

' "Excuse the poor writing but I was pretty emotional, I guess, even a little shook.

' "Your Son."

'The rest of my son's letter goes on to describe what the routines of his life in Vietnam are like. He described an uneventful ambush he participated in, and he got excited about a new-type rifle he had been issued. Beyond that, there are personal matters which he discussed.

'Needless to say, I was very much disturbed to read this letter. My 16-year-old daughter had read it before I did and when I went to her room to ask her if I could read the letter, I found her crying. I asked her the reason, and she replied by handing me the letter.

'I have not been a dove as far as the Vietnamese war is concerned, though I have not been a strong hawk either. But I think that the American people should understand what they mean when they advocate a continuation and even an escalation of our war effort in Vietnam.

'They should understand that war doesn't consist only of two armies made up of young men in uniform, armed and firing at each other across open fields, with bugles blowing and flags waving. The American people should understand what a war such as this does to our young men whom we send overseas to carry out our government's foreign policy.

'I guess what I am saying is that whatever course American public opinion backs should be supported by knowledge and understanding of the concrete results of that course and not by illusions.

'A GI'S DAD.'

I

FOREWORD

At 5 P.M. on December 24, 1966, as my daughter and I were finishing decorating the Christmas tree, I received a phone call from London asking me if I could leave within twenty-four hours to go to North Vietnam. I was to be a member of the first investigating team for the International War Crimes Tribunal which had been set up in Paris by a score of world-renowned leaders of the arts, the law and the peace movement.

The Tribunal had been conceived by the British philosopher Bertrand Russell, and it was the Bertrand Russell Peace Foundation that first financed its operation. Once in motion, however, the Tribunal had become independent of the Foundation and was headquartered in Paris. The French philosopher-novelist-playwright Jean-Paul Sartre was its Executive President, and the Yugoslav writer Vladimir Dedijer was Chairman and President of Tribunal Sessions. Among other members of the Tribunal were the Austrian philosopher Gunther Anders; the Italian international lawyer, deputy and professor of sociology at Rome University, Lelio Basso; the French author Simone de Beauvoir; the American Civil Rights leader Stokely Carmichael; and the American pacifist Dave Dellinger.

The Tribunal was not to be a legal apparatus but a moral body. The American press spoofed it as a mock trial, pointing out that all of its members were opposed to the war in Vietnam and were therefore already committed to establishing America's guilt—since the purpose of the Tribunal was to decide whether or not war crimes were being perpetrated by American forces in Vietnam. A *New York Times* editorial, for example, insisted that the Tribunal was composed in such a way as to guarantee a guilty verdict.

Jean-Paul Sartre tackled this criticism in a cover-story interview in France's leading non-Communist radical weekly, *Le Nouvel Observateur*, on November 30, 1966. He admitted that all of the Tribunal members opposed imperialism and that all were committed to work for a just and unexploited world. He also stated that the Tribunal members were convinced that the United States was fighting an imperialist war in Vietnam. But, he stressed:

'At Nuremberg in 1945 appeared for the first time the notion of political crime. That notion was, to be sure, questionable since it involved imposing the law of the victor on the vanquished. But the condemnation of the leaders of Nazi Germany by the Nuremberg Tribunal made sense only if it implied that any government, which in the future committed similar condemnable acts according to such-and-such article of the laws established at Nuremberg, could be similarly tried. Our "tribunal" now proposes to apply to capitalist imperialism only its *own* laws. . . . We are not concerned with whether or not a particular United States policy is guilty in the name of history of acts against humanity, but simply to say whether or not this policy does fall under existing laws.'

Concluded Sartre: 'We will invent no new legislation.'

What the Tribunal had to show, then, was that by America's own laws, its actions in Vietnam violated its own morality. Thus the fact that all of its members were committed to an anti-imperialist position did not put into jeopardy the truth of the Tribunal's ultimate verdict.

My own position fitted perfectly into these over-all concepts. I have always been opposed to interventionism of any kind, and specifically to the war in Vietnam, and I have often said so in speeches, articles and books. But these articles or books do not mean I was not an objective reporter. In fact, my freelance writing was well known to the editors who had hired me as a professional journalist for over a decade. I had been a Latin American editor at *Time* magazine for almost four years, for example, and *Time*, which supports America's interventionism in Latin America, knew full well that I did not. I had also worked for the *New York Times* in Latin America, again despite our editorial differences, and had been the Latin American editor at *Newsweek* for almost three years after my book, *The Great Fear in Latin America*, was published. That book documented my conviction, which was certainly not *Newsweek's*, that Latin America becomes poorer and poorer every year not in spite of the Alliance for Progress and the influx of capital from American corporations, but because of them.

Contrarily, when the London office of the Tribunal asked me to join the first investigating team, it was fully aware of my past affiliations with *Time*, the *New York Times* and *Newsweek*. The Tribunal members also knew that I would go to Vietnam as a professional journalist, which meant that I would report what I saw as I saw it, and that I might write about it for American newspapers or magazines opposed to the Tribunal. Nor was I ever requested to clear any of my writings with any Tribunal official. In fact, my very first article, which was written in Paris in February 1967 upon my return from Vietnam and which appeared in the March issue of *Esprit*, a Catholic monthly edited by the noted thinker Jean-Marie Domenach, pointed out that Hanoi had not been bombed as systematically or as extensively as I had expected. In any case I was not going to be a member of the Tribunal, nor, in fact, did I even testify when the Tribunal met in Stockholm in May 1967.

I left New York on the evening of Christmas Day, 1966, and arrived in Paris the next morning. From there, two days later, with the other members of the first investigating team of the Tribunal, I went on to Phnom Penh, the capital of Cambodia. Finally, on December 30, we began our final flight to Hanoi, aboard an antique Boeing 307 bearing three huge letters on its silver bodice—CIC.

Set up by the Geneva Convention of 1954 to oversee Laotian and Cambodian neutrality and investigate acts of aggression between North and South Vietnam, the ICC, as Americans call the Commission Internationale de Controle, maintained weekly flights between Saigon, Phnom Penh, Vientiane (Laos) and Hanoi, so that its members—official delegates of Poland, Canada and India—could have access to the various zones of Indochina. The company operating ICC planes was French-owned, the Compagnie Internationale de Transports Civils Aériens, and was under contract to the ICC. But it operated for profit. All of its crew members were French—except one of the two hostesses, Simone Gi Gustain.

Part Chinese, part Vietnamese, Simone had been married to Albert Gustain, who had been a steward aboard another ICC plane. It had crashed October 18, 1966. Since Simone was totally dependent on the income of her husband and since she was anxious to continue in his place, all parties concerned (the ICC, Saigon and Hanoi) waived the regulations which forbade citizens of either side in the Vietnamese conflict to participate in the operations of the 'neutral' ICC. 'I guess they had pity on me,' she told me, 'although, technically, I'm French by marriage.'

My colleagues on this first investigating team included Jean Pierre Vigier, a French physicist who had worked with Juliot-Curie and was now professor of theoretical physics at the Sorbonne. As a colonel in the French Resistance and later as an aide to General LeClerc, the liberator of Paris, Vigier had become an expert on experimental arms and weaponry. Another member was Léon Matarasso, the noted French lawyer, whose main purpose on the team would be to verify the legal aspects of American aggression. A third member was Malcolm Caldwell, a Scotsman who taught at the London School of Asian Affairs. And the fourth, Setsure Tsurushima, professor of agrarian economy at Osaka University in Japan, was on leave for the academic year to research specific agrarian problems in Southeast Asia. We were accompanied by Roger Pic, a first-rate French photographer who had been to North Vietnam before and who had made two excellent films on the war.

The six of us boarded the ICC plane in Phnom Penh on December 30, 1966, at 11 A.M. There were four other passengers, all members of the ICC. Conversation aboard was mostly about New York Timesman Harrison Salisbury and the effect of his articles corroborating North Vietnamese charges of extensive American bombing of civilian centres.

We arrived in Vientiane, the capital of Laos, at 1.55 P.M. and were told that we would have a three-and-a-half hour layover, because only at night can the ICC plane travel to Hanoi with minimum risk of being shot down by American fighters or Vietnamese militia. Laos is supposed to be neutral, but at the airport we found that neutrality to be very one-sided. For one thing, our passports were confiscated, although we were in transit and did not leave the airport; we could see that their numbers were carefully recorded and a Canadian ICC official told us that this was done at the request of the American Embassy, to which the information would be conveyed. For another, the airport was crammed with American military craft, and during one hour that we sat there checking operations, we calculated that an American plane took off or landed every three minutes. These planes were not only reconnaissance craft but also light bombers and troop transports actually carrying military personnel.

At 5 P.M., while we were still waiting in the lounge overlooking the runways, a Royal Thai airliner arrived. By then the airport was full of Americans, many of whom were going to board that plane to go to Bangkok and Hong Kong. 'We're advisers here,' one told me. 'We're going off on R & R (rest and recuperation).' 'But are you regular G.I.'s?' I prodded. 'Sure,' he said, and showed me his ID card. 'The only thing is, we're not allowed to wear our uniform in public.'

Finally at dusk we got under way. We landed in Hanoi at 7.50 P.M. There were no other planes on the runway.

Surprisingly, Hanoi was all lit up. Isn't that dangerous, I asked our host, a vivacious, sentimental, tiny little man of fifty-six years named Pham Van Bach, President of the Supreme Court of the Democratic Republic of Vietnam. 'Not at all,' he answered in perfect French (he had been trained in Bordeaux and Paris). 'Our alarm system warns us when planes are thirty kilometres away and that gives us time to switch our lights off. All it takes is one switch per block.' Later, as we travelled through the provinces, we had a chance to see that alarm system at work. At night it operated by yellow or red lights every two kilometres. In the day time it was by siren, bamboo drums, even tin pots. It may be primitive but, incredibly, it seemed indeed to warn the population thirty kilometres ahead of the planes.

Driving to the centre of town that night, we got our first glimpse of North Vietnam's amazing system of transportation. We did see some jeeps, Land-Rovers and trucks (made in Russia, China, France, England and Japan), all heavily camouflaged, and even some huge trailers carrying Russian missiles; but the roads were mostly crammed with bicycles (mainly Chinese-made), each lugging so much material that only the wheels and the drivers' heads were visible. We were told that each bike could carry as much as one ton. True or not, they did in fact seem to transport everything from sacks of rice and logs of bamboo to bricks and sections of rails.

To get to Hanoi proper, one must cross the Paul Doumer bridge, built by the French at the beginning of the century. Two kilometres span across the Red River, the bridge (called Long Bien by the Vietnamese) has car lanes on both sides and a rail track in the middle. At night it is so jammed that it took us longer to cross it than it would have taken us to drive across the George Washington Bridge on a July Fourth weekend, but most of the traffic, again, was made up of heavily-laden bicycles. We also noticed a dozen men on foot carrying sacks of cement in the traditional Oriental manner: two equal-weight loads hanging down in baskets from the ends of a bamboo pole slung over the shoulders. I have no idea how much two or four sacks of cement can weigh in Vietnam, but to see those thin little men, never more than 5 feet or 5 feet 2 inches tall, strutting at a reasonable clip with such burdens made me realize that the Vietnamese could never be pushovers.

We were not put up at the old Metropole Hotel (called the Hotel Reunification by the Vietnamese), which is where foreigners are traditionally lodged, but at a villa not too far off. Like the Metropole, however, it was an old colonial-style mansion, with huge rooms, tile floors, solid heavy mahogany furniture, low hard beds surrounded by mosquito nets, and ugly yard-wide fans hanging from the ceiling. The fans didn't work, but there's no need for them in winter; the temperature rarely rises above forty degrees and often falls to thirty-two at night, with the humidity very high. Like all sub-tropical countries, North Vietnam is not prepared for the cold—there's no central heating anywhere—which means that we were always a bit uncomfortable. I never saw Harrison Salisbury without a sweater, for example, and the late Rev. A. J. Muste usually wore two sweaters plus an overcoat. As for myself, I often went to bed wearing a sweater, and my feet never completely warmed up during the sixteen days I was in North Vietnam.

But no foreigner could complain about the reception. We had Russian-made Volga cars, with drivers and translators, at our disposal. We ate very well. Our first meal was typical; it included fish, omelette, meat, cheese, fruit and both a sweet red wine made from berries and a dry white rice wine. The cooking was French-style and was always varied; it was so plentiful that we only half-jokingly complained that it would look rather awkward if we came back from the war having gained weight. If we wanted to wander around by ourselves we did, and communication was not much of a problem since almost every educated Vietnamese speaks French, as do I myself; French is still taught as the second language.

In so wandering around Hanoi the next day, we were struck by how different a city looks when there are almost no kids around. Out of a population of 800,000 in the city proper, no less than 200,000 children had been evacuated. Still, the city was full of life. The long, wide, tree-lined boulevards were bustling with bicycles and lots of pretty girls riding sidesaddle on the back of the bikes. Charming, coquettish, extremely graceful, easy with their smiles, Vietnamese girls are often described as the most beautiful in the world and none of us had any arguments. But even the girls reminded us that the country was at war; as members of the People's Militia, many walked or rode armed with rifles.

The war didn't seem to affect their spirit. Along the lovers' lane framing one side of the Small Lake, where youngsters fish for sweetwater shrimps, the girls walked hand-in-hand with their boy friends or husbands or comrades, chattering, giggling at two-men minstrel shows or listening to groups of young soldiers singing folk songs while awaiting transportation. In Reunification Park, which borders another small lake, couples stopped also to admire the hundreds of different trees and flowers, brought from each province of Vietnam, or else looked across the water to the seventeenth-century Ngoc Son (jade mountain) temple rising elegantly from a small artificial island and connected to Hanoi's main street, along which old refurbished French trolleys still run, by a quaint, curved wooden bridge put up in 1885.

But the war could not be escaped. At 3 P.M. on that first full day in Hanoi, New Year's Eve, 1966, the alarms went off, and like all Hanoians, we walked briskly to the shelters. They exist everywhere. In backyards, in parks, along the many lakes, and in every street. The big ones are made of cement and bricks and are covered with earth on which people have planted banana trees. The small ones, made of cement pipes, are sunk into the ground—individual shelters two feet in diameter, five feet deep and with a cement cover. These individual shelters are spaced out five to ten feet apart along both sides of every street in Hanoi, and as I saw later, in every North Vietnamese city.

For our first air raid we were at the villa and so were guided to a fairly large collective shelter in back, under a group of trees that looked like oaks to me but were obviously too short. We stood by the entrance looking at the MIG's above us, all 17s, circling in carefully spaced patterns, loud but graceful as they glided in and out of the clouds. Then the MIG's disappeared and we heard a thunderous bang which rattled my heartbeat for a few seconds. 'A missile shot,' explained one of our waiters who was next to us at the shelter's entrance. I looked around hoping to see it rise, but instead noticed an anti-aircraft battery on top of a nearby school. I then looked harder and suddenly realized that such batteries were on the roofs of every tall building, the hotels, the ministries, even the opera house, a small replica of Paris' famed Opera. Atop the polytechnic institute, a modernistic, poured-concrete and glass edifice built by the Russians for 1,700 students and now completely evacuated, I spotted a whole series of batteries. The peaceful, idyllic city had become one massive fortification.

But we were there to work and the alarms did not stop us. We had begun at 8 A.M. on December 31, the day after we arrived. For four hours, members of North Vietnam's War Crimes Investigating Commission explained to us that they had prepared various documents dealing with all aspects of America's aggression in North Vietnam, as well as documents on the various services (health, education, etc.) which illustrated their concern for the welfare of the population. These documents were turned over to us; we were asked to study them and then to present our needs and our methods for carrying out our own investigation.

Because of the New Year's truce, we were to interrupt our working sessions in Hanoi the next day to journey southward, but we were told we would return to Hanoi by the end of the truce, continue to study documents for a few days and then begin our individual investigations to verify a few of the charges made by the North Vietnamese Government.

In the following pages, I shall quote extensive excerpts from these documents. Most were in English when handed to me; some were in French and these I have translated. I shall then present, as eyewitness testimony, my investigation of some of the incidents related in these documents. I shall also include photographs as corroborating evidence. I took most of the photographs (the ones I obtained from the North Vietnamese Government are noted as such). I was allowed to shoot anything without prior permission, except for bridges, anti-aircraft batteries and missiles. In exchange, I agreed to let the Vietnamese develop my film, as they had requested, with the understanding that they were free to blank out any photograph that violated their national security. Altogether, I took more than 450 photographs. Of those included in this book, some are over-exposed and others under-exposed because the Vietnamese developing process has not been perfected, but all are clear and not one has been blanked out or retouched.

As the reader will notice, the North Vietnamese documents are not written in a polished, cool, reflective style: they are usually awkward, occasionally naïve, often fiery. Certainly they lack the gentility to which we are accustomed; our newspeak euphemisms for human injury and death, for the ravaging of a land and its people, would seem strange indeed coming from the Vietnamese. The reader must remember that the Vietnamese are constantly under attack. They can never forget that they are at war, a war which in their eyes is the result of sheer imperialist lust on the part of the United States. The North Vietnamese did not start it and they are too small to stop it. Hence they are angry, and one way of expressing that anger is to shout insults. But the names are always levelled at 'Giac My', the American aggressors, never at the American people, and I consider that noble. We Americans have never made such a distinction—in Vietnam, Korea, the Dominican Republic, Germany, Mexico or anywhere else where we've been at war.

This being the case, it would be understandable if the Vietnamese documents had turned out to be hysterical, full of exaggerations and misstatements. Instead, in the instances I was able to verify, they were accurate. To be sure, I could verify little, and much of what I could, the Vietnamese wanted me to verify. Theoretically, therefore, they could have been prepared. They could have coaxed witnesses. They could have dashed around from 10 P.M. at night, when I told them I wanted to see Vinh Phuc, for example, to 5 A.M. the next morning, when I got there, and shot beebee guns into every house, tree and pole, then spread around a few hundred American-made 'guavas' so I would see them wherever I went. Also, they could have doctored up a few score of X-rays and they could have shipped in every Vietnamese child with a head wound to make me think he had been a pellet victim. But could they have repeated the same procedure in every district of every province I visited? Even if they are as sophisticated as Washington, could have they have faked so much so often? And then, if they were as sophisticated as all that, would they then have prepared such unsophisticated documents? And finally, would they have faked a bombing attack on a non-military target, on their own people, just because I was there? Just to convince me? Yet unless the Vietnamese had concealed an arms or munitions factory underground (with no road leading to it), I saw all there was to see in the vicinity, and there was nothing but the small hostel where I stayed, mud huts and rice paddies.

One might expect both the government of North Vietnam and the United States government to exaggerate their claims; some observers sympathetic to the North Vietnamese feel the truth lies somewhere in between; others accept what the Vietnamese say; I will present the documents and testify to what I saw.

There is no way to prove that *all* the charges, relevant statistics* and the extent of destruction cited in the documents are factual. The reader is likely to find some of the information incredible. Is it possible that the most powerful nation in the world is systematically applying unprecedented vicious destructive force on the people of a land no larger than New York State merely to break their will? Again, I will only tell what I saw—and what I saw convinced me that while the documents may seem at times fantastic, it is in fact the reality which is fantastic.

My group of investigators decided to select a series of examples from each document which we wanted to verify ourselves. We presented a list of these examples to our hosts and transportation was then arranged for us to visit them. We were denied permission to visit places below Vinh, which is two-thirds of the way from Hanoi to the demarcation line between North and South Vietnam, for safety reasons; our hosts, who were constantly preoccupied with our safety, felt that going below Vinh would expose us to such extensive and intensive bombardment that our lives might be seriously endangered. Otherwise, we were denied no area in North Vietnam.

In addition, when we arrived to investigate one specific reported crime in an area where there were reported to have been a whole series, we usually asked to see others, thus giving the Vietnamese no

* A useful external frame of reference for the figures cited in the documents is provided in a *New York Times* (August 5, 1967) dispatch from Saigon. The story reports a record number of 197 missions over North Vietnam on the previous day, and continues: 'Under the information rules in Saigon, the number of aircraft involved in the missions is not disclosed. A single mission normally involves two to five aircraft. The spokesman said he presumed the record number of missions also involved a record number of planes.'

If each of the planes dropped only one bomb, and if the spokesman's presumption is correct, then nearly 1,000 bombs would have been dropped on North Vietnam on that day alone. Of course, each plane dropped more than one bomb— and many strafed and fired rockets as well.

The bombing figures stated by the North Vietnamese Government (and cited in the documents in this book) are derived from reports filed by officials on the spot at the time of bombing. Naturally, no one else can confirm or deny the figures as stated.

time to prepare for our coming. So, for example, in my particular investigation of the areas surrounding Haiphong, I asked to verify the strafing of Chinese ships coming into the harbour. Then, after having done this, I asked to visit the suburb of Cam Lo where the systematic bombing of a civilian centre with no military objectives within five miles of the target area had been reported in one of the North Vietnamese documents. Thus I went to Cam Lo unannounced and had the opportunity of speaking to scores of witnesses without prior arrangement.

All in all, our team travelled 2,000 miles through North Vietnam. We visited eight out of the twenty-six provinces and the four major cities—Hanoi, Haiphong, Nam Dinh and Thanh Hoa. Among us we must have talked to literally hundreds of witnesses. I personally recorded in my notes almost one hundred. These witnesses included cadremen, officials, teachers, medical men, soldiers, and at least fifty ordinary peasants, workers and fishermen. Though travelling from one military district to another could be done only by permit and with guides in official cars or jeeps, we were free to run around as we wished, unaccompanied, once inside a particular district.

I personally was caught in bombing twice, both times in Thai Binh province, which is southeast of Hanoi and directly east of Nam Dinh. One, I shall never forget as long as I live. Léon Matarasso and I had arrived in a small isolated village at about ten at night, having left Hanoi at dusk, around 6 P.M. We met various provincial leaders for dinner at a small hostel and had just finished eating and were about to retire when the alarms went off. We were led to a collective shelter in back of the hostel, which was the only building not made of mud within a three-mile radius. Assuming that American planes would not bomb this area, since it produced only rice and was not even defended by a single anti-aircraft battery, we stood with our Vietnamese hosts at the entrance of the shelter, talking and smoking—but with one ear tuned in to a Vietnamese officer holding a walkie-talkie. Suddenly the officer said something in Vietnamese and the others asked us to put out our cigarettes and step into the shelter. The Vietnamese officer yelled another order sharply, whereupon the others pushed us down near the centre of the shelter and threw themselves on top of us. At that moment I heard a tremendous explosion. The shelter trembled and dust came down from its roof. I have never been so scared in my life or, rather, I realized then that I had never been really scared before. The bomb, a 1,000-pounder, had hit twenty-five yards away.

I managed to keep my sense of composure and even joked about how close we ourselves had come to becoming evidence for the

Tribunal. But my heart felt literally caught in my throat. We then went to our room to get a couple of hours sleep and, as usual, were visited by the doctor. All foreigners in Vietnam are accompanied by a doctor whenever they travel outside of Hanoi. During my stay in Vietnam I thus got the chance to meet twelve different doctors, all of whom spoke French fluently, though only one had been trained outside the country; the others had learned their skills as well as their French in hill or jungle schools during the war against the French.

Such was the particular doctor who came to visit us that night. As usual, he asked me how my bowel movement had been that day and, also as usual, took my blood pressure. He turned pale and said, 'Oh mon Dieu, it is 100/170. I better give you a shot of tranquillizer.' I argued with him, explained that I was just a little bit nervous. He insisted that I had better take something, since theoretically my veins could burst at over 150. I continued to argue with him, insisting that I would be fine within a couple of hours, repeating that I was just a bit nervous. He asked me why and I said, 'Well . . . er . . . ahhh . . . that is, the bombing, you know.' He jumped back, bowed apologetically as he withdrew from the room, saying, 'Of course, how stupid of me, of course, naturally.'

The doctor had been one of the eight Vietnamese who had thrown themselves on top of me. But to him it had all been routine. I spent the next two hours not only nervous but also ashamed and, in the darkness, jotted down these naïve but, obviously, most sincerely felt words in my notebook:

It is past midnight now and we have to get under way at 4. If only Americans knew what being under a bombing is like. My heart is pounding so much I feel it's going to burst. To these people it is all normal. They take it in their stride. Tonight they wished me and all of the American people well. They won't crack, these people. They are firm, resolute, brave, disciplined. They go about their business, produce goods, build up their communities and, whenever there are planes (and one day last week there were seven raids in one day on the town nearest here), well, they simply man the anti-aircraft batteries or, if there are none around, grab their rifles and start shooting. Or else they go, unashamed, into the shelters to save themselves for the next day. Courage here is so simple, so honest, so humble. It doesn't take big reflection. It's we Americans who look upon it as a great thing. We wait for an extraordinary event. A man who sacrifices his life for others. Our courage is individual. Theirs is collective. It is taken for granted, it is a courage of a whole people. It goes unheralded, except insofar as the whole nation is proud.

41

The other bombardment I lived through was less dramatic personally but no less revealing of the Vietnamese. It occurred when an American plane overflew our area long enough for the all-clear signal to bring us out from our shelters. Then it suddenly returned. We had no time to go back to the shelters, and so took cover wherever we could. I was on one side of a wide paddy with a few officials and various Militia girls. On the other side of the paddy, in a cluster of shrubs and trees, were a whole group of Militia, armed with rifles and submachine guns.

The plane dropped a few bombs, hitting no one, then veered suddenly towards us, away from the cluster of Militiamen. Without waiting for orders, two girls next to us spontaneously jumped to their feet and rushed across the paddy towards the cluster, thereby attracting the F-105 which dived after them and strafed them. In so doing, the American pilot changed his direction and headed towards the cluster. At the right moment the two girls, one of whom was sixteen, the other fifteen, dropped into the shallow water of the paddy. Their comrades opened fire. They hit the plane, which burst into flames and was brought down by the pilot into the paddy.

Everyone shrieked with joy as they rushed out to capture the pilot, who came out of his cockpit unharmed. It seemed as if everyone had to be in on the capture, and therefore had to be armed; thus, I saw young children and old men and women pick up rocks, knives, hoes, anything around, as a symbolic weapon. I spotted one child, who turned out to be eleven years old, charging the pilot with a spoon in his hand.

But no one was angry. The pilot unzipped his Buck Rogers uniform, let it drop to the ground, put up his hands and stood, straight and tall. No one harmed him, and he was quickly handed over to military authorities, who had arrived on the run and who could not allow me to interview him without clearance (which they requested and which came through too late; I was by then on the road again).

I asked various people in the 'capturing' group why they felt no animosity toward this man who, after all, had tried to kill them even though not one of them was directly involved in the war effort. Each one answered in a different way. But they all meant the same thing. The pilot was a victim, they said, just like themselves. They made a distinction between the American people and the American aggressors, the latter being only those who make policy back in the States and those who profit from that policy through their vested interests in the economic control of Southeast Asia—or, as they would say, in the poor countries all over the world.

This distinction between 'Giac My' (American aggressor) and the

American people was stressed by everyone, from President Ho Chi Minh and Prime Minister Pham Van Dong to peasants and workers. It is the same distinction that the Vietnamese made between the French 'people' and the French 'colonialists', a distinction which allows them now to respect the French and their leader, General Charles de Gaulle. It is this distinction which ultimately, when they are free and at peace, will allow them, they say, to respect the American Government.

It is because the Vietnamese want to live in peace and want to respect and be respected by the American people—and ultimately by a fair and non-interventionist American Government—that they spent so much time and effort preparing their case against American crimes and aggression. They are convinced, they told me, that the American people would not condone such crimes and aggression if they knew the truth. And they prepared documents to prove their case.

The documents, my evidence and the photographs will speak for themselves. I went to Vietnam as a reporter and this is a reporter's dossier. While the very nature of what there is to report will make this book polemical, it is primarily intended to be a historical document. I hope it will be taken as such now and in the years to come when this tragic period is analysed with calm, objectivity and honesty.

II

HANOI

By mid-1967 the United States had officially admitted that Hanoi, the capital of North Vietnam, had been bombed heavily and repeatedly. But the United States was still insisting that even within Hanoi the targets were strictly military. The Government of North Vietnam, on the other hand, claimed that most areas bombed were visibly civilian—and always had been. That controversy was crucial, for, if the United States was wrong, Hanoi's charge that the United States war effort was terroristic and criminal would be justified.

Though the Vietnamese had periodically complained that American bombers had raided Hanoi prior to December 13, 1966, the issue began to gain wide publicity in the United States on December 15, 1966, when a *New York Times* headline announced: 'Military Targets Hit Within Hanoi, US Aides Concede'. The article went on to point out, however, that 'the State Department said that in its view there had been no bombing of the city of Hanoi itself, because there had been no deliberate attacks on civilian areas of North Vietnam's capital'. That in itself was remarkable enough, as if what isn't deliberate doesn't exist.

Still, doubts were created. And, said the *Times*, 'the Government here did not confirm or deny a report by Tass, the Soviet press agency, that in a raid yesterday American planes struck workers' housing units within the city limits of Hanoi'. Actually, the Tass report, picked up in Moscow by the Associated Press, had specified that the raid, which lasted 'about an hour and a half', had been directed at 'the right and left banks of the Red River, the embankment and the area of the bridge linking Hanoi with its suburb Gia Lam'.

The *New York Times* also carried an item from Rome that day, December 15, 1966, which quoted the dispatch filed with *Unita* (the Italian Communist daily) by the Italian correspondent Antonello Trombadori. Dated December 13, it read:

At 11 A.M. local [Hanoi] time the criminal American aggressors

44

carried out an atrocious terrorist bombardment on the centre of Hanoi, hitting deliberately two quarters inhabited by 500 workers' families. It was a massacre of which it is not yet possible to give the exact dimensions. The quarters attacked are no farther than 400 meters [1,300 feet] from the historic centre of the city and from our hotel. We are, thus, eyewitnesses of the criminal raid. There participated in it six large planes, which for half an hour loosed heavy-calibre bombs, incendiaries and napalm. Exact figures are still lacking, but one can say without doubt that this new crime, coldly planned and carried out, constitutes a new qualitative rise in escalation.

On the newsstands that day was the December 16, 1966, issue of *Time* magazine. In a special box evaluating the raids on North Vietnam, *Time* insisted that the Administration's object 'is not to bomb North Vietnam back "to the Stone Age", as retired Air Force General Curtis LeMay once proposed'. That is why 'the US has purposely avoided attacking certain targets because they are too close to urban residential areas, would cause suffering among the civilian population or would not significantly affect the enemy's short-term ability to continue fighting'. The question: Was this true?

For the next few days the debate quietened down. And then, on Christmas Day, 1966, as I began my own journey to Hanoi, it was propelled once again to the front pages of the world's dailies as Harrison Salisbury, an assistant managing director of the *New York Times*, reported from Hanoi: 'There is damage, attributed by officials here to the raids, as close as 200 yards from this hotel [the Thong Nhat, meaning Reunification, formerly the Metropole Hotel, which is in the dead centre of Hanoi].' Salisbury went on to detail the areas which he had personally inspected—the Pho Nguyen Thiep Street where thirteen houses and the Phuc Lan Buddhist pagoda were destroyed; the Ba Dinh quarter, where the Chinese and Rumanian embassies were damaged by air-to-ground rockets; Hue Street, which was hit December 2, 1966; and the suburban village of Phu Xa, where anti-personnel fragmentation bombs were dropped on August 13, 1966. Salisbury concluded: 'It is fair to say that, based on evidence of their own eyes, Hanoi residents do not find much credibility in United States bombing communiques.'

At that point, the State Department capitulated—or so it seemed. It told the *Times* that 'the possibility of an accident' could not be ruled out and, as the *Times* said, 'if the bombing had caused civilian injury or damage, the United States regretted it'. But as Salisbury's files began to come in, documenting case after case of extensive bombing of civilian targets—in Hanoi, Phu Ly, Nam Dinh—

Washington hardened again. On December 27, Murray Marder of the *Washington Post* complained that, as a result of Salisbury's reports, 'North Vietnam will admit more Western newsmen in an evident attempt to undermine the Johnson Administration's claims that its policy is to avoid bombing civilians.' The story was topped by an incredible four-column headline reading 'Hanoi Exploits Bombing of Civilians', as if the rules of war demanded, as I. F. Stone quipped in his *Weekly* (Vol. XV, No. 1, January 9, 1967), that 'civilian casualties should be quietly buried in unmarked graves'.

After Marder, it was President Johnson's turn. Speaking through the acting White House press secretary, George Christian, Johnson said on December 28 (as reported in the *Times* on the 29th) that he was satisfied that 'the bombing of North Vietnam by American planes had been directed only at military targets'. Christian insisted that 'no civilian targets had been approved by Mr Johnson and that his orders had been obeyed'. The implication, of course, was that either the military had disobeyed the President, which no one could believe, or else that Salisbury was a liar.

The next day, the *Times'* military editor, Hanson W. Baldwin, softened that implication by writing (December 30, 1966):

> Privately, Pentagon sources agree with [Salisbury's] reports from North Vietnam that civilian residential districts have been hit in the raids and that an undetermined number of North Vietnamese civilians have been killed or wounded.... [But] the targets in North Vietnam, the officers insist, have been military targets; the inevitable damage done to residential areas has been due to the proximity of those areas to military targets and the impossibility of putting all bombs and rockets squarely on target. Residential and populated areas have never been deliberately chosen as targets, all hands agree.

In his article, however, Baldwin pointed out that United States planes drop about half a million tons of bombs on Vietnam *per year*, 'somewhat more than the Army Air Forces expended against Japan in the Pacific during World War II'—the *whole* of World War II.

Naturally, this did not help the Pentagon's claim that most of these bombs hit only military targets. So it had to revert to raw arguments. Salisbury had to be blasted, and it was Arthur Sylvester, then Assistant Secretary of Defence for Public Affairs, who did it. As reported by Neil Sheehan in the *Times* of December 30, Sylvester scoffed at Salisbury's reports as full of 'misstatements of fact'. In effect, said Sylvester, Salisbury was a liar.

With that, the hawks let loose. Chalmers M. Roberts of the *Washington Post* (January 2, 1967) said that Salisbury was Ho Chi

Minh's 'chosen instrument' to subvert America's war effort. Crosby Noyes of the *Washington Star* attacked (January 4) 'an important segment of the press' for its 'utter lack of identification ... with what the Government defines as the national interest'. *Time* (January 6) lamented Salisbury's 'uncritical' reports. And *Newsweek*, never to be outdone by its paceleader, concluded (January 9) that 'to American eyes it [Salisbury's coverage] read like the line from Tass or Hsinsha [misspelled in the original]'.

Meanwhile, on December 30, 1966, the day the Pentagon called Salisbury a liar for having reported that the United States had bombed civilian centres in Hanoi and other North Vietnamese areas, I myself arrived in Hanoi. The next morning at 8 A.M. we began working, and were given a series of documents to study. One of them was the following:

Document No. 1
On US Air Attacks Against Residential Quarters in Hanoi, Capital of the Democratic Republic of Viet Nam, and Its Suburbs
Published by the Ministry of Foreign Affairs, Democratic Republic of Viet Nam,* Hanoi, December 1966. Printed pamphlet; in English.

On December 14, 1966, the US military spokesman in Saigon denied that US aircraft had struck at targets inside Hanoi on December 13, 1966, and stated: 'Our policy is to hit strictly military targets; during the past 24 hours the military targets which were hit have been hit before.'

After the December 14, 1966, bombing of Hanoi, the US military spokesman in Saigon reiterated the same contention.

On December 14, officials of the US Defense Department said 'there was no evidence so far that US planes bombed residential areas of Hanoi yesterday', and claimed that the damage reported by the press could have been caused by Vietnamese surface-to-air missiles.

At the press conferences held on December 14 and 15, 1966, McCloskey, US State Department Press Officer, did not reply directly to the question: 'Has the United States bombed Hanoi?' and reiterated that it was still US policy 'to avoid populated areas and civilian targets' and to limit the bombing to 'military-related targets'.

The US State Department announced that US aircraft struck at 'military or military-related targets' while the US Military Command in Saigon said that they hit only at 'strictly military targets'.

---

* This is the accurate name of the country, abbreviated as DRV; South Vietnam is properly called The Republic of Viet Nam.

First of all, it is to be recalled briefly that Hanoi, capital of the Democratic Republic of Viet Nam, covers an area of 580 square kilometres with a population of about 1,110,000, including 600,000 in the city proper.

For administrative purposes, Hanoi comprises:

—The city itself which is subdivided into four quarters: Hoan Kiem, Ba Dinh, Hai Ba and Dong Da.

—Three urban centres related to the city; Van Dien in the South, Gia Lam and Hen Vien in the North.

—The periphery which includes four districts: Tu Liem, Thanh Tri, Gia Lam and Dong Anh.

The US rulers have admitted the bombing of Van Dien and Hen Vien, but denied the air raids on Hanoi proper.

In point of fact, US aircraft have repeatedly attacked civilian targets, populous places in all the four quarters of Hanoi:

On December 2, 1966

—They fired missiles at Hue Lane (Hai Ba Quarter), destroying or damaging dwelling houses, killing one civilian and wounding 7 others.

—They fired a missile at the 'March 8' Textile Mill (Hai Ba Quarter), damaging part of a building.

On December 13, 1966

—They bombed Giang Vo Street (Dong Da Quarter), killing 7 civilians, wounding 30 others, and destroying 9 dwelling houses.

—They fired many missiles on La Van Cau Block, Phuc Tan Street (Hoan Kiem Quarter), killing 4 civilians, wounding 10 others and reducing to ashes 300 light constructions.

—They fired a missile on Pho Nguyen Thiep Street near Dong Xuan Market (Hoan Kiem Quarter), killing 4 civilians, wounding 11 others and destroying 13 dwelling houses.

On December 14, 1966

—They fired rockets at two places in Hang Chuoi Street (Hai Ba Quarter) causing some damage to dwelling houses.

—They fired a rocket at the Medicine and Pharmacy Faculty in Le Thanh Ton Street (Hai Ba Quarter) causing some damage to the buildings.

—They bombed a flat, the Trade Union Cadres Training School, the Water Conservancy Institute in Tay Son Street (Dong Da Quarter), killing 5 civilians, wounding 11 others and causing heavy damage to many houses.

—They fired missiles at Khuc Hao Street in the quarter of foreign embassies (Ba Dinh Quarter), causing some material losses to the premises of the embassies of the People's Republic of China and the Socialist Republic of Rumania.

Following the December 15, 1966, statement of the Government of the People's Republic of China condemning the US bombing of Hanoi, the spokesman of the Foreign Ministry of the People's Republic of China issued on December 17, 1966, a statement exposing the US crime of attacking the Chinese Embassy:

'On the afternoon of December 14, the United States sent large numbers of pirate planes to carry out renewed wanton bombing raids on Hanoi, capital of the Democratic Republic of Viet Nam, and *brazenly dive-bomb the Chinese Embassy in the Democratic Republic of Viet Nam, causing serious damage to its premises. The Hanoi office of the Hsinhua News Agency near the Embassy was also damaged.*'

In its December 16, 1966, statement condemning the US bombing of Hanoi, the Government of the Socialist Republic of Rumania also pointed out:

'*In the December 14, 1966, raid, the premises of the Embassy of the Socialist Republic of Rumania were also subjected to a provocative attack.*'

In its December 16, 1966, statement condemning the US bombing of Hanoi, the Government of the People's Republic of Poland denounced the repeated US air attacks on the 'Viet Nam—Polish Friendship School':

'*Some days later, they again bombed the Viet Nam—Polish Friendship School.*'*

On December 17, Vietnamese and foreign journalists were led by Ambassador Chu Chi-wen to the buildings of the Chinese Embassy which had been hit by US missiles; they were also shown missile fragments bearing US markings. The Bureau of the International Commission for Supervision and Control in Viet Nam comprising Mr R. Sethi, Head of the Indian Delegation, Chairman, Captain J. Knzyanowski, Head of the Polish Delegation, and Major P. Wilson, Head of the Canadian Delegation, and foreign correspondents in Hanoi have seen on the spot the damage caused by US bombs, missiles and rockets in a number of places inside the city. On December 15, the IC Bureau was led by Ambassador Ion Moanga to the places hit by US missiles in the Rumanian Embassy and it was shown missile fragments bearing US markings.

It was US bombs, missiles and rockets that caused losses in terms of human lives and property inside Hanoi on the 2nd, 13th and 14th of December, 1966.

In the places mentioned above, fragments of US rockets and missiles were recovered. For instance, US missile fragments were

* This school was bombed by US planes on the 2nd, 13th and 14th of December, 1966.

found in the Chinese and Rumanian embassies with the markings
ANR 158, 10.001—1.556.622, 10.001—1.570.372 and the word
'Confidential'. There were other fragments with the markings
'Reaction Motors Division'. Big craters caused by US bombs can
be seen in the compound of the flat, the Trade Union Cadres
Training School, the Water Conservancy Institute in Tay Son and
Giang Vo Streets (Dong Da Quarter). . . .

On December 31, 1966, I made my first visit to a bombed area
within Hanoi proper. This was the Hoan Kiem district, less than five
minutes from the centre of town but only a few hundred yards from
the western approach to the Long Bien (Paul Doumer) bridge span-
ning the Red River. The district had been hit, said the Vietnamese, on
December 13, with missiles, incendiary bombs and percussion or 'wind'
bombs, the kind that flatten buildings by exploding above them.

Such bombs are also used to 'blow down' bridges, though they
rarely do. Conceivably, the United States planes had aimed for the
bridge's approaches. But why? If the target was the bridge, would
not the planes aim their bombs directly at it—and it is two kilometres (1·2 miles) long? In any case, the US Air Force claims a
margin of error of no more than 200 yards—for dive bombers. And
all the planes raiding the north of North Vietnam *are* dive bombers
(B-52's would be sitting ducks for Vietnamese missiles).

Two streets in the Hoan Kiem district had been severely damaged.
One was Phuc Tan, a dirt street lined with mud-walled, thatched-roof
houses. A whole block of that street had been obliterated. Charred
remains of three hundred houses were visible, and here and there a
bomb crater remained unfilled. Otherwise, it looked like an abandoned cemetery, with the remnants of a chimney or of a huge collective
water jug standing crookedly like decaying tombstones (Photo 1b). It
was a good place for kids to play, however, and there were quite a few
around. But none spoke French, and I could not get a clear picture
of what had happened on December 13 from them—except that
their homes had disappeared and that they had been in shelters
when the explosions 'shook the ground'.

Next, I visited Pho Nguyen Thiep Street, again crowded with
working-class homes, but made of bricks this time. A narrow paved
street, it had been hit by a bullpup-type missile which, exploding
above ground, had shattered all the windows in the neighbourhood.
Directly under the explosion, on both sides of the street, thirteen
houses, of one, two and three storeys, had collapsed (Photo 3)
killing four and wounding eleven. I wandered around in the rubble
for a while, then headed for Hue Street, which had been bombed on
December 2. I spotted a twelve-year-old girl standing meekly by a

batch of twisted bricks. She lived right behind the damaged house, she told me in halting French, and will always remember that day when there was a tremendous bang and 'my house trembled like it had bad fever'.

Getting back into our Russian-made Volga sedans (which looked just like Chevys), we drove on to the centre of town, passing by the Quynh pagoda, a Tao Buddhist temple, which I was told had been hit twice: on April 17, 1966, and on December 13. I jumped out of the car to photograph it, its strange statues frozen in tiny, glass-and-wood house-like cases amidst the rubble and under a roof of lonely beams, the tiles having been blasted away (Photo 4a). Then we visited Khuc Hao Street (Ba Dinh district), an elegant tree-lined, tile-sidewalked street housing chic French colonial villas which had been converted into embassies. It was there that, on December 14, a United States air-to-ground missile had struck the Chinese and Rumanian embassies. The United States had denied the raid, positing instead the theory that the embassies had been hit by a Vietnamese missile which had fallen short.

We were requested not to photograph the embassies, but the buildings had obviously been bombed. Part of the railing around them was bent and there were shrapnel holes all along the walls. Three days later, I mentioned this to Jacques Moalic who, as Agence France Presse correspondent in Hanoi, was the only permanent representative of a non-socialist newspaper or agency. He told me: 'As soon as I heard about the bombing on December 14, I rushed to the embassies. At the Rumanian Embassy I saw a piece of the missile. It was clearly American and had American markings.'

Moalic explained that:

By then I was used to the fact that you have to whip around town for information yourself if you want it. There's nobody, no information bureau, that calls you up—as in Western capitals. For example, I came across the first bombing by accident. I was bicycling around town when I suddenly saw a crowd and realized that some of the bangs I had heard earlier had been caused by bombs dropping on the city. When I had heard them I had called the Foreign Ministry's press department but someone there had told me no, no bombs fell on the city that we know of. Yet here they were.

I have travelled relatively little so far [he went on]. In fact, I gather that in your three days you have travelled more than I have. But I have seen enough to make some conclusions. For example, I have seen one small town, five kilometres from any possible military objective, completely wiped out. It could not have been by accident. I am convinced that, at best, American airmen are told to dump their bombs anywhere before returning. Or, if they are told to hit any military objective they can, it comes to the same thing because there are no military objectives. Everything is small and decentralized. Thus, the Americans hit everything and anything.

Finally, on that first full day of work in North Vietnam, December 31, 1966, I was shown one more bombed site: the Medicine and Pharmacy Faculty in Le Thanh Ton Street (Hai Ba district). A complex of three cement buildings ten minutes from downtown Hanoi but still within the city proper, it had been bombed December 14. When I arrived, Militia girls were still trying to fill the huge water-clogged bomb craters (Photo 4b). They joked and laughed, invited us to use the holes for a swim and generally seemed in a jovial mood. Yet on the 14th they had fired their rifles at the attacking planes and, always armed, were ready to do so again on a moment's notice. It was only later that I understood that this is true of all Vietnamese. Gay, friendly, warm, they are all the more resilient because they love and enjoy life.

But they also suffer. On January 3, 1967, I spent the whole day wandering through the General Surgical Hospital of Hanoi, talking to doctors, nurses and patients or their parents. I was especially moved by the children and found that most if them had been wounded by fragmentation bombs. These bombs terrified me.

The main fragmentation bomb is the CBU—cluster bomb unit. It consists of a 'mother bomb' filled with 640 'guavas', baseball-size secondary bombs which are released by the mother at about half a mile off the ground. These guavas in turn explode on the ground, sending 260 steel pellets about one-fifth of an inch in diameter (plus the metal holding these pellets together) in all directions with great force for some twenty yards. The pellets do no harm to concrete, to brick buildings or to weapons, but they tear into human or animal flesh. Since the trajectory of each pellet is a forward spiral, once inside a body it keeps boring, often travelling up legs or arms or through chests and stomachs, tearing the insides. These bombs are used mostly in the countryside.

When Barbara Deming, a pacifist who had toured North Vietnam in early December, first reported that these anti-personnel bombs were being used extensively in Vietnam, the Defence Department laughed it off. One Pentagon spokesman retorted that the Department 'never commented on enemy propaganda', while another ridiculed her by saying, 'all bombs fragment' (*Washington Post*, December 29, 1966). In fact, however, the Pentagon had bragged about such bombs earlier. A UPI report from Saigon dated June 1, 1966, had said:

> US Air Force planes using a new secret-type bomb turned eight square miles of North Vietnam into a raging inferno yesterday in the greatest bombing mission of the war, it was disclosed today. Reliable sources said the American planes dropped a powerful anti-personnel bomb among their explosives. It had been used before against North Vietnam but its use was not made public until today. The bomb shoots out thousands of lethal pellets. [As printed in the *Washington Daily News*, June 1, 1966.]

Besides, the United States Air Force officially considers such bombs, which hurt mostly ordinary people, a fundamental weapon. In a manual entitled *Fundamentals of Air Space Weapons* issued by the Air University of the United States Air Force and dated May 20, 1966, the Air Force distinguishes four kinds of targets: political, 'psycho-social', military and economic. In an underdeveloped country such as Vietnam, says the manual, political centres move around and may be hard to locate; military objectives again are movable; psycho-social (health installations, schools, churches) targets, however, are 'of great importance to the underdeveloped country' and are easy to locate.

In any case, I myself saw pieces of hundreds of anti-personnel fragmentation bombs all over Veitnam. I even brought one home; it is in my possession. More tragically, I saw hundreds of victims of these pellet-spewing bombs. And in Hanoi's General Surgical Hospital, I saw scores of children still suffering or permanently damaged by them. One was a ten-month-old boy called Le Dinh Loc who had been wounded in Hanoi on December 13 and still carried a small sliver of a bomb (no one could be sure if it was part of a frag-mentation bomb of the CBU type or not) in his head. His mother had died in the raid. His father, who was at the hospital, told me:

> My name is Le Dinh Hoi.* My family included five children. My wife was killed. This is my last child. I had gone to buy bread. On my way back I saw many planes bombing my area [Hoan Kiem]

* The first name, 'Le' in this case, is the family name. The middle name is a title or a word denoting sex; 'Van' is most usual for males, 'Thi' for females. The third name is the given name. Women do not change their names when they marry, but children take on the family name of the father. (All Vietnamese words are of one syllable. 'Nguyen', which looks to Westerners like two and is as common in Vietnam as Smith in the United States, is pronounced something like 'Gyen'. Haiphong is really Hai Phong and Hanoi Ha Noi, but these two cities' names, because they are well known to the rest of the world, have informally adopted Westernization, as has Viet Nam itself. My own name, as it appeared in the Vietnamese press, was Gion Gie Ra Xi.)

along the Red River. I ran home, saw my home burning. I found my wife dead. She had lost a leg and blood was flowing everywhere. In her arms was this child. I picked him up and realized that he was wounded but still alive. My house was 900 metres from here. [The 'here' was in the centre of town.]

The next child I saw was a one-year-old girl named Nguyen Thi Thanh who was also wounded in the head (Photo 5a). Her mother Ngo Thi Ky, twenty-nine, was with her. She told me that she 'had gone to work, leaving as usual my child with the neighbours. At 3 P.M. I heard the bombing and I rushed home. Everything was destroyed. I could not find my child—or the neighbours. Then I heard they had all been wounded and I rushed to the hospital. I learned that she was badly wounded in her head, that the brain was actually sticking out of her head through a gash. But they saved her.' (Dr Nguyen Van Duc, a surgeon and the head pediatrician at the hospital, who accompanied me on this part of the tour, told me that the child would remain paralysed for life.)

All day long (and all night long in my nightmares that night) I kept seeing these children, suffering, crippled, helpless. One had been struck by a pellet which had entered one temple and exited through the other, blowing out both eyeballs in the process; the child was technically alive, though, of course, blind and also incurably deranged. Others, like Nguyen Van Quang, twelve (Photo 5b), had been wounded in various places by pellets, including in his head, from which the pellet could not be removed. Some were lucky; they would return to normal. But all stared with haunting eyes that drilled through me even when they never looked at me.

I also talked at length to adult patients, including Le Thi Khuong, a co-op member, who told me how she had been working in Haiphong until July 31, 1966, when she returned to her husband's native village to give birth to a child.

The village is Hiep Hoa, eighty kilometres north of Hanoi. On the day I arrived on maternity leave, on July 31, 1966, there was a raid. It was a Sunday, I remember very well. My husband was home and heard the planes. He told me to take shelter but I couldn't, so I lay down on top of my first child, a boy of three. He was crying. After the bombs went off, he kept crying and was bleeding from his head. My husband rushed up, noticed the blood and ripped some cloth to put on the boy. Then he discovered that the child was not bleeding. *C'était moi!* Only then did I realize that I was very much in pain. First-aid men came at that point and took me to a district post where I was given shots. Then the ambulance arrived and I was taken to the district hospital. One hour later I gave birth to this boy. He did not cry when he was born and I thought he was dead. But he was not. Then the doctors realized that he was wounded and therefore that I must be also, inside my womb. Suddenly I became frightened that I would die. They operated on me for an hour and I remember very well that as soon as the operation was over the American planes came back, bombing and strafing. The doctors tell me that in three years I shall be able to have children again. [But the doctor, Dr Dang Hong Khanh, a neurosurgeon, told me that her child will never be normal.]

A few days later I passed through Thiep Hoa. The town had indeed been heavily bombed—repeatedly. As far as I could see, it had no factories, no military posts, no strategic objective, and, of course, could in no way be interpreted as a transportation centre for shipments of troops or material from Hanoi or Haiphong to the south—since it was quite north of both.

On January 4, 1967, I continued my tour of bombed Hanoi with a briefing at City Hall. The mayor, a young former textile worker and Militia leader who had fought at Dien Bien Phu, showed me, on a map of Hanoi, all the places that had been bombed in the sixteen raids since April 17, 1966. Suddenly I spotted a pattern. The bombed areas made a perfect circle around the Presidential Palace. 'Could the real target have been the Palace?' I asked. 'Perhaps,' answered the mayor, 'but I doubt it. If they had wanted to actually hit it, they would have come closer—even with our defences. No, I think it was just example bombing.' I then drew lines from each bombed site to the Paul Doumer (Long Bien) Bridge, and calculated the distance. Some were a few hundred yards away. But others were as far off as fifteen kilometres (nine miles). Obviously, the bridge wasn't the target either.

It didn't add up. Altogether, I was told, 1,167 bombs had been dropped on Hanoi—plus 3,000 fragmentation 'guava' bombs on the outskirts. On December 2, 1966, the raiding party had consisted of 27 planes. On December 13, 40 planes. On December 14, 61 planes. Through December, 54 people had been killed (85 since April). Considering the fact that the population concentration-rate is 935 per square kilometre in the outskirts, 14,000 per square kilometre in the urban sectors, and in the centre, around the small lake, 38,000 per square kilometre, the low casualty rate seemed miraculous. In fact, more houses had been destroyed than people killed. The reason was simple: Vietnam's alarm system, which is first-rate except along the coast (where planes from carriers can strike with little warning), warns the population in time for it to get to shelters; and because of the firm discipline, almost everyone does get to the shelters before the bombs fall.

After the briefing, I was taken to the village of Phu Xa, a small agricultural centre some five kilometres up the Red River from Hanoi proper but still within its administrative jurisdiction. Phu Xa was a Catholic village of seventy-five families, organized into four cooperatives raising bananas, rice and cocoons for silk. It had been destroyed at 12.17 P.M. on August 13, 1966, but was now partly rebuilt: mud huts topped by rice-straw roofs surrounding the main square or plaza where Vu Va Luy, his wife and their five children, killed on the spot August 13, were buried. The tombstone read: 'In hatred toward the American aggressors who massacred our compatriots of Phu Xa, hamlet of Nhat Tan, on August 13, 1966.'

The town had been extensively bombarded by fragmentation pellets. On the ground I saw part of a mother CBU, kept in place as a sort of reminder. On its khaki shell it bore the inscription, in English, 'Loading Date 7–66'. Twenty-four people had died during the raid and so had 13 pigs and 164 chickens; 1,296 kilos of rice had been destroyed. I asked our guide, Le Van Yep, who was one of the co-op leaders and a Catholic, to comment on Cardinal Spellman's statement, which had just been reported in Hanoi, that American troops were fighting for Christ and that he hoped they would continue to ultimate victory. Le Van Xep thought for a while, then said softly: 'The Cardinal must be mistaken. Christ does not teach aggression.'

I kept wandering around. Among the effects in bombed houses, I noticed pots, pans, furniture and clothes, all pierced by pellets. I also saw the charred remains of a statue of the Virgin and a partly burned photograph of Pope Paul.

Later that day we headed south, along National Route No. 1, which was built by the French to connect Hanoi with Saigon. Toward the edge of Hanoi, but still within city limits, we left the highway, which had been heavily bombed but quickly repaired, for a dirt road. After a few hundred yards, we came to a small hamlet that had been almost completely destroyed. Raided December 2, 13 and 14, it had once housed the Vietnam-Polish Friendship School, donated by the Polish Government. The school was battered—and empty. The children had been evacuated. At the entrance, the posts still stood. A smart-alecky kid had written on one of them something to the effect of 'Hooray, no more school.' (Photo 7a.)

Behind the school, the village (Tu Ky) had been completely devastated. While I was walking around in the rubble, I noticed an old woman piling up bricks. I went to talk to her. She wasn't as old as she seemed—fifty-seven. Her name was Nguyen Thi Sang (Photo 7b), a peasant, and she told me that her entire family of ten—from her four-year-old grandchild to her son and daughter-in-law—had been killed in the December 14 raid. 'I saw it happen from the field over there,' she said. 'The planes flew above us three or four times, then dived. One of the bombs hit the shelter where my family was.' I asked her why she was picking up the bricks. 'My house was destroyed. I have to rebuild it.' Asking her to forgive my cruel question, I prodded: 'Your family is gone, the Government will take care of you now, why do you want to rebuild your house?' She smiled sadly, closed her eyes, then replied: 'Well, I may live for a while still and I want my own home. . . . No, that's not why. I guess it's because I know that after I'm gone, someone else will come here and live in my house. That's the way we go on. The only way to live is always to start again. . . .'

III

HO, PHAM AND FOUR POINTS

On January 11, 1967, at 10 A.M., we were led up the long, white, marble stairway of the Presidential Palace—once the French Governor General's home—to meet Prime Minister Pham Van Dong. It was to be an informal meeting of only a few minutes. Instead, it lasted, over tea, berry wine and tangerines, almost three hours.

Awaiting Pham's entrance, sitting on comfortable leather chairs in the huge, marble-walled reception room, we were struck by the easy, relaxed nature of the Vietnamese. Some were our translators, others our guides; they had never met Pham before. Yet they seemed quite at home, as did the military aides, the Cabinet members, the local photographers. When Pham entered, all stood, but that was as formal as it ever got. Appearing to be in his early forties (he was then sixty), wearing a grey 'people's suit' (and, judging by the sleeves, two sweaters under it) and black half-boots, he strutted in with a huge smile and a ready handshake. He made the rounds himself, firmly gripping our hands with both of his, saying a few kind words to each of us—while cameras flashed. Then he sat down in an armchair and asked us questions: how we were, how we ate, how we slept, whether travelling by night in open jeeps in this cold didn't bother us too much, etc.

Suddenly, he rose, beamed with joy, walked briskly toward the door and, extending his arms, greeted his President, Ho Chi Minh, who had arrived for—to us—a surprise visit. He was also dressed in a simple 'people's suit' made of white cloth. He was wearing 'Liberation sandals', the same kind—rubber soles cut from discarded tyres, tied to the foot by bulky straps—worn by most Viet Cong soldiers in the South. Looking tired but well-disposed, Ho, who was seventy-seven, also greeted us individually. Pham made the introductions, remembering not only our names but also our nationalities and our professions—and there were fourteen of us in all, four investigators (Caldwell had returned to England by then), Pic, the Australian journalist Wilfred Burchett, and eight Japanese war crimes investigators.

Full of wit, with an easy style, Ho stayed only a few minutes and spoke exclusively in French. He read (with glasses) a telegram he had received from Bertrand Russell, joked about the fact that all fourteen of us present came from former or current aggressor nations (Japan, France, Australia, the United States), and finally, and very seriously, said: 'What you saw in the North must be multiplied by the hundreds for you to have an idea of what goes on in the South. Our intention is to fight to the end. Since we are offered either slavery to the United States or victory, we have no alternative.' Then, wishing us well, he bade farewell to each of us and left.

Pham Van Dong then settled back in his chair and told us: 'Alright, let's speak frankly, about anything you wish, but among ourselves.' We did, for about an hour, and then I asked him if he would say, for the record, under what conditions negotiations could start. After quipping that journalists always want things 'for the record', he said that as long as the bombing continued, negotiations were out of the question. I interpreted that to mean that if the bombing did stop, negotiations could get under way immediately. I asked Pham on what basis. On the four points, he said.

He was referring to the resolution passed in April 1965, at the second session of the 3rd National Assembly of the Democratic Republic of Viet Nam. I had seen that declaration. In fact it was included in a document which had been given me earlier by the Vietnamese. In it the history and the reasons why the Vietnamese were fighting the United States in Vietnam were clearly yet briefly spelled out. The following is that document abridged:

Document No. 2
US Intervention and Aggression in Vietnam During the Last Twenty Years.
Published by the Foreign Affairs, Democratic Republic of Vietnam, Hanoi, 1965. In English.

I

FIRST US INTERVENTION IN VIET NAM

After accomplishing the August 19, 1945, Revolution and taking over power from the Japanese Fascists, the Vietnamese people founded the Democratic Republic of Viet Nam, a State with full sovereignty, independence, and territorial integrity from North to South.

In an attempt to reconquer Viet Nam as well as the whole of Indo-China, the French colonialist aggressors started their 'dirty war' at the end of 1945. Under the leadership of the Government of the Democratic Republic of Viet Nam headed by President Ho Chi Minh, the Vietnamese people dealt at the aggressors repeated heavy blows.

For its part, since the end of World War II, the United States has nurtured the design of conquering Viet Nam and Indo-China as a whole, and turning this region into a US military base with a view to carrying out its schemes against the socialist countries and the national liberation movement in Indo-China and South-East Asia. Soon after the triumph of the August Revolution in Viet Nam, it sent to North Viet Nam down to the 16th parallel 200,000 Chiang Kai-shek troops under Lu Han's command as an instrument for intervention in Viet Nam. It will be recalled that at that time, US Generals Gallagher and MacLure made frequent visits to Viet Nam for behind-the-scene activities. In December 1945, despite the fact that the Democratic Republic of Viet Nam had been proclaimed an independent country with a unified Government exercising its authority all over the territory, the then President of the United States bluntly declared that it was necessary to place the Indo-Chinese states under UN trusteeship. It is clear that ever since that date, the United States has schemed to conquer Viet Nam, Laos and Cambodia through the US-manipulated UNO.

After being driven out of the Chinese mainland, from 1950 onward, the United States, taking advantage of the French colonialist aggressors' ever heavier defeats, has gradually increased its intervention in Viet Nam and other parts of Indo-China, endeavouring to help the French pursue their aggressive war, and at the same time seeking to kick them out.

On March 16, 1950, an aircraft-carrier, 2 cruisers and 71 aircraft were sent by the United States to Saigon for a show of force. This stirred up a sweeping wave of indignation among the Vietnamese people. On the following day, South Viet Nam guerrillas mounted a mortar attack against the US navy units. On March 19, 1950, a huge demonstration attended by more than 500,000 people was held in Saigon-Cholon, and the US ships and planes were forced to leave South Viet Nam.

On May 8, 1950, US Secretary of State Dean Acheson and French Foreign Minister Robert Schuman met in camera in Paris and agreed that the United States would increase military and economic aid to France and her puppets.

On June 27, 1950, immediately after the start of the aggressive war against the Democratic People's Republic of Korea and the occupation of Taiwan by US Navy, US President Truman declared that he had ordered to increase military assistance to the French forces and those of the 'Associated States' of Indo-China and to dispatch there a military mission which was to cooperate closely with these forces.

On July 15, 1950, the first US military mission headed by Major

General Graves B. Erskine and John Melby, Head of the South-East Asia Division of the US State Department, arrived in Saigon to survey the situation of the French forces and the possibility for the United States to use military bases in Indo-China.

On August 10, 1950, the first shipment of US arms arrived in Indo-China.

On December 23, 1950, the United States signed with France and the Indo-Chinese 'Associated States' a 'mutual defence' treaty which was in reality an instrument for intensifying US intervention in Indo-China.

Early in 1951 it set up under this treaty the Military Aid Group (MAAG) in Saigon.

Since then, it has engaged in an ever deeper intervention in Indo-China. The US and French Staffs closely cooperated in pursuing the 'dirty war'. Hundreds of US military advisers and hundreds of thousands of tons of arms and war materials were sent to Indo-China. US aid to the French in Indo-China rose from 314 million in 1950–1951 to 1,000 million US dollars—approximately ⅘ of the total war expenditures of the French in Indo-China—in 1953–1954. All in all, from 1950 to 1954, US aid to the French in Indo-China amounted to 2,600 million dollars.

Explaining the reason behind the increasing US intervention in Indo-China, President Eisenhower told a meeting of Governors of the various States on August 4, 1953, that if Indo-China was lost, 'the tin and tungsten that we so greatly value from that area would cease coming'.

In July 1953, it was decided at a meeting of US, French and British Foreign Ministers that increased military aid would be given the French on condition that the latter would carry out the Navarre plan—which was in fact a US plan—for stepping up the war in Indo-China, and that US aid would be given directly to the Bao Dai puppet administration. The French Government had no other choice than to accept these conditions.

When the Viet Nam People's Army began attacking Dien Bien Phu at the beginning of March 1954, the prospect of defeat of the French Expeditionary Corps became clear. US Secretary of State J. F. Dulles declared that henceforth Indo-China would be included in the 'inviolable area' of US strategy. President Eisenhower also threatened that the United States would take part in the Indo-China war if the situation became alarming. The US scheme consisted in taking advantage of the opportunity to take in hand, prolong and expand the Indo-China war. The United States strove to involve Britain and other countries into the war along with it. A plan called 'Operation Vautour' was worked out jointly by the Americans and the French for a massive bombing of North Viet Nam by hundreds of US Air Force planes. Meanwhile two aircraft-carriers of the US 7th Fleet came to the Bac Bo Gulf.

But the United States could not realize its plan of directly intervening in the Indo-China war and expending it in face of the tidal wave of struggle of the people in France and in the world for the restoration of peace in Indo-China, and in face of the disapproval of its allies. The historic victory scored by the Vietnamese army and people at Dien Bien Phu forced it to go to the Geneva Conference to discuss a settlement of the Indo-China question.

Then, the United States sought every means to sabotage the negotiations at the Geneva Conference. However, the Conference went ahead and wound up successfully; peace was restored in Indo-China on the basis of the recognition of the sovereignty, independence, unity and territorial integrity of Viet Nam, Laos and Cambodia.

The great victory gained by the peoples of Viet Nam, Laos and Cambodia at the 1954 Geneva Conference marked the complete failure not only of 'the dirty war', but also of the first US intervention in this country.

II
SECOND US INTERVENTION IN VIET NAM
SYSTEMATIC SABOTAGE OF THE 1954 GENEVA AGREEMENTS

The 1954 Geneva Agreements stipulate that:

—The participants in the 1954 Geneva Conference on Indo-China shall respect the sovereignty, independence, unity and territorial integrity of Viet Nam, Laos and Cambodia, and shall refrain from any interference in their internal affairs.

—Viet Nam, which is temporarily divided into two zones with a view to facilitating the elimination of the state of war, and in substance the repatriation of the French Expeditionary Corps, shall be reunified through nation-wide free general elections to be held in July 1956.

—It is prohibited to bring foreign troops into either part of Viet Nam and establish foreign military bases therein; the regrouping zones of the armed forces of both parties must not join any military alliance or be used for the resumption of hostilities or the furtherance of an aggressive policy.

While the Government of the Democratic Republic of Viet Nam has always been strictly implementing the Geneva Agreements, the United States has embarked on an entirely opposite course with the purpose of pursuing its intervention in Viet Nam.

While at the Geneva Conference W. Bedell Smith, Head of the

US Delegation, gave a solemn undertaking that the United States would refrain from the threat or the use of force to disturb the execution of the Geneva Agreements, US President Eisenhower stated that:

'*The United States has not itself been party to, or bound by, the decisions taken by the Conference.*'

On September 8, 1954, the United States drew Great Britain, France and a number of other countries into signing the Manila Treaty, founded SEATO, an aggressive military *bloc*, and included South Viet Nam, Cambodia and Laos in its 'protection area'. This brazen act, which took place barely two months after the conclusion of the 1954 Geneva Agreements on Indo-China, testified to the US scheme of systematic sabotage of the Agreements.

The United States on the one hand endeavoured to gradually kick the French out of Viet Nam, and on the other made every effort to help the Ngo Dinh Diem puppet administration to 'stabilize the situation', with a view to using South Viet Nam as a springboard for aggression against the Democratic Republic of Viet Nam.

It secured firm control over the Ngo Dinh Diem Administration by means of assistance programmes which mounted to 1,600 million US dollars for the period from 1954 to 1960, a network of 'advisers' and missions dubbed 'Military Aid Advisory Group (MAAG), US Operations Mission' (USOM), and the 'Michigan State University' mission (MSU), which fully control the military, administrative, economic and financial affairs of South Viet Nam. In fact, South Viet Nam has been turned into a US new-type colony, Ngo Dinh Diem said in 1957 during a visit to the United States:

'*The frontiers of the United States extend to the 17th parallel.*'

After wiping out the armed forces of the opponent religious sects, Ngo Dinh Diem organized a fraudulent 'referendum' to depose Bao Dai (October 23, 1955), founded the so-called 'Republic of Viet Nam' (October 26, 1955), and held rigged elections to set up the so-called 'National Assembly' of South Viet Nam (January 23, 1956).

In execution of the scheme for the permanent partition of Viet Nam, the Ngo Dinh Diem Administration rejected all the proposals made by the Government of the Democratic Republic of Viet Nam on the holding of consultations and general elections for the reunification of Viet Nam in July 1956 as explicitly stipulated in the Geneva Agreements.

The United States and the Ngo Dinh Diem Administration went ahead with ever more serious violations of the military provisions of the Geneva Agreements. The United States set about building up the puppet army, bringing into South Viet Nam arms and other war materials, establishing a network of military bases and strategic highways, in feverish preparation for a new war.

From 1954 to 1960, the United States boosted the strength of the puppet regular army to ten infantry divisions fully armed with US weapons, and organized new navy and air force units. It also trained and equipped about 200,000 men of the regional troops, police force and militia of the South Viet Nam Administration.

By the end of 1960, it had built in South Viet Nam 57 airfields, i.e. nine times more than in 1954, and the 32 km.-long and 100 metre-wide Saigon–Bien Hoa autobahn—which was in fact a camouflaged air base—three new naval bases and many strategic highways linking up the various military bases in South Viet Nam and connecting South Viet Nam with military bases in Laos and Thailand.

The United States has also illegally brought into South Viet Nam hundreds of thousands of tons of weapons and war materials. Clandestine at first, these operations were later on carried out openly and uninterruptedly. In 1960 alone, the value of US arms introduced into South Viet Nam amounted to 74,000,000 US dollars.

From a staff of 200 men at the end of the war in Viet Nam, the US military mission MAAG swelled to 2,000 men in 1960. This mission assumed command of the South Viet Nam army, from the Defence Ministry down to army battalions.

In view of the repeated clamours of the Ngo Dinh Diem Administration about 'Marching North' and 'Filling up the Ben Hai river',* it is obvious that the military buildup in South Viet Nam had no other aim than to prepare for an armed aggression against the Democratic Republic of Viet Nam, and to oppose, in accordance with the US plans, the independence and neutrality of the Kingdoms of Laos and Cambodia.

On US orders, the South Viet Nam Administration has cease-lessly smuggled spy-commandos into North Vietnam for espionage and sabotage activities. 1958, 1959 and 1960 witnessed hundreds of violations of the air space and territorial waters of the Democratic Republic of Viet Nam by South Viet Nam air and naval craft. At the instigation of the United States and the South Viet Nam regime, the pro-US Phoui Sananikone clique of Laos undertook harassing actions on the Viet Nam–Laos border, and even staged armed provocations in Huong Lap (Vinh Linh area), a part of the territory of the Democratic Republic of Viet Nam.

* The Ben Hai river flows along the 17th Parallel.

(a) A barber at work on a Hanoi street (notice the cement covers for the individual shelters)

(b) Hanoi's Phuc Tan Street, where 300 houses were obliterated during a raid on December 13, 1966

2 (a) A Russian-made SAM
missile   (DRV *photograp*

(b) An anti-aircraft battery
(DRV *photograp*

3 Pho Nguyen Thiep Street, hit by a bullpup missile on December 13, 1966

(b) Militia girls filling the bomb craters at Hanoi's Medicine and Pharmacy Faculty

4 (a) Hanoi's Quynh pagoda, hit April 17 and December 13, 1966

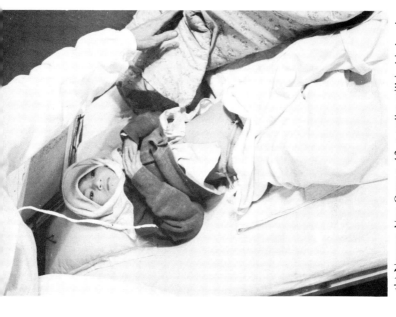

(b) Nguyen Van Quang, 12, a pellet still in his head

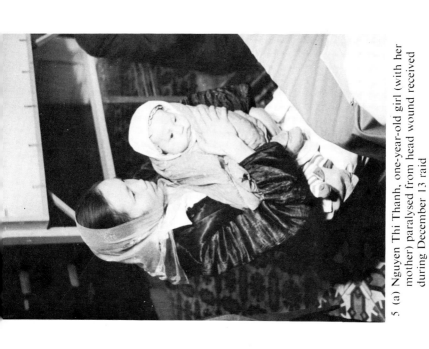

5 (a) Nguyen Thi Thanh, one-year-old girl (with her mother) paralysed from head wound received during December 13 raid

6 Seated: Vigier, the Prime Minister, Burchett, Matarasso, the author. Behind Vigie
Pham Van Bach, Chief Justice of the DRV's Supreme Court, and between Pham V
Dong and Burchett is Dr Pham Ngoc Thach, the Minister of Health

(Photo by Roger

7 (a) Remains of the Vietnam-Polish Friendship School, bombed three times in December 1966. Chalk sign, written by students with a sense of humour, says something like 'Hooray, no more school'

(b) Nguyen Thi Sang, whose family of ten was wiped out at Tu Ky on December 14, 1966, picking up bricks to rebuild her house. 'The only way to live is always to start again . . .

8 (a) The Phu Ly dispensary

(b) Tran Thi Doan, mayoress of Nam Dinh

9 (a) A Nam Dinh Street
(DRV *photograph*)

(b) A Nam Dinh Street

10 (a) Phat Diem Church

(b) Tran Dai Nghia and grandson adopted by Cuban novelist Alejo Carpentier

(c) Sisters Vu: 'They tell you lies. But they know the truth'

1 (a) Haiphong (DRV *photograph*)

(b) Chinese ship at Haiphong Pier (in foreground the bow of a Russian ship)

12 (a) US Navy jet shot down over Haiphong and exhibited at the Museum

(b) Cat Ba island inlet (DRV *photograph*)

Military personnel of the Ngo Dinh Diem Administration were illegally brought into Laos to participate in the US-fomented civil war in that country. The United States and its South Viet Nam agents fostered the reactionary Khmer Serei clique, plotted the murder of the King and the Queen of Cambodia, and attempted to overthrow the Royal Cambodian Government headed by Prince Norodom Sihanouk. Furthermore, South Viet Nam and Thailand made frequent harassments and provocations along the Cambodian borders.

Also on US orders, the Ngo Dinh Diem Administration carried out large-scale and unimaginably savage repressions against the patriots who stand for freedom, peace and national reunification. Former Resistance members were arrested, subjected to inhuman tortures and massacred. Jails mushroomed, hundreds of thousands of patriots were detained; in addition, there were many other prisons and concentration camps camouflaged under such names as 'prosperity zones' and 'agricultural settlements'. A series of fascist laws were promulgated of which the ill-famed 10/59 Law prescribed death sentences without trial against any suspect. By the end of 1960, tens of thousands of people had been murdered, and hundreds of thousands of others tortured to infirmity.*

The above facts show that the United States has been systematically sabotaging the Geneva Agreements on Viet Nam, violating the clauses on the reunification of the country, the military provisions and those dealing with the democratic liberties of the people.

The US policy of intervention has trampled upon the deep aspirations of the people of South Viet Nam and of all Viet Nam for peace, unity, independence and democracy. Even the rights to life and peaceful labour have not been respected by the ruthless fascist dictatorial policies of the Ngo Diem Administration. Therefore, exercising their rights of self-defence and self-determination— which are the inalienable rights of all peoples—the undaunted South Viet Nam people have resolutely risen up against the US imperialists and their agents.

The patriotic movement in South Viet Nam has rapidly developed into a mighty tidal wave which threatens to sweep away the positions of the United States and its agents. Once again, the US policy of intervention in South Viet Nam has sustained disastrous failure.

. . .

On August 5, 1964, the United States launched the first attack, bombing and strafing many localities along the coasts of the

* See Appendix C—J. G.

Democratic Republic of Viet Nam. To create a pretext for this new act of war, it sent the destroyer *Maddox* of the 7th Fleet into the territorial waters of the Democratic Republic of Viet Nam for provocative activities from July 31 to August 2, 1964, and engineered the so-called 'Tonkin Gulf incident' on the night of August 4, 1964.* In the bombing raids of early February 1965, the pretext invoked was 'tit-for-tat retaliation' for the attacks launched by the Liberation Army and guerrillas in South Viet Nam. In April 1965, after the 'tit-for-tat retaliation' argument was exposed, the United States resorted to the 'continuous retaliation' argument to justify its round-the-clock indiscriminate bombing of populated areas, which it called 'escalation' from one parallel to another. The tempo of these piratical attacks was also increased. According to figures officially announced in Saigon and Washington, the US Air Force launched:

In February 1965: 3 attacks with about 250 sorties
In March 1965:   18 attacks with 716 sorties, and the dropping of over 1,200 tons of bombs
In April 1965:   98 attacks with 2,202 sorties, and the dropping of 1,700 to 1,800 tons of bombs. . . .

In addition to rockets, 20 mm guns, and bombs of 500, 750, 1,000 and 2,000 pounds, the United States has also used napalm, white phosphorus bombs, radar-guided Bullpup air-to-ground missiles. On April 25, 1965, it even went to the length of spreading toxic chemicals on Con Co islet.

These are cynical premeditated war activities, brazen violations of the sovereignty and territory of the Democratic Republic of Viet Nam, undeniable violation of the 1954 Geneva Agreements on Viet Nam and all norms of international law. They pose a heavy threat to peace in Indo-China and South-East Asia. That is the reason why the US air and naval attacks on the territory of the Democratic Republic of Viet Nam have been sternly condemned by the peoples of the whole world and by many governments.

The Johnson Administration has repeatedly asserted that US aircraft strike only at 'military targets'. This is a sheer lie since US and South Viet Nam aircraft have bombed and strafed hospitals in Dong Hoi, Ho Xa, Nghia Dan, primary and secondary schools in Vinh Linh, Dong Hoi, Can Loc (Ha Tinh), pagodas and churches such as the Quynh Tam church (Nghe An province), markets such as the markets of Ho Xa (Vinh Linh), Dung, Soi (Nghe An), Tu Tru (Thanh Hoa), bus stations at Vinh (Nghe An), private-owned fishing-boats, and peaceful villages. Each US raid is marked with most odious crimes.

* See Appendix B—J. G.

To defend the sovereignty and territory of their country, and the security of their people, the anti-aircraft units, air force, navy, militia and self-defense units of the Democratic Republic of Viet Nam have resolutely fought back and dealt at the US aggressors ever heavier counter-blows. From August 5, 1964, to May 31, 1965, the North Viet Nam army and people sank or set on fire 8 enemy commando boats, shot down 302 planes, and damaged hundreds of others. On the single day of April 4, 1965, the anti-aircraft units, air force, navy, militia and self-defense units of Thanh Hoa, Quang Binh and Vinh Linh shot down 37 enemy planes, causing the United States the heaviest losses in one day in North Viet Nam for the past period.

While carrying out air strikes against the mainland and some offshore islands, the United States has also used the 7th Fleet and warships of the South Viet Nam stooge administration to provoke, menace, inspect ships and junks sailing in international waters off the Vietnamese coasts or visiting DRV ports. On March 21, 1965, the merchant-ship *San Spyridon*, flying the Lebanese flag and carrying goods for civilian use from Hai Phong port to Europe, was strafed by US and South Viet Nam aircraft, which caused many killed and wounded. On March 24, 1965, the Soviet merchant-ship *Ljma* was also threatened by US planes while sailing in international waters off the Vietnamese coast. . . .

III
THE SO-CALLED US WILL FOR PEACE

The US Government has put forward one argument after another, and published a 'blue book' and a 'white paper' in an attempt to cover up its aggression in South Viet Nam.

Since April 7, 1965, US President Johnson has repeatedly stated that the United States has come to South Viet Nam 'to defend freedom', 'to allow the people of South Viet Nam to guide their own country in their own way'. He has also accused North Viet Nam of 'aggression against South Viet Nam'. He has said that the United States is ready to engage in 'unconditional discussions' to find a peaceful settlement of the war in Viet Nam.

Is the US Government 'defending freedom' in South Viet Nam?

As everybody knows, after World War II, the Vietnamese people seized power from the Japanese Fascists, and founded the Democratic Republic of Viet Nam, a unified country exercising sovereignty from the Viet Nam–China border down to the southernmost end of Viet Nam. But the United States actively helped the French colonialist aggressors with dollars and weapons to carry out 'the dirty war' for the purpose of imposing once again the colonial yoke on the Vietnamese, Khmer and Laotian peoples. After the conclusion of the 1954 Geneva Agreements, when Viet Nam was temporarily partitioned into two zones, the South Viet Nam people longed to see South Viet Nam achieve independence, democracy, peace and neutrality. But the United States has set up a fascist regime under the Ngo Dinh Diem brothers and, later on, under a succession of military dictators; it has sabotaged the peaceful reunification of Viet Nam as provided for in the Geneva Agreements. It has brought into South Viet Nam nearly 50,000 [by 1965] troops from the United States and thousands of mercenaries from a number of satellite countries to wage, together with the Saigon puppet army, an undeclared war, thus encroaching on the sovereignty and territory of Viet Nam. It is crystal-clear that the United States, instead of 'defending freedom', is carrying out an armed aggression in South Viet Nam; it does not 'allow the people of South Viet Nam to guide their own country in their own way', but is stifling their deepest and most sacred aspirations, in an attempt to turn South Viet Nam into a US military base and new-type colony....

Is it true that the United States is ready to engage in 'unconditional discussions' with a view to finding a peaceful settlement of the conflict in Viet Nam?

It will be recalled that, not long ago, President Johnson demanded, as a pre-condition to any negotiations for a settlement of the South Viet Nam question, that North Viet Nam should 'stop its aggression against South Viet Nam'. This time, he proposes 'unconditional discussions' presumably because he wants to give better proof of his 'will for peace', and even of his desire 'to raise the living standards' of South-East Asian peoples. The US ruling circles probably hope that Johnson's April 7 speech might mislead the world's peoples into taking this as the sign of a change in the US policy.

Unfortunately, the April 7 speech is full of contradictions:

—It is a fact that US and puppet troops are fighting against the South Viet Nam Liberation Army and people which are led by the South Viet Nam National Front for Liberation. The United States talks about its desire to hold 'discussions' with a view to finding a peaceful solution to the South Viet Nam question, but it refuses to recognize the South Viet Nam National Front for Liberation as the sole genuine representative of the South Viet Nam people. It is obvious that the United States wants neither peace nor 'negotiations'.

—The United States says that it wants a peaceful settlement of the war in Viet Nam but, at the same time, it declares that 'it will not withdraw, either openly or under the cloak of a meaningless agreement'. A peaceful settlement which does not include the withdrawal of US and satellite troops from South Viet Nam cannot be regarded as such by sound-minded people. It only means that the United States, which has launched an armed aggression against South Viet Nam, is insolently asking the heroic South Viet Nam people to lay down their arms and surrender to those on whom they have inflicted defeat after defeat. This is the kind of 'negotiations from a position of strength' repeatedly mentioned by the US ruling circles, from Johnson to Dean Rusk and McNamara. But they should not have any illusions about it. The indomitable South Viet Nam people deeply love peace but they are determined to struggle against the US imperialist aggressors; never will they lay down their arms until they win final victory.

—The United States says that it wants to seek a peaceful settlement of the war in Viet Nam because it 'wants peace quickly to be restored' but it deems it 'necessary to increase its response and make attacks by air'. While President Johnson says that the United States 'will strive not to extend the hostilities', Maxwell Taylor, the initiator of the theory of 'special war', who is now the plenipotentiary representative of the US Government in South Viet Nam for carrying out this kind of war, bluntly states that 'no limit exists to the potential escalation of the war', and that 'America may directly enter the fighting ground if necessary'.

While talking about peace, the United States continues to intensify the war in South Viet Nam and to extend the war with its air force and navy to North Viet Nam. This may lead to unforeseeable consequences. It is clear that the US aggressors and warmongers are using double talk to cover up their new dangerous military adventures in this area.

Over the recent period, the United States has brought into South Viet Nam the major part of the third division of marines commanded by Major-General Williams R. Collins (this is stationed in the bases of Da Nang, Phu Bai and Chu Lai, a new air base now being built about 100 kilometres south of Da Nang); the whole 173rd brigade of paratroops commanded by Brigadier-General Ellis Williamson (this is stationed in Bien Hoa and Vung Tau bases); many support units such as those of engineers, artillery, Hawk anti-aircraft missiles. On April 10, 1965, the United States set up in Saigon the Support Command No. 1, a body responsible for ensuring material supplies for the operations of US army corps.

The United States has also ordered its satellites to send troops to South Viet Nam as cannon-fodder. The South Korean puppet government has sent 2,000 troops; Australia has sent a battalion of 800 men; the Philippine authorities are plotting to send 2,000 mercenaries to South Viet Nam.

With regard to arms and equipment, the United States has introduced into South Viet Nam many modern means of warfare such as F.104 Starfighter and F.4C Phantom jet fighters, radar-equipped E.C.121 planes, Incendiegel bombs, and even big guns capable of firing tactical nuclear shells, etc. On many occasions, it has even used air bases in Thailand for the bombing and strafing of the territory of the Democratic Republic of Viet Nam. With a view to intensifying the bombing of North Viet Nam by night and in the forthcoming rainy season, it is sending to South Viet Nam many A.6 Intruder jet fighters specially equipped for this purpose.

While US reinforcements in troops and weapons are flowing in, the US Seventh Fleet with the Ranger, Hancock, Coral Sea and Midway task forces keeps operating in, and south of, the Bac Bo Gulf, multiplying provocations against ships plying in this area or visiting the harbours of the Democratic Republic of Viet Nam.

The aggressive and bellicose features of the US Government are further laid bare by the following arrogant action: on April 24, 1965, President Johnson designated the whole of Viet Nam and the waters adjacent thereto up to 100 miles from the Vietnamese coasts, and part of the territorial waters of the Chinese People's Republic around the Paracels islands, as a 'combat zone' of the US armed forces This is in essence a move towards a blockade of the Democratic Republic of Viet Nam and, at the same time, a preparation for larger-scale military adventures.

In fact, the United States is frenziedly intensifying the aggressive war in South Viet Nam, stepping up the war of destruction with its air force against North Viet Nam, and menacing the territorial waters of the Democratic Republic of Viet Nam with its naval forces, in an attempt to turn defeat and weakness into victory and strength, get out of its present impasse in South Viet Nam, and obtain at the conference table what it cannot win on the battle-field.

The so-called 'will for peace' and 'economic aid' recently mentioned by Johnson are but familiar tricks of psychological warfare of the US imperialists designed to soothe and deceive public opinion, and cover up their attempt to extend the war and enslave the Indo-Chinese and South-East Asian peoples. But such tricks, however perfidious, can fool no one. The US rulers know better than anyone else how many countries have courageously renounced the noose of 'US aid' and how many US personnel carrying out the 'food for peace' and 'alliance for progress' programmes have been expelled from Asian, African and Latin American countries.

IV
THE SOUND BASIS FOR SETTLEMENT
OF THE VIET NAM PROBLEM

The South Viet Nam army and people, starting with almost bare hands, have scored great achievements, recorded glorious victories and driven the US imperialists and their agents into a corner. In an attempt to retrieve this critical position, the US imperialists are embarking on new, extremely dangerous military adventures, thereby threatening peace in Indo-China and South-East Asia more seriously than ever.

In its March 22, 1965, statement, the Central Committee of the South Viet Nam National Front for Liberation exposed the US imperialists' policy of aggression and war, demonstrated the inevitability of their defeat, and made clear its stand on the South Viet Nam problem:

'The South Viet Nam people and their armed forces are resolved never to loose hold of their arms so long as they have not reached their basic goals, viz., independence, democracy, peace and neutrality. The South Viet Nam people are determined to go on striking hard at the US aggressors and their lackeys, and they are sure to win final victory. All negotiations at this moment are entirely useless if the US imperialists still persist in refusing to withdraw from South Viet Nam all their troops and war materials of all kinds and those of their satellites, and to dismantle all their military bases in South Viet Nam, if the Vietnamese traitors continue to surrender to the US imperialists the South Viet Nam people's sacred rights to independence and democracy, and if the South Viet Nam National Front for Liberation—the only genuine representative of the 14 million South Viet Nam people—is not asked to say its decisive say.'

The whole Vietnamese people and the Government of the Democratic Republic of Viet Nam warmly hail and support this correct stand of the South Viet Nam National Front for Liberation.

The Government of the Democratic Republic of Viet Nam has always held that the correct implementation of the 1954 Geneva Agreements on Viet Nam is the correct way of settling the South Viet Nam problem.

On April 8, 1965, at the second session of the 3rd National Assembly of the Democratic Republic of Viet Nam, Prime Minister Pham Van Dong once again made clear the position of the Government of the Democratic Republic of Viet Nam regarding the present situation in Viet Nam.

'The unswerving policy of the Government of the Democratic

Republic of Viet Nam is to strictly respect the 1954 Geneva Agreements on Viet Nam, and to correctly implement their basic provisions as embodied in the following points:

1. Recognition of the basic national rights of the Vietnamese people: peace, independence, sovereignty, unity and territorial integrity. In accordance with the Geneva Agreements, the US Government must withdraw from South Viet Nam all US troops, military personnel and weapons of all kinds, dismantle all US military bases there, cancel its 'military alliance' with South Viet Nam. The US Government must end its policy of intervention and aggression in South Viet Nam. In accordance with the Geneva Agreements, the US Government must stop its acts of war against North Viet Nam, cease all encroachments on the territory and sovereignty of the Democratic Republic of Viet Nam.

2. Pending the peaceful reunification of Viet Nam, while Viet Nam is still temporarily divided into two zones, the military provisions of the 1954 Geneva Agreements on Viet Nam must be strictly respected: the two zones must refrain from joining any military alliance with foreign countries, and there must be no foreign military bases, troops and military personnel on their respective territory.

3. The internal affairs of South Viet Nam must be settled by the South Viet Nam people themselves, in accordance with the programme of the South Viet Nam National Front for Liberation without any foreign interference.

4. The peaceful reunification of Viet Nam is to be settled by the Vietnamese people in both zones, without any foreign interference.

This stand unquestionably enjoys the approval and support of all peace and justice loving governments and peoples in the world.

The Government of the Democratic Republic of Viet Nam holds that the above-mentioned stand is the basis for the soundest political settlement of the Viet Nam problem. If this basis is accepted, favourable conditions will be created for the peaceful settlement of the Viet Nam problem and it will be possible to consider the reconvening of an international conference of the type of the 1954 Geneva Conference of Viet Nam.

The Government of the Democratic Republic of Viet Nam declares that any approach contrary to the above stand is irrelevant; any approach leading to a UN intervention in the Viet Nam situation is also irrelevant, because such approaches are basically at variance with the 1954 Geneva Agreements on Viet Nam.

Hanoi, May 1965

Are your four points pre-conditions? I asked Prime Minister Pham Van Dong. He smiled and answered:

Our four points are a position of principle, the basis for solving the Vietnam problem. If you want a serious solution, you must come back to our four points; they are the most reasonable and fair. The four points are an expression of our will, of our people's will. Let there be no illusions on this question: they represent a whole, each dependent on the other.

He had studiously avoided the word pre-condition. I wanted to press him. He noticed it and laughed good-naturedly, then quickly went on, speaking in a flowing cultured French (Pham studied in a Lycée Français as a child in Saigon, his native town):

Your military think that with fire and steel they can win. They are wrong. The problem of Vietnam poses a problem of universal conscience. That is why we have such moral strength. So much so that we can defeat steel and fire. Our fight is now a fight of all the peoples of the world against foreign domination. The question is to mobilize the peoples of the world to oppose United States aggression.

At that point, I decided to raise the question of international brigades. I knew from Salisbury, who had already interviewed Pham, that the Prime Minister did not see much value, militarily, in such brigades. But there was the political aspect. 'May I ask you an indiscreet question or rather preface a question with an indiscreet evaluation?' I asked him.

'Go ahead. If it is too indiscreet, I shall answer diplomatically,' he said, roaring with laughter.

I then said something to the effect that the whole world knows that the Socialist countries have not committed themselves enough to the Vietnamese struggle, that the split between major Socialist powers is hurting the DRV and the United States is taking advantage of it, that Vietnam is being isolated in a way by its own friends who buy off their consciences with a bit of material and military aid. In this light and since he himself had just said that his fight is a fight of all the peoples of the world against foreign domination, that is, American domination, should he not accept international brigades. They would certainly come from all Socialist countries which would tend to unify them, at least on the Vietnam question. Also they would come from those areas where the United States does dominate most, in Africa, Latin America, Asia.

Pham became very serious. He looked at me squarely and replied:

We agree that since, in fact, it is the people who are confronting the United States' attempt to dominate the world, then surely the time must come, will come, when we shall accept those people, accept international brigades, both armed and civil.

He paused, then added:

It is not just our destiny which is at stake here but that of all the peoples of the world—in a word, of all humanity. Let each man take conscience of what happens here and draw his own conclusion.

Pham Van Dong then talked about the South:

It has always been the South which has been invaded. It has been suffering for decades. The South has always been the centre of imperialist wars. We must re-win it completely. We are a very united people. We are united by the heart, however, not by directives. We love, respect and admire our southern compatriots. But it is not true that the NLF is directed by us. I learned of the Pleiku affair [the base of Pleiku had just been bombed three times in one day by the NLF] at the same time as your Pentagon did.

He returned to the South again later:

These atrocities you have seen here in the North are nothing compared to those in the South. If you say this, no one will believe you, but in the South, puppet troops often kill and disembowel the people. In the name of the dead as well as of the living, we will all wage this fight to the end.

We talked off the record again for a while, then walked out to the patio in back of the Palace. Finally, Pham Van Dong shook our hands warmly. As jovial and friendly as he was, one could feel that he was a man of steel, a tough, dedicated professional. To me he said: 'I know it is especially hard for you Americans who are honest and courageous, who try to tell the truth. We greatly admire you.' Then he embraced me.

IV

TO AND FROM NAM DINH

While still in Paris, I had read about Nam Dinh in a dispatch from Salisbury printed in the International Edition of the *New York Times*. He had written then that a significant portion of that city had been destroyed by American bombing raids. The Pentagon had taken up the issue with him, insisting that only military targets had been hit. On December 30, 1966, the day I arrived in Hanoi, Salisbury had filed another story on Nam Dinh. 'Are there or have there been military objectives in Nam Dinh?' he asked in print (December 31). His answer:

> The railroad runs through town and presumably there are freight yards and depots. There are a textile factory and a rice mill, both of which this correspondent saw. Both are operating, but the textile mill has been severely damaged. There is also a silk mill, which officials said had been destroyed. . . . Are there other war plants in town? This correspondent cannot say. He saw intensive destruction of civilian housing and ordinary business streets in considerable areas—damage so severe that whole blocks have been abandoned. These areas lie largely, but not entirely, in the vicinity of the textile plant. There is severe damage all over town. The bombed areas of Nam Dinh possess an appearance familiar to anyone who saw blitzed London, devastated Berlin and Warsaw, or smashed Soviet cities like Stalingrad and Kharkov.

I had brought the first three Salisbury *Times* pieces with me and when I met him, at the Reunification Hotel on December 31, he asked me to show them to him. He hadn't seen them yet, though he had heard of the Pentagon's reaction. 'Arthur Sylvester claims that Nam Dinh is strategic,' Salisbury told me. 'He insists that if you go down Main Street you'll see all those anti-aircraft batteries, and that's proof the city is important. Well, that's like saying that the guy who arms himself to fire back at you when you've already fired at him really intended to kill you all along.' I told Salisbury that I was going to Nam Dinh the next day. 'Take a good look down Main

Street and see how many anti-aircraft batteries there are,' he said. 'I sure as hell didn't see any.'

The next day, New Year's Day, at four in the morning, we started off for Nam Dinh. The road, Route No. 1, was crowded with trucks, bicycles and pedestrians. The truce was on, so I for one didn't expect an air raid, but the Vietnamese apparently did. Or else they had become so accustomed to travelling in the relative safety of night that they did so even on Truce days. In any case, by 6 A.M. the sky became light, the road lost much of its traffic—and we arrived at Phu Ly.

Phu Ly used to be a throbbing little agricultural and artifact centre, a provincial headquarters with 7,600 inhabitants. Today it has none. It used to have 1,230 houses. Today it has 245, and they have been abandoned. Tran Van Chi, Phu Ly's former mayor who had become mayor of the neighbouring town after moving there late in 1966, told us a little of his town's history. Phu Ly had been razed completely to the ground by the French in 1954—before Dien Bien Phu. Rebuilt after the Vietnamese victory, it was bombed by Americans for the first time on November 7, 1965. Since then, 1,124 bombs had been dropped on the city in eight raids. The school, the Catholic church and the dispensary (Photo 8a) had been destroyed.

Aghast at what I saw, I couldn't believe that Phu Ly didn't really hide some military objective. I asked to be driven up and down each street in a jeep; not one was paved, not one revealed a building (or building ruins) big enough to have sheltered a major factory. I then asked my driver to circle the town three times—at 300 yards, 700 yards, and 1,200 yards. The only possible objective I found, besides Route No. 1, was a small railroad bridge 1·2 miles from the school. The bridge had obviously been downed, then repaired. Later, I heard that the United States considered Phu Ly a rallying ground for supplies going south to the National Liberation Front. If so, it could have amounted to no more than a temporary stop, like a truck stop at some all-night diner along the old Boston Post Road.

Continuing on Route No. 1 from Phu Ly to Nam Dinh, we were struck by the extent of bomb damage along the open countryside. Almost every farm house near the road had been demolished or damaged or was surrounded by bomb craters. Every bridge (and the Red River delta of Vietnam is so thoroughly riddled with streams, canals and affluents that each mile of road has at least one bridge) had been knocked out—and repaired. In our relatively short ride, we must have crossed almost a hundred. Some were made of steel, repaired in wood. Others had been of stone, now were bamboo. Near Nam Dinh we crossed one bridge made completely out of cables; when planes attacked it, the cables on one side of the river were released and the bridge disappeared.

Route No. 1 showed traces of having been bombed extensively—but nowhere did we have to make a detour. There were bomb craters everywhere, but each hole had been filled and was quite navigable. Along the sides, at regular intervals, piles of rocks, dirt and rails awaited the next bombing.

We arrived at Nam Dinh's House of the People at 8 A.M. There to greet us with a speech, breakfast and documents was Tran Thi Doan, aged forty, the city's petite, pretty, charming mayoress (Photo 8b). She told us that Nam Ha province, of which Nam Dinh is the capital, was the largest in North Vietnam. Its population was 1·7 million. The city itself had been North Vietnam's third largest, but it was now mostly evacuated. One-third was in ruin, she said, 'as you shall see for yourselves'. While we were talking, one of her aides distributed the following document:

Document No. 3
REPORT ON US WAR CRIMES IN NAM DINH CITY
Prepared by the Administrative Committee of Nam Ha Province for the Committee for the Investigation of the US War Crimes in the DRV. Mimeographed; dated October, 1966; in English.

In their air war of destruction against the DRV, the US have perpetrated innumerable crimes: Massacre of civilians, destruction of property, devastation of populated areas, many prosperous towns and villages in North Vietnam. Nam Dinh city is one of their victims.

It is a densely populated area with a population consisting of 93,000, mostly of women and children crowding an area of over 5 square kilometres. Nam Dinh's population density is very high: 17,000 people per square kilometre. The city lies in the middle of an expanse of paddy fields on the right bank of the Red River, south of the Dao Canal, south-west of the Day River, and 30 km from the sea coast.

Nam Dinh is also a well-known textile city. After the last devastating nine-year war, it spent eleven years restoring and expanding its Textile complex. A series of new factories have been built. Nearly all of the population of Nam Dinh are workers and handicraftsmen working in factories among which is the Textile complex which employs 13,000 workers of whom 70 per cent are women. Handicraftsmen alone number nearly ten thousand.

Nam Dinh is also a famous cultural centre of North Vietnam. It boasts ancient historical sites and natural beauty spots such as the 'Scholar Campus', the Scholar Lane, The Vixuyên Lake, etc.... The talented poet Tran Ke Xuong was born there. Continuing

Nam Dinh's cultural tradition, general education schools have been vigorously developed. Nam Dinh city has two schools of the third level, six schools of the second level and twenty of the first level, with a total enrolment of 24,066 pupils. Besides there are many vocational schools such as an assistant-doctor school, technical school No. 3, School of Architecture, etc. Nam Dinh city has a big polyclinic with modern equipment and numerous beds, sanitary stations, maternity houses, nurseries, kindergartens, cinemas, theatres, and other public utilities. The workers' living quarter is one of the city's biggest installations.

Up to July 20, 1966, in 1,135 sorties, the US carried out 270 strafings and dropped over 2,000 bombs of all types* (some localities received thousands of shrapnel bombs), fired 1,800 rockets and hundreds of missiles on many villages, dykes, etc.

On January 17, 1965, at 10.37 A.M. (local time) a reconnaissance plane flew over the city at the altitude of sixteen km. On May 14, 1965, four jets carried out another reconnaissance flight over the city.

After a few months of reconnaissance, on June 28, 1965, at 7.30 A.M. (local time) when it was cloudy and raining hard, two F.105s and two F.4Hs from eleven km south of the city launched two Bullpup missiles on the living quarters of the textile workers. The first surprise attack killed ten civilians including two old men and three children, and wounded twelve others. During this raid, five members of the family of weaver Hoang Thi Sinh were killed (three children among them).

From early 1965 to September 20, 1966, the US conducted thirty-three air raids over Nam Dinh city (eleven times in 1965 and twenty-two times in the first nine months of 1966).

The Americans bombed and strafed many densely populated districts of the city like Hang Thao, Hoang Van Thu, Hang Cau streets, the workers' living quarters and so on. They bombed the Textile complex when the weavers were working and blew up the dyke protecting the city. The US went to the length of destroying hospitals, schools, nurseries, kindergartens and even churches and pagodas.

In their bombings and strafings of the city they have used various ultra-modern planes such as A.4A, A.6A, A.3J, F.105, F.4H, RB.57. . . . They have showered over Nam Dinh more than 700 bombs totalling 200 tons, including MK.81, MK.82, MK.83, MK.84 . . . , fired fifty-four Bullpups and 248 rockets. Particularly, in the two raids of August 4, 1965, and May 31, 1966, the Americans flew in as many as twenty-seven planes of all types, and poured more than one hundred bombs on the city each time.

* By November 1966, the total was 4,934 bombs.

US pilots have resorted to surprise attacks. From the 7th Fleet, US Navy aircraft made a quick dash through thirty km from the coast to the city, flying at various low altitudes and in different directions along the basins of the Red River and Day River, or at times very high, hiding themselves amidst dark clouds in rainy days or in morning mist. Most disastrous for the civilians were the fourteen night raids between mid-1965 and September 20, 1966.

During the thirty-three abovesaid air attacks against Nam Dinh, the US caused many losses in lives and property to the city's inhabitants. 89 persons were killed, among them 23 children, 36 women; and 405 wounded, among them 81 women, 44 old men and 41 children. 881 dwelling houses (accounting for 13 per cent of the city housing) with an area of 86,847 square metres, were detroyed, leaving 12,464 inhabitants homeless.

Many industrial and handicraft enterprises were attacked like the Textile complex.

While strafing Nam Dinh's populous quarters, the US did not spare hospitals, schools, nurseries and kindergartens. The city's hospital was bombed twice, and its consulting room, maternity room and X-ray room damaged. Tran Quoc Toan, Nguyen Van Cu, Ho Tung Mau schools were also destroyed. A kindergarten in the Textile complex was bombed time and again; many buildings razed to the ground and equipment damaged. Fortunately, all the children had been evacuated to safety. As public welfare facilities, hospitals were built in special areas with visible Red Cross marking; schools and nurseries bore no sign which might cause them to be mistaken for military targets. Churches, pagodas, holy sites with religious symbols have been strafed, damaged and wrecked by US planes.

Following are some typical air raids in which the US bombed and strafed several populated quarters:

(a) The April 14, 1966, air raid over Hang Thao street was one of the biggest.

Hang Thao street was a populous one, with a population of 17,680. People had evacuated before April 14, 1966, and there were only 2,300 left. They were workers and handicraftmen who had to stick to their factories, enterprises and cooperatives to live and work.

Before attacking Hang Thao street, US aircraft had carried out seven reconnaissance flights over Nam Dinh.

—At 10.35 A.M. (local time) on December 1, 1965, two F.8Us flew in from the South West;

—At 7.02 A.M. (local time) on December 12, 1965, two A.4s flew in from the South East direction of the city;

—At 10.32 A.M. (local time) on December 18, 1965, six aircraft flew over the city;

—At 2 P.M. (local time) on January 12, 1966, two F.4s flew over the Southern part of the city;

—At 3.35 P.M. (local time) on February 4, 1966, two four-plane formations operating in the South East and South West, twenty kilometres from the city, dropped anti-radar materials on the city;

—At 1.05 P.M. on February 18, 1966, two F.8Us flew from the South West to the North, nine kilometres from the city;

—At 1.06 P.M. on February 7, 1966, an unmanned plane flew over the city.

At 6.30 A.M., when those who had just come back from a night shift were still sleeping, those who were about to work were having breakfast, women were getting ready for their shopping or for their house work, and children were getting ready for the kindergartens or infant classes, two US planes came flying at low altitude along Ninh Binh Highway No. 10 and into Hang Thao, Hang Cau, Tran Hung Dao streets and Ben Thoc area, dropped eight MK.84 bombs killing forty-nine people, among them 15 children, 8 old men, 20 women, wounding 135 people and destroying 240 houses on an area of 31,440 square metres in which 810 households with 4,129 people were living.

—Mr Tran Dang Van, 30, married to Nguyen Thi Kim Dung, living at No. 28 Hang Thao street, was manager of Van Tuong Tailoring Cooperative. On April 14, which was the anniversary of his father's death, his brothers and sisters gathered at his house. On April 14 morning, Van went to his shop. Having finished feeding her baby, his sister Hoi was getting ready for her shopping. Her husband Xanh was sitting in a hammock, fondling his first baby, Vo Thi Thu Ha, who was five months old. The two sisters were busy buying things for the anniversary of their father's death at Dragon Market, when suddenly they heard a terrible bomb explosion. Seeing high columns of smoke in Hang Thao street direction, they rushed home. In their street they saw demolished houses and corpses all over the ground. What remained of their houses was only heaps of debris. Dung rushed to the tailoring cooperative's shop; it was also demolished. Together with the cadres of the district, she calmly cleared the ruins and it was not until 8 A.M. on April 15, 1966, that she found her husband's body still holding a pair of scissors in a hand. As for Hoi, together with her relatives, she cleared the debris of her house and at 9 A.M. on April 14, 1966, she found Xanh's corpse, still holding little Thu Ha, both wrapped up in the hammock. Ham Dinh citizens will never forget what Hoi said: 'I didn't expect that the death anniversary of my father would also be that of my husband, brother and child.'

—Mrs Nguyen Thi Quy, 36, became a widow in 1963, when she was expecting her fourth baby, Kieu Dung. She worked hard to bring up her four children: Nguyen Cao Thang, 11; Thanh Huong, 8; Thanh Thuy, 6; and Kieu Dung, 3. In May 1966, she evacuated her three daughters to Ninh Cuong village, Truc Ninh district. Thang went to Thanh Hoa to live with his great uncle. She remained in the city to produce joss-sticks. After some months, as she missed them very much, her mother agreed to let her bring back her three daughters to the city to spend some days with her.

On April 14, no sooner had Mrs Quy gone down to the kitchen to take the pot of soup, than a bomb exploded by her, wounding her in a leg. With the help of a stick she came up to see what had happened to her children but found no trace of them. The people in her street had to spend a lot of time digging out their corpses buried in the ground.

(b) A month after the air raid on Hang Thoa street, on May 18, 1965, US aircraft attacked Hoang Van Thu, a populous street next to it. Hoang Van Thu street was formerly called the Chinese quarter. The street was inhabited by 1,734 households with 7,856 persons. The houses there were built long ago, with some accommodating up to ten households comprising nearly 100 persons. In the street were many handicraft shops, eastern and western medicine shops, thread-producing co-ops, the Thanh Quan Temple of the Chinese residents and the municipal church. The Municipal Administrative Committee had evacuated most of the inhabitants and had air raid shelters dug. On May 18, there remained in the street only 230 persons. At 11.04 A.M., when the population was either lunching or resting and when it was raining heavily, the street was flooded and water filled up all air-raid shelters, foxholes and trenches, two F.4Hs flying at a 600-metre altitude dropped eight thin-shelled bombs causing many casualties. The victims did not have time to take shelter. Mr Duc, 38, a worker at a rice-husking mill, had just returned from his work. He was preparing lunch in the kitchen when he was thrown out by a bomb explosion in the middle of his house. The second bomb blast in front of the Cathedral threw him back into the first bomb crater full of water. His corpse was taken out five hours later from water and ruins. He died leaving a widow and three orphans. Mr Hung, upon hearing the bomb blast, hastily jumped into a trench full of water. A wall fell down into the trench and he got drowned, leaving a widow and two orphans. Among thirteen persons killed and eleven wounded, was Nguyen Van Vinh, 25, who had survived after the previous air raid on Hang Thao street. He moved to Hoang Van Thu street after his house was destroyed.

The air raid on Hoang Van Thu street resulted in great material losses: 372 houses which accommodated 1,129 households consisting of 5,555 people were destroyed or heavily damaged. The Cathedral area was bombed, the Jesus stone-cavern collapsed. The Lac Thien Temple and the meeting hall of the Chinese residents were demolished.

(c) The surprise night raids inflicted heavy losses on the population inside and outside the city.

—At 9.24 P.M. (local time), on September 12, 1965, two A.6As released sixteen bombs on the Textile complex killing six workers and wounding twenty-eight others at work.

—At 00.50 A.M., on July 4, 1966, two A.6As flew in and dropped fourteen bombs, wounding eleven civilians and killing a medical worker of the 4th living quarters in his sleep.

—At 11.38 P.M., on July 30, 1966, two A.6As dropped twenty-six bombs on Phu Long hamlet, My Tan village, in the outskirts of the city, killing twelve persons, including a whole family of seven, and wounding ten others.

(d) US attacked factories and enterprises which produced daily necessities for the people. They carried out nineteen air raids on the Textile complex on which they dropped more than 100 bombs, causing heavy losses.

(e) The US also attacked the dyke surrounding the city. On May 31 and July 14, 1966, they dropped six bombs on the two-kilometre long dyke which protects the city against floods, damaging many sections. The population in the city spent twenty days removing 1,209 cubic metres of earth to repair the damaged parts. One day later, the water-level of the Dao River rose to 0·4 m above street level and continued to rise to 0·9 m. During the last days of July, 1966, when the water level kept rising, at 11.38 P.M. on July 20, and at 2.28 A.M. on July 31, 1966, US aircraft repeatedly struck at this dyke.

The US have been dealt telling counter-blows: fifteen jet planes have been downed, many others shot ablaze, a number of US pilots captured. Along with the fight against US air attacks, the town folk have actively increased production so as to safeguard their lives. In the first six months of 1966, the evacuated city plants and factories have all fulfilled and overfulfilled the State plan.

Mayoress Tran accompanied us on our tour. Gentle, soft-spoken, rather shy, she seemed at first somewhat ill-equipped to be a cadre-woman. She took us to one of the workers' districts that had been heavily bombed (Photo 9a), explaining that 17,000 people used to live there before April 14, 1966, when US planes levelled the area. At the main crossroad of the district, a monument had been erected for those killed that day. Talking to people who grouped around us, we met Tran Thi Mai, a textile worker, who told us that two of the dead were her children.

We continued on foot, walking through the city. We saw street after street totally demolished (Photo 9b). Then we crossed a wide avenue which made me think of Salisbury's Main Street. 'Before we leave,' I told the mayoress, 'I must see your principal street.' She smiled and said, 'But you are on it.' I looked around: There were some fairly swanky villas, lots of shelters—but no anti-aircraft batteries. 'Where are your defences?' I asked the lady mayor. 'We have millions of defenders,' she replied, 'every man, woman or child who can carry a gun will defend our country.' I was about to try again, to be more specific, when suddenly the alarms went off.

'It can't be,' I blurted, 'It's Truce!' She laughed at my naïveté as she shouted her first order. And now I saw a leader. With amazing rapidity but without creating panic she cleared Main Street of all traffic, hustled us towards shelters and gently but firmly coaxed everyone around to the right places. At first I was led to an individual shelter, but I couldn't quite fit into it so I was moved on to a collective one. There I ran into Wilfred Burchett, the Australian newsman who was with us on the tour. 'Couldn't fit, eh? You must be as fat as I am,' he joked. Burchett, who had covered Asian wars for two decades, was well equipped. He not only had two cameras strapped around his neck but also a tape recorder on one arm. He decided to record the noise created by the raid and stood at the entrance of the shelter, microphone in hand, while I peeked out at the street to photograph Nam Dinhians crouching by their individual shelters ready to jump in at the appropriate signal from their cadremen. I then spotted an anti-aircraft battery atop a three-storey brick building across the avenue. I could see the muzzle of the cannon turning slowly away from us and I wanted to photograph it but was not permitted to do so. The amazing thing, however, was that I did see only one—at a moment when all cannons must be raised.

The raiding party turned out to be a lone pilotless reconnaissance plane. After a few minutes we heard a thunderous explosion; a missile had brought the plane down. At 10.10, twenty minutes after the first siren warning, the all-clear sounded and we quickly resumed our walk.

Not far from Main Street, we again entered a heavily bombed district. As we walked through it, I spotted an old man with a small child (Photo 10b) and approached him. Unless it had been planned that way, my interview with him was completely accidental. His name was Tran Dai Nghia. He told me how his only daughter, his son-in-law and two of their three children (plus two other children playing in their house) had been killed during one of the raids. 'I hate Johnson,' he said. 'He killed my family. Please denounce his crime.'

Nghia, who was sixty years old, worked in the textile plant and was now taking care of his only surviving grandson. But he was getting help, he said, from a Cuban named Carpentier. I asked the mayoress if this Cuban might not be Alejo Carpentier, the great novelist, who had visited Vietnam shortly before me. She said yes. (In February I had the occasion to see Carpentier, who was then and is at this time of writing Cuba's cultural attaché to France. He verified the story.)

For three hours, all I saw was bombed-out houses, schools, hospitals, dikes, blocks upon blocks of rubble. I saw the famous railroad siding which the Pentagon claimed was a major military target. It was no bigger than the station at Mamaroneck. The rail line, which follows the river, had been repeatedly struck, but was always quickly repaired. It was functioning perfectly that day. Around the Cathedral, in the centre of town, three-hundred houses were down. Near the textile mill, a half-dozen brand-new low-cost housing projects had been melted to the ground, while others, hit dead-centre, had been cleared of inner walls—and of people. The outer walls still standing, swaying ominously in the January breeze, were pock-marked from countless rocket bursts. The mill itself, slashed on one side, was still operating. The large rooms had been emptied of most of the machinery, but a few workers were busy producing cloth. A trench leading outside to safety had been cut right through the floor.

As I left Nam Dinh that day, heading east towards the sea, I could not help thinking that the city had been the victim of old-fashioned World War II saturation raids. As we drove on, I kept asking myself, 'What is so goddam militarily important about a textile mill?'

The road from Nam Dinh to Ninh Binh is a major thoroughfare going south. Expectedly, therefore, it had been heavily bombed. But from Ninh Binh to Phat Diem, it became increasingly narrow. It was asphalted only near Ninh Binh and it certainly was not a transportation route since it came to a dead end at Phat Diem. Yet it too had been blasted. Every house along the way was crippled, every bridge had been hit—and repaired.

Phat Diem is a two-mile-long, one-mile-wide Catholic centre; of its 5,700 inhabitants, 4,200 were then Catholic. There were fifteen churches in town and one pagoda-styled Roman Catholic cathedral, fronted by a grey, cement-lined lake, which gave it a second exposure. Producing fishnets, artifacts, but mostly fish and fishermen, Phat

Diem is twenty kilometres (twelve miles) from the sea, connected to it by small canals or feeder rivers never more than sixty feet wide. At best, these rivers and canals could give access to small gunboats. But the bridges across these waterways were low and fixed, making it impossible for ships without collapsible masts to pass. Naturally, as in any fishing village, the waters surrounding Phat Diem were usually crammed with junks and sampans.

To the United States Air Force, however, Phat Diem was a naval base. Thus, from March 1965 to January 1, 1967, its planes bombed it fifty-seven times. Five of the fifteen churches have been destroyed (Photo 10a), hundreds of people have been killed. I was told by inhabitants that on Sunday, April 24, 1966, American bombers struck the church of St Francis Xavier while mass was in progress, killing seventy-two, wounding forty-six. The church certainly did look as if it had suffered a major blow.

Being so close to the sea, Phat Diem did not benefit much from Vietnam's normally effective alarm system. Planes from Seventh Fleet ships, coming in low to escape radar nets, could be upon the city in seconds. On July 10, 1966, for example, ten planes attacked the town at three o'clock in the morning, catching most people in bed. All of the witnesses I talked to, including two sisters, Vu Thi Phoi and Vu Thi Thanh (Photo 10c), refused to believe that the United States can really justify its claim that Phat Diem was strategic. As Vu said:

They fly over us almost every day, we only count when they fire at us or drop bombs. But every day, as they fly to bomb Ninh Binh or Nam Dinh, they come over us very low. They can tell. They know we don't even have a single factory here, not a single ship with a cannon on it. They have raided us fifty-seven times, bombed us and strafed us, yet not once has a ship fired back—except for our fishermen who fire rifles. Why? Because our ships are only poor fishing junks. They're not armed. The American Air Force knows this. They tell you lies. But they know the truth.

V

HAIPHONG

Travelling to Haiphong during the night of January 7–8, 1967, from Thai Binh province was a formidable adventure in logistics. The roads, often no more than just hardened soil, were never paved. Each river or canal we had to cross presented new dimensions of Vietnamese ingenuity. Once we had to abandon our jeep, cross the river in a small rowboat and pick up a second jeep on the other side. At another place where crossings were dangerous even at night, we used a canoe while our jeep was being ferried over on a raft.

Shortly afterward, around 11 P.M., we saw the sky light up ahead. We were hustled off to a bunker shelter (built by the French in 1953), then after the all clear drove on for eight miles to still another river. It was that bridge that had been bombed while we were in the bunker. 'Please go to the command post for a cup of tea,' said the officer. 'We'll call you as soon as the bridge is repaired.' I looked at it; it was completely destroyed. I was certain we'd be stuck for the night. Less than two hours later, however, the officer returned. 'You may cross now,' he said. A whole new bridge, forty feet long, had been built—out of bamboo. And it was sturdy enough for two loaded trucks which were ahead of us.

Altogether, we must have crossed twenty waterways that night—via floating bridges, suspension bridges, cable bridges, rope-ferries, boats of all kinds. When we had to wait, people were warm and friendly, always offering us tea, bananas and tangerines. It took us six hours to travel fifty miles, but it was a worthwhile experience.

We began by touring Haiphong. A city of 960,000 people (230,000 in the city proper), it appeared to me as by far the most active spot in all of Vietnam—and January 8 was a Sunday. Factory chimneys were spewing smoke, fishing sampans were floating up and down the canals, and the port was bustling (Photo 11a).

In 1954, Haiphong had only seven factories. By 1967, it had become the second industrial centre of the country, with eighty regular and five-hundred shop-type factories. Most of the population, however, lived from fishing, using the Cua Cam River, a Red River tributary, to go out to sea (as did the regular ships). The port itself had been enlarged since Vietnam's independence so as to be able to receive ships of more than 10,000 tons. On January 8, the ships in dock were Russian, Chinese (Photo 11b) and Polish. Most were loading coal, which North Vietnam exports. The port master told me that in the last three months ships from non-Socialist countries which had come into Haiphong had included ones from Greece, Norway, Sweden, England and France.

On the way to City Hall, we stopped for a few minutes at the Museum, in front of which an American Navy jet shot down over Haiphong was displayed (Photo 12a), and at the city's Exhibition Hall. On view at the time were over three-hundred paintings by contemporary Haiphong artists. All but four of the three-hundred were typical Social-Realist works, depicting American aggression and the Vietnamese's efforts in combating it. The remaining four were still-lifes. At the entrance to the Hall was a huge, twenty-foot-wide banner with gold letters sewn on red cloth. It read: 'Our nation is very beautiful, our people are very heroic, our work is very glorious; our arts must render, must sing all this in order to contribute to the common effort.' It was signed: Phan Van Dong, Prime Minister.

When we talked to Pham, we brought up the show. He asked us what we thought of it and we replied that we found it somewhat regrettable, considering Vietnam's great artistic tradition, that every artist had felt obliged to paint in Western styles. Pham agreed; but, he said, we are all under attack, all fighting together against an aggressor, all dependent on each other. Isn't it normal, under such conditions, that artists cannot—indeed should not—think about their own fulfilment? After all, it is the fulfilment of their motherland which is at stake. Against this monolith, this hyper-mechanized, extraordinarily technical machine which seeks to kill us, we have only human beings. Should not every human, then, join the effort for all?

At Haiphong's City Hall, on January 8, 1967, Léon Matarasso and I sat down with various members of the city's War Crimes Investigating Committee. They told us the following facts (in French, transcribed from my notes):

Document No. 4
US RAIDS ON HAIPHONG
The city proper of Haiphong has not yet been bombed, but greater Haiphong has, and very extensively. During 1966, 1,500 bombs and 1,000 rockets have been dropped in the area, also various air-to-ground missiles and, on four occasions, fragmentation [CBU] bombs. These were dropped on Cat Ba Island, just off the port, a

fishing centre. From March 26, 1965, to January 8, 1967, Cat Ba has been bombed 256 times. In July 1966, greater Haiphong was raided twenty-one times; in August, 123 times after more than 400 reconnaissance flights. In this period [July and August] 349 people have been killed, 698 houses destroyed. In Cam Lo village, west of the city proper, thirty-six people were killed, including sixteen children, during one raid on August 2, 1966. That village is in no way militarily strategic; it is eight kilometres [five miles] from the centre of Haiphong.

American planes have continuously harassed and often attacked ships coming into or leaving Haiphong, while in international waters. No foreign ship has been attacked within Vietnamese waters. On October 31, 1965, United States planes attacked the Chinese freighter 'Nam Hai No. 146' while it was cruising seventy miles out of Haiphong. On April 19, 1966, the Polish freighter 'Broniewski' was hit by cannon fire as it made its approach. On August 1, 1966, the Soviet ship 'Ingvor' was strafed. On August 2, 1966, it was the Soviet ship 'Medin' which was hit. On August 29, 1966, two Chinese commercial ships, No. 1018 and No. 1019, were bombed and strafed for three solid hours while en route to Haiphong; No. 1018 was sunk, No. 1019 was badly damaged. Many sailors were killed.

The three main lighthouses guarding Haiphong harbour have been raided fifty-six times, the major one forty-five times. On January 2, 1967, this lighthouse was under attack almost continuously between the hours of 0700 and 1800.

The major bombings in the Haiphong area include: the hamlet of Truong Thoa, on December 23, 1965; An San on December 5, 1965; Lap Le on November 1, 1966; and Cam Lo on August 2, 1966. Cam Lo, with a population of 3,512 in 759 houses, was raided at 0600 when twenty-three planes dropped twenty-eight explosive bombs and numerous rockets, killing thirty-six, wounding thirty-three, destroying one infirmary.

Cat Ba, an island of more than 10,000 people, mostly fishermen [Photo 12b] and peasants, was first struck August 5, 1965. Many fishing boats were sunk. From then until November 1966, there have been 128 attacks on the island, including seventeen on August 28, 1966. In total, 238 private dwellings, thirty-seven public buildings, fourteen hospital buildings and two schools have been destroyed. One kilometre-long section of the capital, in which 5,000 people lived, was completely obliterated [Photo 14a]. Twenty-three fishing boats have been sunk.

When the Haiphong officials ended their general remarks, two witnesses were brought in, Le Thi Moi, thirty-five, and Hoang Xuan Xuong, twenty-seven, both members of the Do Son fishing cooperative situated on the beach of Haiphong. Neither could speak French, hence their testimony was translated by a Vietnamese official. Mme Le, wearing the white headband of mourning, spoke first:

My husband is a fisherman. He is always at sea. On August 12, 1966, United States planes bombed our cooperative and strafed the sea waters in front of us, but no one was hurt. The next day, as my husband was navigating one of the cooperative ships going out to sea, another raid took place. I had brought, with others, the nets that morning and was still on the shore. So I saw the raid. My husband was not hurt. In the afternoon, I left the cooperative to evacuate my mother and my six children. I had become convinced, because there were so many raids on the cooperative, that they would be safer somewhere else. When I returned at 7 P.M., I heard that the planes had returned during the afternoon and that my husband had been killed at sea. His body had been retrieved and was on his bed when I got home. He was buried at 1 A.M. and the planes were still flying above us. My husband was a fisherman. His ship was not armed.

Mr Hoang, a fisherman with two children, spoke next:

We had been attacked many times before, but we kept on fishing. We still keep on fishing.* On November 23, 1966, four American planes attacked our fishing boats. First they dropped four bombs but they fell ten metres away. They turned and came back and dropped six more bombs. That time, they hit two of the three ships in our group, including mine. Four among us were wounded, three in the head and me in the leg. Then the planes left. Our ship was sinking but we made it close enough to shore before it sank so that our people rushing out from shore could save us. So we all survived. We are still fishing, all four of us.

I asked him details of the co-op:

We have forty-five ships in the cooperative in all. The biggest is eleven tons, the smallest five tons. None of the ships are armed, nor did we shoot at that time because we still did not carry rifles. Now we do. We were two kilometres off shore at the time of the attack. So far, we have had two ships sunk outright, many damaged but repaired. Of the 245 fishermen in our cooperative, three, including the husband of Le Thi Moi, have been killed.

Where was he when Mme Le's husband was killed, I asked. 'I was

* Rare is the country whose population eats more fish than Vietnam—J.G.

on a ship not too near his. I saw two planes drop four bombs, then strafe his ship.'

The witnesses left and we were asked what we wanted to verify while there was still light. I said that first I wanted to go back to the port. We did. I went up to the Chinese ship, asked if I could inspect it. Just from the deck, I was told, and no camera. The deck was indeed pock-marked from machine gun and cannon fire. One of the crew members, who spoke French, told me that this is normal. 'Every ship is strafed,' he said, meaning every Chinese ship.

Next I walked over to the Seamen's Club, which is right in the port area. Built during colonial days, it features a bar, a dance floor, pingpong tables, a barbershop, novelty and artifact stores. I spotted a group of Russian sailors drinking something clear-coloured, which I took, thinking in a movie-type cliché, to be vodka. It was, but Vietnamese-made—out of rice. The Russian sailors seemed to be enjoying it. Two spoke English. 'Have you ever been strafed?' I asked. 'No,' one answered, 'but always buzzed, always provoked.'

Rejoining Matarasso, who had gone to verify the bombing of Lap Le (which was quite extensive and had no visible military objective, he said), I asked to see Cam Lo. It took us twenty minutes to get there because of the heavy late Sunday afternoon traffic, but once close to it no explanations were needed. Huge expanses of land looked as if a mammoth bulldozer had systemically churned it up—except that scores of houses had once rested on it (Photo 13). We toured the area; the only possible target was a small house-tile factory complex, which had not been hit. Just about everything else had, however, from tiny mud huts to the marketing cooperative (Photo 14b). A monument to the dead had been erected at the village square; the people referred to it as 'the hate monument.'

Matarasso and I spoke to many of the people of Cam Lo that afternoon and evening—to widows and orphans, militia men and peasants, workers and fishermen. But one will forever remain engraved in our memory. She was a pleasant, attractive, thirty-two-year-old worker at the tile factory. Her name was Nguyen Thi Bau. When I met her, she was with her seven-year-old son, Phan Ngoc Bao. Before August 2, 1966, her husband, Phan Ngoc Can, forty-two, had been a district judge. They had four other children: Phan Thi Ngoc Ha, thirteen; Phan Ngoc Huan, eleven; Phan Ngoc Hanh, eight; and Phan Thi Ngoc Hiep, four (Photo 15a). Thus, their youngest and oldest were girls.

She began, calmly, softly, obviously under full control:

My husband and I were married on December 23, 1952. We had a very happy marriage. Our oldest girl was thirteen, so we could both work. When we came home in the evening, our kids always received us with joy. They would prepare the meal before we arrived and, over dinner, give us a report on their day's activities. Since I usually got home first, we often walked together part of the way to meet their father. Sometimes, if it was still early, he would take them to the river behind our house for a swim. Our oldest was a good swimmer and the next two were pretty fair. Our children were good students at school; they won many commendations from the teachers. We were a happy family.

We were sitting on some rocks and debris in the area where scores of houses had been demolished. She continued, still outwardly calm, still speaking softly, still quite in control:

And then came the second of August 1966. I went to work at 5 A.M. that day, taking my youngest child, my little four-year-old girl, with me. I had asked my oldest to come to the factory to take her back later. On the way to work, I had bought ten loaves of bread and would ask the oldest to take them back with her. She showed up at the factory at 5.20, but it wasn't time for me to start yet, so we talked for a while. I asked her if papa had left. She said no, that he had a special meeting that day and would go to it directly, so he didn't have to leave home until 6.30. I then told my daughter to hurry home with the bread so he could have some before leaving. She did, and at 5.30 I started my work. I work at the oven where the roof tiles are baked.

A few minutes after I started working I heard the alarm. Like everyone at the factory, I went to the shelter. Then I heard the planes and a lot of explosions. I asked a Militiaman where the bombs had fallen; I knew it must have been fairly near since our shelter was shaken. The Militiaman told me it was in my neighbourhood and told me to rush home. I did, and as soon as I turned the corner over there [pointing], I saw it—our home had vanished.

She rose. We did too. She walked slowly toward a hollowed spot in the ground. 'That's where my house used to be,' she said, still calm, her voice still clear. Then she continued:

Our house had been razed to the ground. But I noticed that my bicycle was at the entrance to the shelter over there. We had built a trench from the house to the garden, so for a second I hoped that everyone in my family had made it. But then I saw my third child, Hanh, being carried on a stretcher. He was dead.

She paused, looked toward the place where the shelter used to be, with Bao at her side walked over to it and, pointing to a small black

91

sign, said: 'That was the shelter' (Photo 15b). Still under control, she went on:

A Militiaman was uncovering it. It had been completely buried with dirt from an explosion a few feet away. The first body to be pulled out was my second child Huan, a boy of eleven. The Militiamen who were digging were all our neighbours. I kept calling for help because I knew that the rest of my family must be in the shelter, perhaps still alive though buried with earth. I ran hysterically from side to side until I noticed my youngest son, Bao, this one, all covered with mud and blood but walking, coming toward me. He called 'Mama, Mama'. I found out later that he had been projected out of the shelter and thus, though wounded on his head, cheeks and legs, had survived. I kept hugging him and then took him to the infirmary post so he could be cared for. He was trembling all the time.

She stopped again, sat down. Then, still composed, she continued:

I had hoped and I was still hoping, even then, that the two girls, my oldest and youngest children, had not had time to reach home with the bread and so might still be alive. With great fear, yet hope, I finally pulled myself together and asked Bao as calmly as I could if he had had fresh bread that morning. He said yes. And so I knew my girls had reached home.

While I was at the infirmary, a Militiaman came to tell me that they had found my husband. He was dead. They had also found a neighbour and his four children and another neighbour's child in the same shelter with my husband. Two of the first four were alive, one with a broken skull, the other with a shattered leg. But they were still alive. So, I thought, might be my daughters.

They kept searching for my girls but they couldn't find them. Maybe, I said to myself, Bao was wrong. Or maybe they had gone elsewhere. That night, I was at my husband's funeral when I finally learned that they had found my girls. They were sitting all the way in back of the shelter, my oldest holding my youngest in her arms—buried alive. My youngest child was clutching a piece of bread in her hands.

She got up to go. Where do you live now, I asked her. 'In a room at the factory,' she replied. I asked if I might see it. She hesitated. 'It's very small . . . well, alright.' And we walked together, she with her only surviving child, Matarasso and I, followed by our guides and Haiphong officials, silently, to the factory, down a small alley, to her room. Two beds, one next to the other; a few bits of clothing and a rice-straw rug on the wall. 'I'm sorry it's so dark,' she said, 'but I keep that rug over the window because it gives out on where we were. I don't want to look out there all the time.'

She sat down with Bao on one of the beds and as we talked instinctively reached for a little red book lying on the bed. She fingered it with such feeling that I asked what it was. 'Nothing,' she said, 'just an old diary.' Whose? 'His.' I asked her if there was a passage from it that she wanted to read us. She hesitated. 'Let's go to the lounge,' she said, and led the way. Once there, she sat down with Bao in an armchair and started reading. Her voice was finally beginning to break:

> Every day I try to draw lessons from my work. I try to understand myself, control myself, find what is good and bad in me to develop the former and curtail the latter. I must study myself endlessly. I must learn from the people, learn *with* the people. I must study the books and the history of my work [law]. I must learn from friends. . . . I must never take pride in success. I must never despair of failure. I must constantly learn from experience in order to keep progressing.

I asked her if I could have the diary photostated, then, glancing through it I noticed that the last three pages were in a different handwriting. Who wrote this, I asked. Her eyes reddened. 'I did.' May I know what you said? 'The first page, those five lines are just a quick note written after my husband's funeral, on August 2, 1966. The next two pages are a letter to my surviving son, written six weeks later.' Would she read them, I asked. She was reluctant to do so. But she did. Her voice broke completely and tears swelled in her eyes, then ran down her cheeks in total abandon. Her first entry was bitter. It read:

> I shall never be able to forget that my husband Can and my children Ha, Huan, Hanh and Hiep were killed by the American aggressors. Nor will the hate that I nurture for these assassins ever be extinguished.

The second passage was quite different. It was addressed to the child sitting next to her:

> Bao, my dear child. You cannot imagine how much I suffer from the death of your father and brothers and sisters, so much that I have to keep reminding myself that I must go on, that I must endure, in order to bring you up. I must survive for if not, with me dead, you would be all alone, without love. And yet, every day of my life is a Calvary, my darling. Can you ever understand how affected I am by the death of Huan, Hanh, Ha and Hiep? My

darling, forgive me, but I would like to die. You are too young to understand, too young to console me. If I could only die, I say to myself, I would no longer suffer. But that would be selfish, and so I shall go on for you and you shall never know how painful it will be for me to live for you.

An hour or so later, Matarasso and I said good-bye to the people of Cam Lo, to our Haiphong hosts, and started the journey back to Hanoi—104 kilometres inland on Route No. 5. It was heavily bombed all the way. 'Well,' said Matarasso, 'at least the centre of Haiphong has not been raided. Did you notice how that city is laid out? Like Venice! Canals everywhere and bridges, so many bridges, and so close to the houses. If your Pentagon decides to go after the bridges, it would be a massacre.'

On April 20, 1967, the United States declared the centre of Haiphong strategic—and began bombing it.

VI

HOSPITALS

One of the most charming, humorous, intelligent, capable men I met in North Vietnam was Dr Pham Ngoc Thach, the Minister of Health. Educated and trained in France, he was a genuinely dedicated public servant, physician and leader, who seemed indefatigable as he rushed around from province to province, checking the damage to hospitals here, the success of inoculation programmes there, the training of medical cadremen everywhere. He was also very proud of this work, and with good reason: Everywhere I went, the health programme seemed to be highly successful. And this despite the fact that everywhere I went it seemed as if medical facilities—hospitals, infirmaries, dispensaries, etc.—were bearing the brunt of all air-raid attacks. Both of these points were made in the following document I was given at the Ministry of Health:

Document No. 5
US CRIMES AGAINST DRV HEALTH SERVICES
Prepared by the Committee for Investigation of US War Crimes in Vietnam of the DRV Health Ministry. Mimeographed; dated October 1966; in English.

Prior to the August Revolution, the Vietnamese people had to live a life plagued by misery, hunger and diseases. All the health organization of the colonialists throughout the country consisted of 47 hospitals, 9 maternity houses in various cities and towns. There was only one medical worker (assistant doctor or doctor) for every 180,000 people; when the labouring people got ill they lay where they were and hoped for the best.

After the successful August Revolution, the DRV State right from the first set to itself the task of improving the people's health. But the newly-founded revolutionary administration had to cope with the French colonialists' new aggression.

After the restoration of peace, public health in Vietnam faced unprecedented difficulties. The people's health was considerably impaired by nearly 100 years of slavery followed by nearly 10 years of war.

The struggle against diseases and for the protection and improvement of the people's health was considered an urgent task which was to promote their living conditions, production and national defence.

If formerly in the countryside, there was not a single medical establishment and in 1955 there were only 200 village medical stations and maternity homes, in 1964 there were, all over North Vietnam, 5,274 medical stations and maternity homes, i.e. 100 per cent of the villages in the delta and nearly 80 per cent of the villages on the highland were supplied with medical stations and maternity homes. There are health centres where the villagers receive medical attention free of charge.

Infirmaries have been set up at construction sites, forestry exploitation sites, factories and mines. There is now one hospital bed for every 100 workers.

Small-pox and cholera were wiped out as early as 1957, infantile paralysis has been in the main done away with. The anti-trachoma work is being expanded to almost all villages. In the mountain regions, malaria has been in the main liquidated.

Various preventive measures against tuberculosis are on the upgrade. Broad masses have been periodically given anti-TB injections. Thanks to this, the ratio of primary TB infections was reduced from 2·5 per cent in 1958 to 0·8 per cent in 1964.

Great importance has also been attached to the anti-leprosy work. The Ministry of Public Health has built several new leper sanatoria, among them Quynh Lâp sanatorium is the biggest, equipped with every kind of device for the best treatment and capable of accommodating 2,600 patients.

Many great achievements have also been recorded in the protection of women and children's health. The death rate of lying-in mothers also recorded a sharp fall from 2 per cent before the August Revolution to 0·04 per cent in 1964 (50 times less). Infant mortality was only 2·58 per cent in 1963 as against 30 per cent in pre-revolution time (an 11-fold fall).

At the end of 1964 every province and district had its hospitals. The number of hospital-beds, including those of village infirmaries, has increased by 16 times as compared with 1954.

In 1964, the number of physicians trained was ten times greater than in 1954.

Since the August 5, 1964, incident* and particularly since February 1965, 74 health services have been bombed, strafed or

* The first US bombing of North Vietnam.

destroyed by the US in their air war against the DRV (up to June 30, 1966).

After a short period of attacks on the communication lines they intensified their strafing of hospitals. Within 3 months, June, July and August 1965, they concentrated their bombing on, and destroyed, 6 big special hospitals and sanatoria, 6 provincial hospitals, and 10 district ones from Quang Binh, Nghê An up to Son La, Yên Bai. The total of the strafings and bombings during those months was as follows:

—In June 1965, they bombed and strafed 28 times the health services in various places,
—In July 1965, 19 times,
—In August 1965, 23 times.

For example, on June 14, they attacked two hospitals in Quang Trach (Quang Binh) and the Ba Dôn sanatorium; on July 25, they strafed the Tuong Duong, Con Cuòng and Nghê An hospitals and the Quynh Lâp leper sanatorium.

US Defense Secretary McNamara has time and again boasted that with US reconnaissance technique they have photographed North Vietnam territory inch by inch and can detect the tiniest targets. So, how could a hospital be taken for an army barrack? Take the Quynh Lâp leprosy sanatorium for example. It was built in a secluded place, far remote from populated areas and highways. The Quynh Lâp Sanatorium was subjected to US air strikes 39 times within 12 months.

Up to now, nearly all the hospitals of the larger provinces have been bombed: hospitals in Vinh Linh, Quang Binh, Ha Tinh, Nghê An, Thanh Hoa, Son La, Yên Bai, Nam Hà, Phu Ly, Bac Thai, Phu Tho, Hoà Binh, and so on. . . . Especially in provinces in the fourth zone from Vinh Linh to Thanh Hoa, besides provincial hospitals which are now heaps of ruins, most of the district hospitals, village medical stations and maternity homes have been attacked.

Many establishments have been bombed 6, 7 times; there were places attacked day and night for 39 times killing doctors who were treating victims of US bombings.

For instance, the Quang Binh hospital was bombed 11 times on:

Feb. 7, 1965	Sept. 19, 1965
Feb. 11, 1965	Sept. 23, 1965
July 24, 1965	Sept. 24, 1965
July 27, 1965	Oct. 9, 1965
Sept. 6, 1965	Oct. 14, 1965
Sept. 11, 1965	

And the Ha Tinh hospital 17 times on:

July 30, 1965	Nov. 11, 1965
Aug. 1, 1965	Nov. 18, 1965
Aug. 13, 1965	Nov. 19, 1965
Sept. 10, 1965	Apr. 20, 1966
Sept. 24, 1965	May 10, 1966
Oct. 5, 1965	May 12, 1966
Oct. 8, 1965	May 14, 1966
Oct. 10, 1956	May 21, 1966
Oct. 13, 1965	

The air raids on the Thanh Hoa anti-TB hospital (July 8, 1965), the Yên Bai hospital for 3 days running (July 9, 10, 11, 1965) and the Quyn Lâp leper sanatorium (from June 12, 1965, to June 24, 1966) are typical.

The Thanh Hoa TB hospital with its 600 beds is one of the large establishments for anti-TB treatment and research in the North, adequately equipped for TB treatment and scientific research. From 1960 to 1964, 1,821 in-patients and tens of thousands of out-patients were given treatment in this hospital. On July 8, 1965, at 7 A.M., while the hospital was busy with its daily chores, 40 US jet aircraft dropped over 100 ton-bombs destroying nearly 50 hospital wards and a number of civilian houses in the vicinity of the hospital, killing over 30 people including 5 doctors and wounding many others. Six hundred patients who were under treatment were deprived overnight of a place where they could have appropriate medical care.

On the days that followed, at 7 P.M. on July 14, 1965, and at 10 A.M. on August 8, 1965, many US planes came to bomb and strafe for hours the remaining houses, killing another 4 civilians.

In Yên Bai province, on an area less than an acre, for three days running (July 9, 10, 11, 1965), US planes dropped hundreds of bombs on hospitals, offices, the province health services, the pro-phylactic hygiene station, the anti-TB station and the health centre for mothers, killing 58 people.

Most of the victims were doctors and medical workers. The US destroyed 30 buildings, thereby depriving 140 patients of accommodation and suitable medical care. There were cases where a mother and her child were bombed right at the moment when they had just arrived at the city hospital for treatment. The con-sulting room X-ray research units, the laboratories, and the treatment wards were all destroyed.

The Quynh Lâp sanatorium was the biggest DRV centre for leprosy treatment and research. It was built in June 1956 and its expansion was completed in 1959. It was situated in an area away from the coastal populated areas of Quynh Luu district, Nghê An province, with its small and big houses fully equipped with modern facilities, capable of accommodating 2,600 patients at a time. For the last five years, 1,000 out of the 4,000 people affected by leprosy were cured and sent back to their families to enjoy a normal life.

At 8 P.M. on June 12, 1965, while the patients were asleep, many formations of US planes came and dropped hundreds of bombs and fired many rockets on the hospital, then for 10 days running they bombed and strafed another 12 times. The US bombs and rockets destroyed and burned down 160 buildings consisting of houses, hospital wards, research units, laboratories, consulting and pharmaceutical rooms, the club, cooperative shops and the power-station. 139 patients were killed and over 100 others wounded.

On July 16, 1965, the DRV Ministry of Public Health issued a statement denouncing such bombings.

But the next year, at 8.30 A.M. and 12 A.M. on May 6, 1966, US planes again came and bombed and strafed the new premises of Quynh Lâp leper sanatorium located at Quynh Lâp village (Quynh Luu district, Nghê An province), causing 30 dead and 34 wounded, of whom 10 seriously.

The Ministry of Public Health once again issued a statement, on May 16, 1966, strongly condemning such raids.

Yet, at 7 A.M. and 10.15 A.M. on June 12, 1966; at 10.30 A.M. on June 19, 1966; and 10.31 A.M. on June 24, 1966, dozens of US jet and B-57 planes again came and bombed and fired missiles and rockets at this new establishment. During these air-raids, 8 patients were wounded and three others killed.

On International Children's Day, June 1, 1966, the mother and children health centre Thanh Hoa hospital, one of the big poly-clinics in the DRV, with 500 beds fully equipped with all kinds of modern devices, was greatly damaged by US planes. This air-raid caused 14 dead and 28 seriously wounded, most of whom were women and children. Nearly 50 two- or three-storeyed buildings were burned down and all the equipments of the laboratories of the pharmaceutical and X-ray rooms and all the patients' wards, the club and lecture hall were seriously damaged.

On June 22, 1966, at 3 P.M., many formations of US aircraft bombed and rocketed the Bac Thai hospital, a hospital of the mountainous region, and destroyed it completely. In this air attack 9 persons lost their lives.

All together, in the last year to June 30, 1966, eighty establishments were destroyed with their special equipments heavily damaged; 76 cadres and medical workers were killed and 27 others wounded; 253 patients massacred, and 236 others injured; 57 civilians living near those hospitals were also killed by US bombs.

By conducting the above-said atrocious bombing and strafing, the US were nurturing the hope to intimidate the Vietnamese medical workers and paralyse every activity of the DRV Public Health Service.

However, contrary to the US wishes and despite those heavy losses, in the years of 1965 and 1966 the DRV Public Health Service grew and became stronger than ever.

—Hygiene and disease prevention activities as well as the anti-US and patriotic movement of prophylactic hygiene developed on and unprecedented scale.

—The care for the health of mothers and children, kindergartens and pre-school classes also continued to develop.

—The bombed hospitals have been reconstructed and even expanded. Up to May 1966, the total number of hospitals has doubled that of 1965. Leper sanatoria and anti-TB institutions have been rebuilt.

—Prevention and treatment of diseases, the combat against various social diseases and other tasks of the DRV Public Health Service have continuously been developing quantitatively and qualitatively.

—The medical personnel has been also increasing; the number of doctors and medical workers has increased by 1·5 times and that of midwives and medical workers in villages and agricultural co-ops has nearly doubled.

Naturally it was impossible for our group to check out but a small fraction of the scores of hospitals destroyed by United States attacks. We were told that from February 7, 1965, to June 30, 1966, there had been 170 such raids.* We did, however, verify a few, including the hospital of Son La (Photo 16a), bombed from the eighteenth to the twenty-second of June, 1965; the hospital of Bach Thai (Photo 16b), hit the twenty-second of June, 1966; and some of the hospitals and medical stations of Yai Bai (Photo 17a), which were all destroyed during five raids on three consecutive days, July 9, 10, and 11, 1965. Most of these hospitals, which are to the west and northwest of Hanoi, had been steeped in the fight to eradicate malaria, a fight that the Vietnamese have been consistently winning.

* For a complete list, see Appendix D—J. G.

In this respect, it might interest doctors (and laymen too) to read the following short document:

Document No. 6
Given me by the Ministry of Health. Mimeographed document; undated (but early 1966); in English.

BASIC ERADICATION OF MALARIA IN LARGE AREAS OF NORTH VIETNAM

By Doctor Professor Dang Van Ngu
Head of the Institute of
Malariology, Parasitology and Entomology

For thousands of years malaria wrought great havoc among our people, chiefly among the minority people of various nationalities living in the mountainous regions. It caused general debility, splenitis and low birth rate, so that there was hardly any increase in population in those parts. At the same time it prevented the people in the plain, the densely populated area, from moving to the mountainous regions to settle down there. Malaria was one of the main factors which exerted a bad influence on our people's life and production.

Under the French domination, it developed more than in any other period. The French colonialists did nothing to do away with malaria. On the contrary, they considered it one of the favourable factors which enabled them to easily rule over our people.

When the resistance war against the French colonialists started, millions of our compatriots were so enraged at the enemy that they left the plain in spite of the malaria and went to the mountainous regions to build up our resistance bases there. In our bases the people and army used various prophylactic and preventive measures against malaria such as proper food, cleaning up houses, using mosquito nets, better drainage, smoking and burning mosquitoes and killing them.

That was why malaria produced no great effect on production and our fighting capacity. On the contrary, many areas known in the old days as places of high ratio of malaria now became relatively healthy during the many years they gave residence to the Government offices and army units.

Immediately after the restoration of peace, our Party and Government made it their urgent task to give our people and cadres anti-malaria drugs to restore their health. After the completion of the plan for economic rehabilitation, right from the beginning of 1958, the Party and Government drafted out the programme for 'basic eradication of malaria in 8 years'. The Institute of Malariology was established with the task of studying measures to put into practice the Party and Government's line.

Thái Nguyên was chosen as a pilot-province because of the complexity of its malarial situation, nationalities, customs, habits and social life. In 1960, after three years of active struggle against malaria, the ratio of malaria decreased more than 30-fold, so that tens of thousands of workers who, in 1961, went to Thái Nguyên from the plain to build up the steel centre were not in the least afraid of being affected by malaria.

The third Congress of the Vietnam Workers' Party included in the first five-year plan (1961–1965) the task of eradicating malaria in the main from the whole of North Vietnam with a view to creating favourable conditions for its complete eradication in the second five-year plan (1966–1970).

After only three years of struggling against malaria on a large scale in the North, the ratio of malaria has decreased more than 100-fold. Formerly, in the mountainous regions, out of 10,000 people there were approximately from 1,000 to 1,500 who were carriers of malaria germs; but at the end of 1964, out of 10,000 there were only 11. Even during the US war of destruction against the North, the ratio is growing much smaller. In the first 6 months of 1965, out of 10,000 mountainous people there were only 6 carriers.

Over recent years, in order to carry out the Party and Government's line of making the mountainous regions catch up with the plain, millions of people and cadres in the plain have gone to the mountains to work either temporarily or as settlers to develop economy and culture there without any anxiety about malaria.

The masses have voluntarily and satisfactorily carried out their daily anti-malaria work. In spite of the fact that they have to encounter the enemy's daily air-raids, all villages in Vinh Linh, Quang Binh and Nghe An provinces give regular attention to curing malarial patients and to isolating the foci of infection.

Those are initial but great achievements of the public health service of our regime under the leadership of the Party and Government. The successes scored in the anti-malaria drive have been an active contribution to the development of economy, culture and higher standards of living, and at the same time have created favourable conditions for national defence. They have been beneficial to the life of the national minorities in the mountainous regions, contributing therefore to the success of our Party and Government's policy as regards nationalities.

It is crystal clear that the work bears a social character for it requires the willing participation of the broad masses after the level of their general knowledge of science and hygiene has been improved. That is why malaria has been eradicated on a grand scale, constituting a further step in our people's cultural life and hygienic conditions.

How were we able to achieve such advances? We must reaffirm that it was thanks to the political regime of our State, to the particular attention of the Party, Government and President Ho concerning the people's health that we succeeded.

We obtained these initial achievements in the anti-malaria programme in the North in the course of our struggle to improve the life of millions of our compatriots, particularly of the national minorities. The anti-malaria teams, the research workers and their staff endeavoured to overcome all difficulties and hardships in serving the people. We also enjoyed the all-out assistance of the peoples of the fraternal socialist countries who shared their experiences, drugs and other anti-malaria essentials.

In the various talks that we had with Minister Pham Ngoc Thach, the names of two hospitals kept recurring: the TB sanatorium of Thanh Hoa and the leprosarium of Quynh Lâp. These hospitals were not unknown to me; quite a bit had been written about their destruction in the liberal press in the United States. The other members of our team also knew about them, and so we were anxious to visit them. We were told, however, that Quynh Lâp was in too dangerous a zone. Besides, it had been so completely destroyed that it no longer served as a leprosarium. All the surviving patients had been evacuated and we could go and see some of them who had been relocated nearer to Hanoi. Thanh Hoa, on the other hand, was within access. It was also dangerous, since United States planes continue to bomb the city regularly. Nevertheless, a trip was arranged. But first, we were given this document:

Document No. 7
THE K-71 HOSPITAL FOR TUBERCULOUS PATIENTS
AT THANH HOA
Published by the DRV Red Cross Society, Hanoi. In English. 1965.

K-71 hospital is built in a picturesque locality some kilometres from the head-town of Thanh Hoa province. It is composed of some fifty buildings in which are housed 600 patients and a staff of 243 members including 32 doctors and pharmacists. A big hall is used for scientific meetings and weekly theatrical performances of movie-shows. Important laboratories are attached to this hospital.

K-71 is one of the essential links in the anti-tuberculous network set up a decade ago by our health service. After the re-establishment of peace in 1954, throughout the country there were in all 80 beds for consumptive persons incorporated in a general hospital. What is to be done to care for hundreds of thousands of patients and to carry out prophylactic work?

Our medical workers have buckled down to a double task, that of finding on the one hand the methods of detecting the disease, of treatment and prophylaxis suitable to a poor country; on the other hand, of fostering cadres and setting up a medico-social organization to cope with the situation. A major part of these researches have been conducted at K-71 with the co-operation of the Central Institute for Tuberculous Patients and other departments.

For the detection of the disease, we make use of radiography but resort mainly to bacteriology. The sole use of BCG-test has given us entire satisfaction since 7 years.

The joint treatment by INH, strepto and PAS proves to be too expensive and difficult to apply in a country which runs short of means; after painstaking researches we have perfected an original method of treatment by INH in conjunction with injections of Filatov's biostimulines in the pulmonary acupuncture zone (omo-vertebral area). Applied in tens of thousands of cases, this treatment has shown as efficacious, if not more, as the association of INH, strepto and PAS. It is not too expensive and can be handled by a rural nurse after a few months' training.

Of late, we have striven to use together the injections of Bacillus subtilis and INH and the results bid fair to be satisfactory.

We have resumed the researches on dead BCG and found that, killed piecemeal in one month at 43 degrees Centigrade, BCG show themselves as immunizing and allergic as the living BCG without having their disadvantages. Applied on a large scale since five years (several millions of vaccinations were given) the killed BCG have revealed themselves most efficacious.

K-71 has actively taken part in all these clinical and immuno-logical researches.

However, these researches do not reflect all the activity of K-21 hospital, which covers all Thanh Hoa province and its 1,700,000 inhabitants. The dispensary of the hospital is a model of its kind in our country and has become the pilot-centre for the organiza-tion of the struggle against tuberculosis in various provinces.

In this extra-hospital organization, we must overcome two major difficulties. First, like all developing countries, we must complement the intra-hospital treatment by large-scale extra-hospital treatment. This can be successful only thanks to a close attendance on the patients. Inspired by an initiative of the dispensaries of the city of Hanoi and the province of Nam Ding, Thanh Hoa province is able to secure this attendance by 'groups of patients'. These are small groups of from 10 to 20 patients according to their living quarter which enables them easily to see one another. They appoint their group leader who is most of the time an in-patient having long stay in the hospital. They give counsel to one another concerning the regular taking of drugs, the strict observance of the regulation on rest and hygiene. The doctor or nurse of the dispensary regularly attends their meeting or gives them all necessary advice or information. Thanh Hoa province has now 725 groups of patients numbering over 10,000 tuberculous patients.

The second major hitch is the problem of shortage of hospital beds which is solved successfully in Thanh Hoa under the form of small rural anti-tuberculous station, consisting of an old communal house or huts built with the assistance of the population. In general each of these stations houses from 10 to 20 tuberculous patients who provide themselves with bedding, bowls, and cooking utensils. The medicines are supplied by the State but the patients have to feed themselves by their own means. Usually the local agricultural cooperative would allocate them a patch of land near their station, and they can use their 'curative agent' labour to farm this land so as to eke out their daily ration. The hospital attendant or sanitary agent of the village works in these stations which are also centres for anti-tuberculous struggle and propaganda for general hygiene. He keeps the BCG vaccination book and at the same time encourages the inhabitants to sink wells and build hygienic latrines.

Thanh Hoa province has made the best use of this initiative. Some stations are run in common by many villages, some others have even become anti-tuberculous stations for the district. Thanh Hoa has now 94 of these stations totalling 1,984 beds.

All this work requires from the doctors of K-71 hospital that they make regular trips to supervise the treatment as well as the prophylaxis of tuberculosis and lung diseases.

Thanks to this organization, Thanh Hoa province was able to make from 1960 to 1963 213,863 vaccinations on newly-born babies and 1,450,388 vaccinations and revaccinations on children and adults (our killed BCG vaccine has made it possible for us to increase the immunity of allergic persons by vaccination and revaccination). Moreover, the prevalence rate dropped from 1·12 per cent in 1960 to 0·61 per cent in 1963.

For more ample details we can mention the case of Quangyen village in which this rate has continually fallen since 1960.

Year	Number of Inhabitants	Ratio of Incidence Radio	Ratio of Bacillary Incidence
1960	3,056	0·88%	0·22%
1961	3,153	0·63%	0·28%
1962	3,251	0·58%	0·12%
1963	3,470	0·37%	0·11%

Thank Hoa province is proud of its hospital for tuberculous patients and the success of the anti-tuberculous struggle won through the zeal of the medical staff of K-71 hospital. The other provinces of our country strive to take advantage of the experience gained by K-71 hospital to intensify their anti-tuberculous struggle. At many congresses of the International Union Against Tuberculosis we have introduced the experience learnt in our country, a sizable part of which comes from K-71 hospital of Thanh Hoa province.

On July 8, 1965, at about 8 A.M., that is the rush hour, 40 American jet planes dropped, for over one hour, more than 100 bombs including 500-kilog-bombs on K-71 hospital, causing casualties among 40 patients and destroying most of its buildings.

On July 14, 1965, around 6 P.M., American airplanes again attacked the hospital, destroying all that was left standing, killing 2 patients and injuring many others.

The city of Thanh Hoa, which is about one-third of the way from Hanoi to the 17th parallel, had been bombed as heavily, if not more, than Nam Dinh. Once the home to some 50,000 people, by January 5, 1967, it was almost completely evacuated. Nearly every stone building in it had been destroyed and the centre of town had been pulverized. It was there that once flourished the 500-bed Thanh Hoa Province Hospital, a sleek, modern complex of eleven blocks, completed in 1964. Now it was nothing but ruins, having been smashed by 1,000- and 2,000-pound bombs for one solid hour on June 1, 1966 (Photo 17b). The hospital director, Dr Tran Van Quy, who showed the hospital to our team, said that he personally had seen the planes dive very low, not only bombing but also firing rockets and machine guns at the buildings and at people trying to run away from them.

Around this hospital were blocks upon blocks of houses and small shops—all in rubble. The area was almost four miles from the Ham Rong (or the 'Mouth of the Dragon') bridge, which was the nearest military 'objective'. That bridge, in fact, had been target No. 1 in the

Thanh Hoa area for American planes since the bombing began. Attacked more than one hundred times, the bridge was battered, pock-marked and worn. Since April 1965, reported *Time* magazine (January 2, 1967), 'Virtually every type of jet aircraft the US Navy and Air Force have in Southeast Asia—F.104s and F.105s, F.4s, A-6s and A-4s—has had at least one crack at it. Hundreds of tons of bombs have been dropped. But the bridge still stands.' The United States admits having lost nine planes over the bridge; the Vietnamese figure is seventy-eight, including thirty-seven in one single day. In the meantime, perhaps because of United States airmen's frustrations at not being able to knock it out, everything else in the area, within dozens of miles, has been bombed, rocketed and strafed.

Such was the case of a little hamlet called Hoan Kim, for example. Six miles off the main road, it was attacked during the night of January 6, 1967. I was not there, but other members of our team, including Jean-Pierre Vigier, the French physicist, and Wilfred Burchett were. They told me how they heard the attack, saw the tracers and inspected the town afterward: of the hamlet's fifty-two houses, eleven were destroyed and twenty-five were badly damaged. They found no possible, even imaginable, military target within five miles of the hamlet.

Nor were there such targets near the Thanh Hoa TB sanatorium. Situated in the low hills outside of the city, seven miles from the nearest concentration of buildings, surrounded by shrubs or rice paddies, clearly marked with red crosses, the sanatorium buildings were unquestionably non-military. Yet they were almost totally destroyed (Photo 18a). As far as I was concerned, Dr Pham Ngoc Thach's charges were fully justified.

Meanwhile, on January 3, 1967, at the Ministry of Health, I interviewed Dr Nguyen Van Oai, one of the surgeons from the Quynh Lâp leprosarium. He told me that:

At 2000 hours on June 12, 1965, I was on duty when United States planes came in from the sea, flying very high. I thought that they had passed by when suddenly the shrieking noise made me realize that they were diving. They dropped twenty-four bombs and rockets. One rocket hit the building I was in, but I was not hurt. Most of the bombs hit the hearby hills and we were plastered by flying rocks and debris. The night nurse was on the floor and had 60 per cent burns, but she survived. Only one man, a leper, died during this raid.

The next day, June 13, we evacuated all the sick. It was a very hot day; the sun was beating hard and the wind, too, was hot. Nevertheless, we completed the evacuation by twelve noon. Those who could walk helped those who could not. But they became very thirsty and in the hills where we had taken the sick, in the caves we were to use for shelters, there was no water. So, many of the stronger lepers and most of the staff returned to the hospital to fetch supplies and especially water, making various trips, giving the water to attendants who would give it to those too ill to care for themselves [Photo 19a], then returning to get more water for themselves and for later. Thus many of our patients and staffers were on the hospital grounds at 1345 hours when American planes returned to bomb and strafe us for almost an hour. This time the centre of the hospital complex was hit and totally destroyed. The carnage was so vast that we had to ask people to come with baskets to pick up pieces of bodies. Of the hundred or so personnel, fourteen women attendants, five nurses, one doctor and three assistants were killed. So were 111 patients on the spot, nineteen later. There were sixty-seven wounded. To save some of them, we had to operate at once and so we set up tents near some caves and did it then and there. I must have been at the makeshift operation table for most of the rest of the day [Photo 19b].

The next day, June 14, some of the patients went back to the hospital to search for their belongings. We tried to stop them, but not very firmly. Even I was now convinced, with the hospital completely destroyed, that the Americans would not return. Yet at 0700 and again at 1400, they struck again, bombing and strafing. They strafed anything that moved, and all of us staffers as well as many patients were dressed in white uniforms. That did not stop them. On the contrary, we stood out against the brown and green surroundings and so became immediate targets. I actually saw patients running on crutches being machine-gunned by the planes.

On June 15, the planes came back again—three times. At 0410, 0610 and 1350. On the sixteenth, they struck at 0700, at 1300 and at 1400. But in these raids, only one man died because by now we were all safely concealed in caves or were away, having been transported elsewhere during the intervening nights. There were two more raids on the seventeenth and one on the twenty-first, and then more all year, thirty-nine in all to June 24, 1966. Altogether 140 people died. But, in a way, the worse aspect is that all the lepers were dispersed. Our research, our treatment, our facilities were all concentrated in one area. Now, each small hospital or sanatorium where these lepers have been distributed has to duplicate the work for a few at a time. The whole thing is absolutely criminal.

Later that day the doctor and I went by one of the clinics in Hanoi where some of the lepers were being cared for. Three of them were there, all relatively cured. They were Hoang Sinh, thirty; Duong Thi Lin, twenty-four; and Vu Thanh Mui, twenty-seven. Each spoke for a few seconds. Mr Hoang said that he had been almost cured prior to the raids and had been working as a nurse:

I was on duty during the second raid, on June 13. I saw the planes make many turns, then start dropping the bombs. I tried to help but then a bomb exploded near me and I lost consciousness. When I came to, I was bleeding a lot and someone was bandaging me.

Miss Duong said that she was taking a walk when the plane arrived the first time:

I hid out and stayed away from the hospital until the next day. Then I returned and the planes came again. They turned and re-turned. They bombed from the northwest, especially the centre. There were lots of bombs. I saw a lot of dead.

Miss Vu remembered mostly the first night 'because of the light'. She thought that:

rockets make a lot of light. I was one who took refuge in the nearby hills. On the second day I was taking a siesta when the alarm sounded. I ran toward the shelter when the bombs hit. There were so many bombs I couldn't see anything.

Dr Nguyen added:

And, you know, the Americans knew very well what they were doing. Our leprosarium was very famous in Asia. Every doctor— and, I'm sure, intelligence agent—knew where it was. Besides, they had often reconnoitred the area. I personally saw seven or eight reconnaissance planes fly very low over our leprosarium before the first attack.

Dr Pham Ngoc Thach, the Minister of Health, later told me that he was convinced that the United States was deliberately and continuously bombing Vietnam's health centres 'in order to demoralize us'. But on the contrary, he said:

we have renewed, restrengthened our efforts. Since September 1965, we have solved the problems of water, trash and vaccination. We have installed a double-compartment system of septic tanks so that no epidemic can start. We have built individual water wells for every five families. We have vaccinated every child in the country against diphtheria. We have decentralized every hospital, yet we have one within reach of almost everyone; just in Thanh Hoa province, we can perform major operations or cope with the most serious disease at any of twenty-two hospitals. Despite the massive bombings, we have had no epidemics in the North. In the South, with supposedly so much help from the most sophisticated technical country in the world, there are epidemics all the time. The reason is simple. We care about our people. The Americans do not.

VII

SCHOOLS

Shortly after returning to Hanoi from Nam Dinh, where I saw various schools completely smashed by United States bombing raids—specifically the large nursery complex (Photo 18b)—the Ministry of Education of the DRV handed me the following document:

Document No. 8
US CRIMES AGAINST DRV SCHOOLS
Prepared by the Committee for the Investigation of US War Crimes in Vietnam of the DRV Education Ministry. Mimeographed; dated October 1966; in English.

The Vietnamese people have a traditional passion for knowledge. However, under the domination of the French colonialists, 95 per cent of the people were illiterate. Each province had only ten primary schools, there were no more than twenty elementary schools throughout the country, and the number of secondary schools could be counted on the fingers of one hand.

After the success of the August 1945 Revolution and the coming into being of the Democratic Republic of Vietnam, our Government paid immediate attention to the struggle against illiteracy which was carried out simultaneously with the struggles against famine and foreign aggression. . . . In the 1964–1965 school-year, there were 30,000 university students in North Vietnam (i.e. fifty times as many as in 1939, the peak year of educational development under the French rule). The Vietnamese language is being used as a medium in Universities. The number of pupils of general education schools amounted to 2,914,277 (i.e. 513 per cent more than in 1939). In addition, nearly one million children under six attended infant schools. 60,000 were trained in various vocational schools into middle-level technicians for economic and cultural branches, and millions of adults while engaging in production or other activities attended supplementary cultural and technical classes.

In spite of many difficulties, the Vietnamese State and people have paid great attention to building educational establishments.

111

There is one primary school for every village and on the average, one elementary school for every two villages, and in many delta provinces each district has a secondary school. In all North Vietnam, there are twenty-eight universities and 140 middle-level vocational schools.

Universities are large-scale projects furnished with adequate equipment for both teaching and scientific research. Most of the secondary schools are two-storey buildings furnished with libraries, laboratories, work-shops, gardens, clubs. . . . The primary and elementary schools and infants' classes were built in finest and most accessible places in various villages. Whenever one sees tall and beautiful buildings among shady trees one can be sure they are educational centres. It is hard to mistake them for 'military targets'.

On August 5, 1964—the day when the US began their escalation war in North Vietnam, they immediately strafed the Xuan Giang primary school in Nghi Xuan district, Ha Tinh province, burning one class-room with many tables, benches and teaching aids. At noon that day, the elementary school on a hill in Hong Gai provincial centre was destroyed by US bombs.

On February 7, 1965, the US raided the secondary school in Dong Hoi provincial centre. On February 8, 1965, three schools built on a hilly slope 300 m. long 232 m. wide in Ho Xa (Vinh Linh) were also air-raided. 132 bomb-craters were found on this area and a number of 200 or 250 pound dud-bombs were collected. Seven pupils were killed. Le Duy Minh, a literature teacher of the 10th form, was killed, leaving his 20-year-old wife and a child.

On February 8, 1965, afternoon, the infants' class of Mistress Nguyen Thi Hoa in Ho Xa district town was bombed, the class-room was heavily damaged and many tables and benches were smashed.

Also on February 8, the Dong Hoi secondary school and the Ly Ninh elementary school in Quang Binh province were bombed

According to still incomplete statistics, by the end of September 1966, 294 schools of the DRV had been air raided, comprising 21 infants' schools, 232 primary and elementary schools, 18 secondary schools, 15 low-level and middle-level vocational schools, 1 Teachers' College, 5 complementary education schools, a low-grade seminary and a high-grade seminary.

The schools subjected to air raids belong to fourteen provinces from Vinh Linh area, Quan Binh, Nghe An, Thanh Hoa provinces in the former 4th zone to the mountain provinces of Son La, Yen Bai, Lai Chau, Tuyen Quang, etc. Thus, the area subjected to air raids has been expanding and the scale of the air strikes has been increasing.

The US have used every type of aircraft, from Skyraiders to up-to-date jet planes such as F.105, F.4H, etc., which took off from the 7th Fleet and from US military bases in South Viet Nam and Thailand.

They rocketed schools in Ho Xa (Vinh Linh) and Thach Khe (Ha Tinh). They showered anti-personnel fragmentation bombs on the Thach Tan school in Thach Ha district, Ha Tinh province, and on the Phu Loc primary school in Phu Ninh district, Phu Tho province. In the August 13, 1966, air-attack against Phu Xa hamlet, Nhat Tan village, in the vicinity of Hanoi capital city, 2,000-pound bombs and anti-personnel fragmentation bombs killed mostly pupils.

In Thanh Hoa, after a temporary suspension of the bombing of North Viet Nam the US resuming the bombing on January 30, 1966, bombed the Hai Hoa primary school, killing or wounding twenty-four pupils. In Nghe An, thirty schools were attacked in 1965. In the first six months of 1966, thirty-one schools were raided. In Vinh city, the network of schools in the populated area was completely destroyed. The US bombed and strafed the Vinh Teachers' College, the elementary teachers' school, the Vinh secondary school and twelve primary and elementary schools in this city.

Ha Tinh is the province where schools have been subjected to the most frequent US bombings. All told, 118 air raids were directed against schools in this province: one raid on August 5, 1964, sixty-four raids in 1965, and fifty-three raids in the first seven months of 1966.

Most atrocious was the bombing of the Huong Phuc elementary school in Huong Khe district, Ha Tinh province, on February 9, 1966. That day at 4.30 P.M. US aircraft flew in when the pupils of the 5th form were attending teacher Thai Van Nham's geography lesson. They quickly slipped into trenches beside their class leading to air-raid shelters. Teacher Thai Van Nham was the last to take shelter. Immediately, bombs rained on the scene, some on the class-room, others on the shelters. Earth filled up trenches and shelters. This air raid killed thirty-two 5th-form pupils and one other. There were pupils who died in the trenches still clasping their class-mates and holding books and pens tight in their hands.

Besides the thirty-three killed, twenty-four more pupils and one teacher were wounded. On March 1, 1966, a press Conference was held by the Ministry of Education denouncing these crimes.

The Huong Phuc school was then the 134th school victim of US bombing. Yet between March 1966 and September 1966, 160 more schools were targets of US bombings and strafings.

It is to be noted that the US *conduct their air raids on schools during class time.*

Many schools other than Huong Phuc have been bombed during class time. Take, for example, the elementary Van Son school, Trieu Son district, Thanh Hoa province. One cold morning in late December 1965, a group of US planes came and dropped six bombs in a line near the school. Soon after that came another group of jets releasing another six bombs in a perpendicular line to the previous one.

The bombs fell on the 6th form classroom. Most of its forty-two pupils were girls from 12-14. These bombs weighed 2,000 pounds each, their craters were 6 metres deep with a diameter of 9 or 10 metres. A number of pupils dispersed through communication trenches into mountain caves. (This village being situated near a mountain.) Several others went in the direction of the fields but as their communication trenches ended before they reached safety, nine pupils among them lost their lives. Whole bamboo groves uprooted and blown up, fell upon the pupils; communication trenches were almost filled up with mud blasted by the bombs.

Here are some more cases: on September 25, 1965, the Primary-Elementary school of Quynh Tien (Quynh Luu district, Nghe An province), already evacuated away from military and economic targets, was beginning its new academic year. The teachers were giving the lessons, when US planes came and dumped bombs on the school. Thirty-one pupils of the 4th and 5th forms were killed or wounded, some killed at their very desks. A school mistress was also seriously wounded. Though many schools had their class times shifted to early morning or evening, they were also bombed and strafed. Schools in the Nam Dinh city were air-raided on May 31, 1966, at as early as 5.20 A.M. So were the elementary and secondary schools of Yen Bai provincial town the same day. The primary and elementary schools of Dan Thuong (Ha Hoa district, Phu Tho province) were attacked at 6.30 P.M. On September 10, 1966, the primary school of Hao Binh (Ha Bac province) was also attacked at 8.45 P.M. while a complementary course was in session; two classrooms completely collapsed. The crèche of Trung Son co-operative (Thieu Nguyen village, Thieu Hoa district, Thanh Hoa province) was attacked at the very moment when mothers handed over their babies to the nurses before going to their afternoon work. Among the seventy killed by US bombs there were fifteen babies in the crèche; some nurses were grievously wounded.

There were localities where US bombing raids were launched against pupils on the way home from school as in the case of the infant class (Hop Thanh village, Trieu Son district, Thanh Hoa province). It was 11 A.M. on an early spring day in 1966, seventeen little pupils, on their way home, had cautiously split into small groups. They were approaching the highway when a group of jets rushed in and fired rockets. No sooner had some of them hidden themselves down the roadsides while six others were making for dug-outs than US pilots released nine bombs from 50 to 100 kg. All the six were killed.

US bombing and strafing of schools have caused considerable losses of life: up to September 1966,* 331 pupils have been killed and 172 others wounded; 35 teachers killed and 32 others wounded.

The province which has sustained the heaviest casualties is Ha Tinh: 118 US air raids on schools have resulted in 101 pupils and 14 teachers killed and 76 pupils and 16 teachers wounded.

Ha Tinh alone has had thirty-seven schools completely destroyed, twenty-six schools in Thanh Hoa are out of use.

Despite the US raids and the daily casualties they cause to our young generations, the Vietnamese Government and people are determined to step up the development and consolidation of our education.

In the 1966–67 school-year all the schools have resumed work as scheduled. The number of schools has increased by 7 per cent, and the pupils by 6 per cent; secondary school pupils by 28 per cent over the previous year.

I had numerous occasions to verify the bombings of schools—beginning with Hanoi itself. But these were big schools in populated areas. What I hadn't yet seen were small provincial schools. And so I asked our hosts if they could schedule a trip to a small hamlet in an isolated section of a strictly agricultural province, where I might stay all day talking to farmers, teachers, students. My hosts arranged for such a trip on January 7, 1967. The village we visited was Thuy Dan in Thai Binh province, below Haiphong. We arrived there at 4 A.M. and remained until after dinner that night. Not only did it give me a chance to investigate the bombing of a small rural school, but it also allowed me to obtain a good understanding of how ordinary Vietnamese people behave under attack. It was there, for example, that I saw the Militia shoot down an American plane, as I described in the introduction.

Thai Binh province is very flat, totally agricultural and completely surrounded by water, either rivers or the sea. It is also interlaced with affluents or effluents of the Song Hong (Red River), which are interconnected by canals. The province is therefore dangerously dependent for its safety on dams and dikes. Only two roads connect the

* See Appendix E—J. G.

province with the rest of Vietnam: Route No. 10, which links Thai Binh city with Nam Dinh, and Route No. 39, which crosses the province and goes on to Hanoi. There are about 1,270,000 people living 900 to the square kilometre, mostly raising rice, producing salt or fishing. During the French occupation there were no industries at all; now home utensils and agricultural tools are manufactured locally.

The first air attack on Thai Binh was on August 13, 1965, I was told. From then until November 20, 1966, it had been raided 881 times (bombs being dropped 227 times, the rest being strafing attacks) in 242 different places by up to seventeen planes per raid. Total number of bombs dropped during this period was 1,399, plus 1,450 rockets, twenty-three air-to-surface missiles and thousands of 20 mm. cannon shots. Provincial cadremen to whom I talked insisted that the vast majority of raids came right after the rains, when shelters were full of water. Schools, they said, are bombed during school hours. Also, though provincial towns are rarely defended with anti-aircraft batteries, American planes always try to catch people by surprise; they feint towards one place, then double back and dive at another.

This, I was told, is the manner in which six planes hit the town of Thuy Dung. Comprising no more than one-third of a hectare, in which forty-nine families in 118 houses were organized in an agricultural cooperative, it was bombed on December 21, 1965, at 5 A.M., catching most people still asleep on a cold day. Six bombs are all it took to kill thirty-one and wound forty-eight.

Then there were the hamlets of Dong Loi and Lac Dao, two kilometres from Thai Binh city. They were first strafed at 2.20 A.M. on January 26, 1966, when two planes dropped four bombs. Finally on June 29, 1966, at 1845, eight planes dropped twenty-four bombs and strafed with rockets, killing twenty-three and wounding fifteen.

And then there was Thuy Dan, a combination of three hamlets producing five tons of rice per hectare (as compared to 1·2 tons during the French occupation). As I spent the morning of January 7 wandering about the town (Photo 20a), I couldn't possibly imagine why it had ever been bombed. All the buildings were made of mud and rice-straw, the roads were of dirt, the fields were flat. As in any strange land, the kids were as curious about me as I was about them. I watched them go to school wearing their regulation anti-pellet hats, which can be made in minutes from rice-straw; I watched them watch me in groups whenever I stopped to investigate something (Photo 20c), or standing barefooted in their doorways. And I watched them scramble to the shelters during the four alarms that shattered the morning calm. There were no cars in town, no electricity, no telephones. The nearest and only possible target in the area was a small hydraulic-pump bridge one kilometre away, four kilometres from the sea, whose function was to regulate the water level in the rice paddies and keep the salt water out.

Yet on October 21, 1966, at 10.30 A.M., Thuy Dan was hit—and hit hard. Six American planes, coming in from the sea, overflew the village, then returned. Two stayed high, four low. One plane dropped two bombs on An Tiem, one of Thuy Dan's three hamlets, killing nine. Then two planes let loose one bomb each, hitting only rice paddies, injuring no one. Finally, two planes let go with two bombs each on the one building that, at the time, was made of cement—the school, which was located at the spot where the three hamlets came together.

'We had just built that secondary school, a complex of one big building of five rooms and eleven one-room bungalows,' explained, through a translator, Thuy Dan's mayor, a peasant who did not speak French. 'The village had footed the bill, either by saving on its budget or, more, by collection. The complex had been finished four weeks before the raid.'

Walking towards where the school used to be, we stopped at An Tiem, where nine people had died. Nguyen Thi Gai, twenty-four, a monitor in kindergarten, crouched on the ground where she used to live. A huge bomb crater had been filled with water, giving it the appearance of a pond. 'Our house was right here,' she told me. She was wearing the familiar white band of mourning:

> There was a trench right outside. I went into the trench with my mother, sister, sister-in-law and aunt when the alarm sounded. We had been eating lunch [which is around 10 A.M. in Vietnam agricultural villages where peasants rise at 4 to 5 A.M.]. Already in the trench were my niece and the neighbour's four children. I yelled 'Quiet, it's coming!' and at that moment the bomb exploded. I was thrown forward and down, along the trench. I thought I was dead, my head against the ground, but I heard my mother crying, so I realized I was still living. My mother was yelling hysterically, 'We're done for, we're done for!' My sister was taking her last gasps. My sister-in-law, who was pregnant, was screaming 'Save me and my child!' Then I fainted. In the hospital I learned that my mother, sister, aunt, sister-in-law, my niece and all four of the neighbour's children were dead.

She told me that her father had died during the 1945 famine, that she is married, but her husband is at the front in South Vietnam.

I then walked to the old school site. On the way I passed some tombstones. One read: 'Teacher Bui Thi Thanh Xuan, twenty-six years old.' Some hundred open yards later I spotted a black, eight-foot-tall 'Stone of Hate'. Carved into it were these words: 'The population of the village of Thuy Dan profoundly remembers this crime by American aggressors who, by bombing, assassinated the teacher and these thirty students of the secondary school of the village of Thuy Dan on 21.10.1966.' There followed a list of the dead and their ages (Photo 20b).

The dead were students of the seventh grade and Bui Thi Thanh Xuan their teacher. She was married and the mother of a three-year-old boy (Photo 21a) who had been evacuated to his grandmother's in Nam Ha province, not too far from where Bui's husband, who had just finished a course at Hanoi's Pedagogical Centre, was teaching. On October 17, 1966, four days before she died, she had written him this letter (a photostat and French translation given me by the Minister of Education):

Darling,
With these first days of cold, I have difficulty falling asleep. I have hence risen to write you. I don't know if you have received my last letter, but I'll write you again. Maybe it disturbs you, but I am so sad, I hope you won't hold it against me, will you?

Yesterday, Sunday, did you go see our little boy? From here I see you well, struggling along those muddy paths, in this cold, to go see him; believe me that I struggle with you. Darling, I have great difficulty passing Sundays. All the comrades go away. I remain all alone, seized by an invincible sadness. For quite a while already it is not only Sundays that pain me. I am rarely asleep anymore when the cock crows. Our boy, I see him in front of me all the time, I think of him constantly, the poor one, at three years old, he must already live far from his father, from his mother, only with the affection of his grandparents.

How is he, our little one? I'm dying to see him, if only for a minute, to see how he is faring. When will I be able to relive those moments, walking with him after my classes?

These days, I have learned that the American planes are concentrating on Nam Ha province, and I feel myself going crazy, I can't stay still, I lose my spirits. I am so far; take care of our boy. I count on you. When I see him again, he will certainly be a big and bright boy, not so?

Tell Grandma that she must dress him warmly, that she must take all necessary precautions so nothing unfortunate can happen. He's a true pearl, our boy, we have put so much love into bringing him up that if something happens to him, our lives will lose all value. Not so?

I tell you all this, darling, in these times of war, to live each on his own makes me apprehensive, for where can one be safe? I feel all alone, I admit, I think all the time about our boy. I cry every night, and I am restless long into the morning. I am not in good shape, as when you last saw me. One must go on, another twenty-eight weeks, until vacation time. . . .

Within fifteen or twenty days, we will have vacation for the harvest. I am set to go see our boy, even for only one day, I have promised it to me. Trips are dangerous, so please don't travel, except to go see our boy. And be careful. As for me, I move the least possible, for if anything happens to one of us, how the other will suffer. What a sad situation. I burn to see you both, but life is such. We must be patient, and I have learned to have a lot of patience. I only hope that you understand me, that we have no misunderstanding.

Six days ago, they bombarded Diem Dien. No victims. Here, all is calm. The planes fly above us without molesting us.

Write me, give me your news. Be well.

I kiss you tenderly.

Four days later she was dead.

At the new school, called 'The School of the Class of October 21, 1966', I interviewed some of the surviving seventh grade students. There used to be fifty-four of them. (The whole school had 347 students, divided into morning and afternoon sessions.) Now, with increases from neighbouring hamlets, there were forty-three. Le Xuan Thang was fifteen. He told me:

That morning we had had three hours of class already. We had just started the fourth hour, reading in literature. Teacher Bui was going to explain an ancient poem from historical times. She had just introduced the general theme and had written on the board 'Explication de texte', when we heard the planes. Our teacher took a look, judged that it was dangerous and gave the order to go to the shelter. We did as she told us, and at once heard a fantastic noise and earth was flying all over us. It was barely over when I heard my comrades in the other shelter yell 'Help! Help! We are going to die! Help! Teacher! Teacher!' I was still hearing the shouts when a second set of explosions went off and then I heard no more cries. I was in an individual shelter. I touched my head and chest and felt all wet, so I thought I was wounded. I used all my strength to lift the earth which was on top of the shelter cover and get out. There was a lot of smoke and I could see that the school, the desks, everything was gone. I ran out and was taken by another teacher,

119

who had rushed up, to the hospital. I had been wounded in three places on my head, but not on my chest.

Nguyen Thi Nuoi was thirty-nine, a peasant in the rice cooperative. Her husband had been killed by the French in 1951 when she was three months pregnant with her son, Pham Van Thanh. 'By the time I reached the school I could only embrace a cadaver. He was only fifteen then, only fifteen.'

Phan Hong Tu was also fifteen, a member of the *Jeunesse de Travail* (the Youth Militia):

As soon as I reached the spot where the bombs had fallen, I started digging. I dug a lot with a small shovel to get the dirt off the school shelters. I found Nguyen Manh Haung, a friend of mine, who had passed out with his mouth full of dirt. I called a nurse who gave him an injection but at that point the planes came back. On orders from the cadre, we all took shelter. I found one on the bank of the canal, five metres from where I was digging. As soon as the planes left I rushed out to my friend Haung. But now he was dead.

Pham Ngoc Han was twenty-six; he was teaching the sixth grade in one of the mud-hut classrooms, 150 metres away from the main building:

As soon as the planes went away we rushed to the main building. It was gone. There used to be two huge trees, one on each side of the building. Now I saw one in pieces on the ground. The other had evaporated. There were four huge craters, and all the big shelters were covered with earth. We tried very hard to uncover them as fast as possible; fifty-two seventh graders were buried. We managed to dig out twelve quickly, unhurt. Then six who were slightly wounded and four more seriously. Finally we found Teacher Bui and the thirty students. They were all dead. My sister was among them.

He showed me her notebook. On the first page there was a drawing of Morrison, called 'Mo Hi Son' in Vietnamese, the American who had burned himself to death in front of the Pentagon in protest against the war in Vietnam. Underneath it another student, Le Xuan Thao, who also died, had written a poem. It read: 'Has occurred the moment when our hearts shine the most. We burn our bodies so that the fire may be the most luminous.'

VIII

DIKES AND FARMS

If a hydrogen bomb were dropped on Vietnam's Red River delta fewer people would die from the explosions than from the destruction of the dikes. In 1945, for example, the dikes were destroyed, partly by Japanese action. The resulting floods caused the death of almost 2,000,000 people. It is no wonder, therefore, that the Vietnamese consider any attack on their dikes as the most vicious and cruel of aggressive acts. And, they say, the United States has already bombed parts of them repeatedly. The document they prepared remains unverifiable except for the particular destruction that I witnessed.

Document No. 9
Report on the Attacks Launched by the United States Against Irrigation Projects and Dike Systems in North Viet Nam.
Prepared by the DRV Ministry of Water Conservation. Mimeographed; October 1966; in English.

In their escalation war of destruction against economic establishments and populous areas in North Viet Nam, the US imperialists have committed an extremely barbarous crime by attacking irrigation projects and dike systems in an attempt to cause famine and floods to millions of people.

Realizing clearly the importance of the problem of water conservation in the development of the economy in general and agriculture in particular, the North Vietnamese people have concentrated their efforts and energy on developing hydraulic works. In the conditions of a tropical agricultural country advancing toward socialism the DRV Government's line is: 'water conservation work is the primary technical task in agricultural development' and 'hydraulic work coupled with co-operativization'.

Since the return of peace in 1954, through over 10 years of exertions in the gradual harnessing and transformation of nature, the Vietnamese people have recorded very great successes in the construction of hydraulic projects. By 1965, 90 per cent of the cultivated area had been watered, of which 80 per cent under rice crops was adequately provided with hydraulic works. The water conservation works has in the main prevented drought in the North Viet Nam delta and plains of the provinces of Thanh Hoa southward; flooding has been done away with step by step.

The vigorous development of water conservation which serves as an important material and technical basis has contributed to strengthening and consolidating the cooperative movement. The successes gained in the field of water conservation have made a decisive contribution to the all-sided, vigorous and steady development of agriculture in North Viet Nam, and the Vietnamese people have put an end to the once chronic famine and achieved self-sufficiency in foodstuffs.

In the transformation and conquest of nature, another very important victory of the Vietnamese people has been won over floods which can be compared with the greatest ones ever known, thus protecting production and the life and property of the people. It should be recalled that during 45 years (1900–1945), due to the colonialist and feudal regime of repression and exploitation, dikes were broken on 17 occasions, causing untold disasters to the Vietnamese people. Typical was the dike breaking in 1945 (prior to the August 1945 Revolution) which caused death and famine to millions of people. . . . (The Red River dike was broken on 17 spots, the flood-stricken area covering 8 provinces.) Realizing the disastrous effect of floods, the Vietnamese people have, during the past 10 years, been sparing no efforts and energy to consolidate and strengthen the networks of river and sea dikes stretching all in all over 4,000 kms.

To accomplish the great water conservation work and to successfully combat floods, the Vietnamese people have, during the past 10 years (1955–1965), removed 1,200 million cubic metres of earth by their own means and with a high spirit of self-reliance. The Vietnamese people attach great importance to hydraulic projects which are of great use to their peaceful labour and existence. They regard them as arteries of agriculture and dike systems as the loving arms of a mother protecting the life of her children. But the us imperialists have deliberately been destroying hydraulic projects and dike systems, thereby threatening the very life of millions of Vietnamese.

Since March 1965 the us imperialists have systematically and brutally been attacking water conservation works in North Viet Nam, and the dike networks of the provinces in North Viet Nam, Red River delta which is North Viet Nam's most populous area and largest rice bowl. Fierce raids were made right at the moment when there was danger of flood.

The US aggressors have systematically bombed and strafed from the key projects and canals carrying water to the fields to the regulating projects of the whole system. Again and again they attacked those projects already repaired by the people after their previous bombings. They even attacked projects under construction where a large number of workers and peasants were working; they dropped a large quantity of fragmentation and napalm bombs killing many people at work, and causing losses in lives and property to the population in the surroundings.

Between March 1965 and December 1965, US airplanes launched over 500 attacks on 150 water conservation works. After resuming their bombings on North Viet Nam, between February and September 1966, they launched over 1,000 attacks on 300 water conservation projects in 19 provinces of the North.

We only mention below three of the worst-hit projects:

(1) *The water conservation system, North Nghe An province:*

The water conservation system in North Nghe An province serves 5 districts and hundreds of thousands of people. It consists of a key project, the Do Luong dam, and hundreds of water regulating projects. Between June 26 and 28, 1965, US airplanes bombed and strafed the Do Luong dam 12 times; on June 5, 6, 7, 8, 12, 15, 1965, and between July 8 and 14, 1966, they continuously raided the sluices 10 times and the water regulating project of the whole system 137 times. They also bombed irrigation canals. Between March 1965 and September 1966, the water conservation system in North Nghe An was bombed and strafed 178 times in all.

The temporarily damaged projects failed to supply water to certain areas at certain periods of time. The US aggressors also caused great losses of life and property to the people in the nearby area. The damaged projects have been repaired at the cost of many people's efforts and material. Being short of water as a result of the enemy's destruction in 1965 the people in Quynh Luu district alone had to spend a lot of labour and money on building 30 new water reservoirs to replace the destroyed ones, with a view to ensuring the seasonal production in time and securing a good harvest in 1965.

(2) *The Chu river water conservation system, Thanh Hoa province.*

This system serves a production area comprising 6 districts with more than half a million people.

Bai Thuong dam, the key-project of the above network, was bombed on April 22, 1965, and has been up to September 1966 strafed 13 times. The big water regulating projects were strafed 41 times, the Northern big canal was damaged 10 times.

Typical are the US imperialists' attacks on the Ban Thach water regulating dam, an important project of the system.

They attacked it 6 times on August 21, 22, 1965, dropped 236 bombs on it and the pumping power station. On August 23, 1965, they repeatedly attacked the project for 7 hours running, with tens of tons of bombs and hundreds of rockets, causing great damage to the water regulating dam, sluices, disastrously affecting thousands of hectares of crops at the time when the peasants were harvesting the 1965 autumn crop.

(3) *The Suoi Hai water reservoir of Ha Tay province:*

The Suoi Hai water reservoir is one of the big water reservoirs in North Viet Nam with a capacity of tens of millions of cubic metres serving 2 districts of Ha Tay province.

US pilots, on September 9, 1965, started attacking the project from 6.45 A.M. to 1.30 P.M., bombed and strafed it 9 times, releasing hundreds of heavy bombs.

—On September 10, 1965, they bombed it 2 times;
—On September 11, 1965, they bombed and strafed it 9 times from morning till afternoon;
—On September 12, 1965, they bombed it 9 times;
—On September 14, 1965, they bombed and strafed it 3 times.
—On September 15, 1965, they bombed it 2 times and on September 16, 1965, one time.

Thus, the US imperialists attacked the dam and the project of this water reservoir 34 times within 7 days, damaging a sluice built across the Tich river and a dam section, destroying much civilian property around the project.

Apart from the hydraulic systems mentioned above, they expanded their attacks on the hydraulic projects in various places of North Viet Nam plains.

In addition:

In the fourth zone they attacked the Cam Ly water reservoir, the Be lake, the Da Mai dam (Quang Binh); the Duc Tho pumping station, the Thuong Tuy water reservoir (Ha Tinh), the La Nga water reservoir (Vinh Linh), the Quynh Tam water reservoir (Nghe An).

Hydraulic works in mid-land provinces were attacked: the Lien Son dam of Vinh Phuc province 2 times on July 20 and 22, 1966; the Tan Dan pumping station of Phu Tho province 1 time and the Lua Viet sluice of the same province 5 times on August 15, 1966; the Cau Son dam of Ha Bac province 4 times between October 7, 1965 and September 4, 1966.

In coastal provinces they attacked the following hydraulic works of Thai Binh province: the Nguyet Lam sluice on July 29, 1966; the Tra Linh sluice on August 4, 1966; the Da Coc and Thai Do sluices on August 8, 1966; 3 salt water blocking sluices of Dong Cao, Thu Chinh, Diem Dien coastlines on August 11, 1966. In Hai Phong, the Co Tiêu sluice was bombed on July 31, 1966, and the Don sluice 2 times on July 19 and 20, 1966.

In the mountainous provinces, the Phuong Hoang water reservoir of Bac Thai province was attacked on July 31, 1966; the Thac Huông dam of the same province was bombed on June 22, 1966; the Nhu Khê water reservoir of Tuyên Quang province on July 25, 1966; the construction site of the Thac Ba dam, Yen Bai province, 14 times between April 23, 1966, and September 19, 1966.

Between May 25, 1965, and September 19, 1965, the Be water reservoir of Quang Binh province was subjected to 59 bombing and strafing raids, sustaining 1,033 bombs and rockets and bullets of various kinds. In 1966, between June 26, 1966, and August 18,.1966, it was the target of 47 air attacks. Most barbarous was the July 11, 1966, attack in which 480 lazy-dog fragmentation bombs were dropped on its construction site aiming at killing workers and peasants at work. On July 13, 1966, they again released 400 lazy-dog fragmentation bombs on top of the dam where workers and peasants were working in great numbers. On July 19, 1966, napalm bombs were showered on the construction site aiming at destroying its property and operation equipment and killing workers there.

The Thac Ba dam of Yen Bai province, a great project under construction in North Viet Nam was bombed for the first time on September 21, 1965. On April 23, 1966, and June 22, 1966, the US aggressors conducted air strikes against places where workers were at work. On July 8, 20 and 21, 1966, they continually bombed the centre of the construction site where workers were busy on the main dam, causing heavy losses: 30 workers killed and lots of equipment damaged.

Between February 1965 and December 1965, 87 important sections of dikes were the targets of US air strikes. In 1966, US bombings and strafings of the dike network were exceptionally fierce and concentrated in July, August, and September when there was great danger of flood.

From February 1966 to June 1966: 55 air raids.

In July 1966: 69 air raids.

In August and September 1966: 136 air raids.

We only mention Nam Ha, Thanh Hoa and Quanh Ninh provinces among many others where river and coastal dikes were subjected to serious bombings and strafings.

The dikes of Nam Ha province were raided 34 times between April and September 1966. Nam Ha is a populous province and a big rice bowl of North Viet Nam. In April and May 1966, it was air attacked 5 times; in July it was subjected to 7 air raids; in August and September, when the water level rose the highest, the number of air strikes was brought to 50. On August 1 and 3, 1966, US aircraft bombed and strafed the Kinh Lung dike and sluice of Nam Dao village, Nam Truc district, when the rising water level was only 2 m below that of the dike; a section of dike was so damaged that its level was only 0·80 of a metre higher than that of the water and the populous area of Nam Ha province was there threatened by the floods of the turbulent Red river.

On August 3, 1966, the same section of the dike was again attacked and the danger of the dike breaking was very serious as some bombs dug 4-metre deep craters in it.

Quang Ninh, a coastal province, was the objective of continual bombing and strafing raids on July 13, August 6 and 17, 1966, on its Ha Dong dike which prevents sea water from flooding 1,200 hectares of newly reclaimed land under rice cultivation. Bombs completely destroyed a 3-metre long dike section which was dug 10 metres deep, thus causing sea water to overflow the whole cultivated area.

Dikes in Thanh Hoa province were subjected to 24 air strikes between March and September 1966. (In August they were bombed 7 times; in September, when there were heavy rains, they were attacked 17 times.)

Northern banks of the Ma river, in two days only, September 21 and 22, 1966, were bombed and strafed 8 times, damaging dikes and dams in hundreds of metre-long sections, blasting away 25,000 cubic metres of earth. In the air raids US pilots dropped lazy-dog fragmentation bombs on the people, who were filling the gaps in the dike and dam network after the bombing, killing many of the workers and labouring people on the top of the dike.

Besides, from July 27 to 31, 1966, since due to the torrential rains of typhoon Ora the water level of the Red River and of the Thai Binh River was mounting, US aircraft strafed 14 times many important sections of dike in Tiên Lang and Vinh Bao districts in the suburbs of Hai Phong city.

In July 1966, Thai Binh province was subjected to 8 bombings, but in August and September alone, the dikes and dams and the sluices were bombed 16 times. Thu Tri dike was bombed many times, and the left and right banks of the Tra Ly dike were the targets of continuous air raids causing great danger. They also bombed the sluices of the Lan, Ngu Thon, Thai Do, Tra Linh and Diêm Dien rivers, etc., causing a great danger of inundation, drought, overflow of sea water to millions of hectares in densely populated areas of Thai Binh province.

I had no way, of course, of verifying these charges: dikes are repaired immediately. Besides, new dikes and dams are under construction all the time (Photo 22a) while others are constantly under repair and not necessarily from bomb damage. Nam Dinh officials, for example, told me that a mile-long section of the dike in their city was breached repeatedly during raids from May 31 to July 14, 1966, but the damage was no longer visible when I saw it. The same was true of Thai Binh, where thirteen sections of the dike along an effluent of the Red River, called Tra Ly, which slices the province in half, had been bombed during 1966. All of the torn-up sections, varying from four to 100 metres in length, were near Thai Binh city, where, I was told, 40,000 people are extremely vulnerable. But all the sections were repaired by January 1967.

That was why the incident in Nam Dinh on December 31, 1966, turned out to be so crucial—as far as my investigation was concerned at least. On that day, at 6 A.M., the United States and the NLF officially stopped shooting for a two-day truce. But at 5.20, forty minutes before the truce went into effect, American planes from the Seventh Fleet struck at Nam Dinh. The United States communique claimed that the raid was directed at the railroad junction and Marc Riboud, the famous French correspondent (best known in the United States for his book *The Three Banners of China*, published by Macmillan) who was then aboard a Seventh Fleet carrier, told me later in Paris that on December 31, 1966, he had actually interviewed an American pilot returning from that very raid. This pilot proudly described to him the run on the junction.

But at 8.45 A.M. on January 1, 1967, I visited that junction. Unless the Pentagon is willing to claim that in precisely 27 hours and 25 minutes the Vietnamese are capable of eliminating all traces of an American bombing attack, then the United States communique and the pilot in question were lying. On the other hand, at 12 noon that day, January 1, 1967, I visited an area that looked devastated and had obviously been bombed very recently. It was a poor section of Nam Dinh on the other side of the river, and the peasants to whom I talked told me that they had been bombed and strafed by very low-flying jets at 5.20 A.M. the day before. Tran Thi Thu (Photo 23a), for example, told me how the planes had suddenly 'appeared from nowhere'; a twenty-nine-year-old practising Catholic, she had lost her husband in the raid.

Bomb craters everywhere were being filled by scores of people; flattened houses were being cleared; and wounds were being cared for. I was personally present, as were other members of our team, when the body of one of the four people killed during the raid was wrapped up in a sheet (Photo 23b) and made ready for a wooden coffin, while relatives and friends moaned (Photo 23c). The dead man was Nguyen Ngoc Hoi, eighteen, and he had been uncovered from under the debris only a few hours before. In fact, it was when a messenger told Mayoress Tran that the body had been found that she invited us to go see it. Not thinking that the United States would later deny that this area had been bombed, she had not planned to take us there in the first place.

But she should have, for the area was completely devoid of any possible military target. There was a small, bamboo bridge nearby (by which we had crossed) and nothing else—except dikes. And it was the dikes which were hit. Fortunately for the population, the water level was very low, and very little damage in terms of floods had taken place (Photo 22b). But the hard mud dikes had definitely been hit.*

Despite such attacks, the Vietnamese claim that their agricultural output keeps increasing:

Document No. 10—Agricultural Production
Given me by the Ministry of Agriculture. Mimeographed document; undated (but early 1966); in English.

Despite the increased fierceness of the war of destruction unleashed by the United States last year, together with the achievements obtained by industry and commerce, agricultural production of North Vietnam made a great step in the direction of intensive cultivation, multiplication of crops, increase in crop yield and stepping up of animal husbandry in harmony with cultivation.
In 1965 the food problem was fairly satisfactorily resolved.
The 5th month rice crop recorded big successes nearly on all

* Since the time of this writing several foreign observers in North Vietnam have reported damage to the dikes as a result of bombing. The *New York Times* of August 1, 1967, carried a brief undescriptive dispatch from Hanoi (Agence France-Presse, July 31, 1967) which tells of French reporters seeing the destruction of dikes on the River Cau. Additionally, Dave Dellinger, editor of *Liberation* (a pacifist monthly), writes in the Summer issue of that magazine: 'I myself saw dam after dam and dike after dike which had been attacked in Nam Ha and Thanh Hoa provinces, when I travelled through those provinces in October and November 1966. I also saw hundreds of peasants laboriously filling in the bomb craters with rocks that they passed from hand to hand, in the manner of the fire brigades of our forefathers, and with sand that they carried in primitive buckets. I saw mountains of material piled ready for such repairs and in other places whole dikes which had been erected near the original ones to serve in emergencies.'

13 Cam Lo, bombed August 2, 1966 (DRV *photograph*)

14 (a) Bombed section of Cat Ba's capital (DRV *photograph*)

(b) Cam Lo's marketing co-op

5 (a) Cam Lo's judge, Phan Ngoc Can, his wife Nguyen Thi Bau and their children: Ha, thirteen; Huan, eleven; Hanh, eight; Bao, seven; Hiep, four. Only mother and Bao survived. (*Photograph by friend of Phan Ngoc Can*)

(b) Bau (with Bao) showing us where her family died

16 (a) Son La hospital, bombed June 18–22, 1965 (DRV *photograph*)

(b) Bach Thai hospital, bombed June 22, 1966 (DRV *photograph*)

(a) Yen Bai hospital, bombed July 9–11, 1965 (DRV *photograph*)

(b) Thanh Hoa province hospital, bombed June 1, 1966 (DRV *photograph*)

18 (a) Thanh Hoa TB Sanatorium, bombed July 8, 14, 1965

(b) Nam Dinh Nursery School

(a) Quynh Lập leper being cared for in the hills after leprosorium was bombed the first time, June 12, 1965. During the next year it was bombed thirty-eight times more (DRV *photograph*)

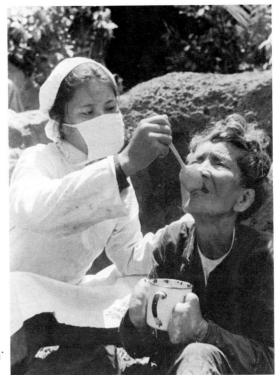

(b) Dr Nguyen Van Oai operating on leper in makeshift operating 'room' after June 13, 1965, bombing of leprosorium (DRV *photograph*)

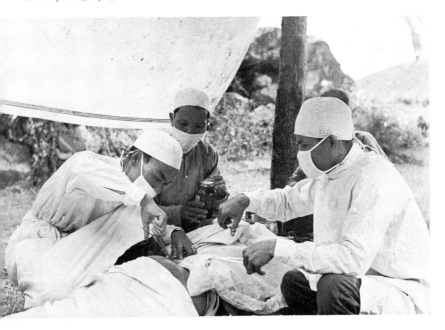

20 (a) Thuy Dan scene

(b) Thuy Dan's 'Stone of Hate'

(c) Thuy Dan children

21 (a) Teacher Bui and son
(*Photograph by Bui's husband*)

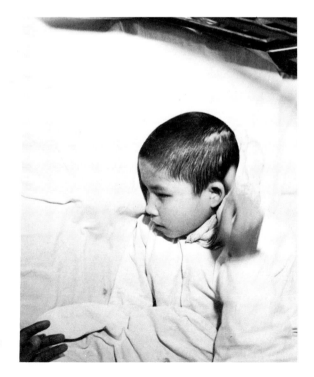

(b) Girl with pellet on the brain

22 (a) A dam in Nam Dinh (DRV *photograph*)

(b) Flooding; Nam Dinh population at work repairing dike 'not hit' by US bomb

3 (a) Tran Thi Thu and child. Her husband died on December 31, 1966, when US raided Nam Dinh dike, which it denies

(b) The body of Nguyen Ngoc Hoi, 18, killed by bombs during raid that 'never took place'

(c) Relatives mourn Nguyen's death

24 (a) Napalm victim Thai Binh Dan (Prof. Tsurishima is on the left, I'm on the right) (*Pic photo with my camera*)

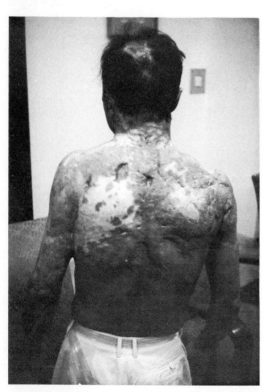

(b) Napalm victim Hoang Tan Hung: 'A yellow liquid still oozes out of my body'

sides and exceeded the planned targets in planting areas, productivity and crop yield (reaching the record figures to date in area and yield). Even in the bumper crop of the 5th month of 1963–1964, no region was able to get the average yield of 2·4 tons per hectare. In the delta and mid-land, 10 districts obtained yields ranging from 2·4 tons to 2·7 tons per hectare. In seven provinces (Thai Binh, Vinh Phuc, Ninh Binh, Hai Duong, Hung Yen, Nam Ha and Ha Bac) over 200 agricultural cooperatives achieved average yields of from 2·5 to 3 tons per hectare and over 100 cooperatives exceeded the mark of 3 tons per hectare. The 10th month rice crop was good though a number of provinces in the delta and mid-land region suffered from water-logging at the beginning and drought in the middle of the planting season and from serious devastation by insect and plant diseases, which exerted a bad influence on the yield. The total yield was 70,000 tons higher compared with that of 1964. In the former interzone alone, the 10th month food production was very successful, especially Quang Binh, and Vinh Linh, though the hardest hit by air raids, harvested two bumper crops in the year. The 10th month crop yield was 20 per cent higher than in 1964. Hanoi suburbs smashed the record with an average yield of 2·674 tons per hectare, the highest ever in North Vietnam. Thanks to the multiplication of crops, some regions could grow three crops in the year on a number of rice fields (the 5th month crop, the autumn crop and the 10th month crop), many regions harvested on the average more than 5 tons per year. Taking the lead was Dan Phuong district which reached an average yield of 5·564 tons per year. The cooperatives which obtained 5 tons upwards existed in all regions: Hanoi had over 70 cooperatives of this kind and Hai Duong over 100. Some cooperatives harvested 6 tons in the year, the most outstanding of which was Tan Phong which obtained 6·910 tons per hectare.

Especially a number of regions which were regularly hit by the enemy recorded outstanding achievements: Vinh Kim village (Vinh Linh), though frequently attacked, obtained an average yield of 5·2 tons a year; Huong Khe district in Ha Tinh province, about 600 times devastated by the enemy who dropped more than 8,000 bombs and fired tens of thousands of rockets, harvested two bumper crops. In the 10th month crop alone, the planting area of Huong Khe increased by 4 per cent and the yield 5,000 tons; Thanh Hoa province which was hard hit also obtained an average yield of 4·95 tons per year, the highest in the past 5 years.

Production of subsidiary crops was fairly good. Though the area fell short of target, the yield was 7·4 per cent higher than the previous year, the year in which subsidiary crops were highly developed. The acreage grown to vegetables and beans of all kinds was 8,000 hectares larger than in 1964. In the towns, the production, supply and marketing of vegetables made notable progress.

Industrial crops and animal husbandry changed for the better.

The area grown to industrial crops increased by about 9·2 per cent over 1964. Jute, mulberry trees, groundnuts, tobacco (for cigarettes and water-pipe smoking) exceeded the targets in planting areas. The yields of jute, groundnuts, tobacco, tea and coffee fulfilled or over-fulfilled the plan, especially groundnuts increased by about 10,000 tons.

Animal husbandry has undergone many changes.

Compared with 1964, pigs increased by 310,000 head, buffaloes by 300,000 head and oxen 170,000 head. . . . While 1964 had seen the installation of 3,454 pigsties, up to September 1965 this number was 4,500.

The successes recorded by North Vietnam last year in agricultural production was the outcome of the efforts of the entire people and the clearsighted leadership of the Party and Government. Correctly applying the directives of the high level 'to fight and get ready to fight at the same time as to step up production and to actively protect production, to eagerly build up the economic potentiality and to strengthen national defence', many localities which were directly involved in the fight were able to overcome difficulties, carry through production and achieve big successes.

The agricultural successes scored by North Vietnam last year testify to the fact that to whatever extent may be the destruction wrought by the United States, the latter could not prevent North Vietnam's agriculture from going ahead. Under the leadership of the Party and Government, the peasants of North Vietnam will obtain more glorious achievements as a decisive contribution to the defeat of the United States.

One of the provinces which produced the most during 1965 (and, according to preliminary reports, 1966 as well) was Vinh Phuc, northwest of Hanoi. I visited it on January 9, 1967, arriving near Vinh Yen at 5.30 in the morning. Over breakfast, a charming and beautiful woman named Vu Thuy Chau, who turned out to be the vice-president of the province's court system, told me that from June 28, 1966, to January 9, 1967, the province had been bombed twenty-two times in forty-three different localities. But the worst raid, as far as attacks on agricultural production was concerned, had taken place a month before, on December 8, 1966.

That day, American planes raided nine sites in four districts of Vinh Phuc, specifically Vinh Yen, the capital of the province. Judge

Vu told us that Vinh Yen is almost exclusively a farming centre; of its 10,000 people, 90 per cent are engaged in agricultural production, 10 per cent in artisan crafts. The town, which is sprawled out over five square kilometres, did indeed appear as she said when we toured it later. There were one market, two pagodas and one Catholic church.

She said that from February 2 to December 6, 1966, eighteen reconnaissance planes had canvassed the area. Then, at 1520 on December 8, a sunny day, sixteen F.105s, flying in various formations and coming in from the northeast, the southeast and the southwest, attacked Vinh Yen (and two neighbouring communes). The first group of planes fired rockets. The rest dropped fragmentation bombs. In all, ten 'mother bombs' were unleashed over the area, meaning that some 2,000,000 pellets (plus their connecting steel) rained over the farmers of a 12 sq. km. sector of Vinh Phuc. In the capital, eight of the nine districts were plastered. All the bombs functioned well; they were of recent vintage, bearing dates of October or November 1966.

When Mme Vu finished, she introduced Dr Nguyen Huu Nghiem, the deputy director of the Vinh Phuc Provincial Hospital, who requested that I read the following document before we examined individual instances of bombing casualties:

Document No 11
Statement issued by the Vinh Phuc Public Health Service Provincial Hospital of the Democratic Republic of Viet Nam, on December 13, 1966. Typewritten; in English.

ON THE DROPPING OF FRAGMENTATION BOMBS (CBU) BY
US AGGRESSORS ON DECEMBER 8, 1966, ON VINH YEN
TOWN AND TWO VILLAGES OF TAM DUONG DISTRICT
At 1520, on December 8, 1966, US aircraft launched an air raid on the town of Vinh Yen and on two nearby villages, Dinh Trung and Thanh Van, in Tam Duong district, killing twenty-six, wounding seventy-seven.

The wounds received by these persons were of various kinds: fractured skull, wounds on head, skin, brain, chest, lungs, arms, legs, belly and soft parts.

There are many cases in which a victim received different kinds of wounds. All the victims were injured by fragmentation bombs which are specifically designed to harm people and domestic animals. Each bomb contains hundreds of steel pellets like bearings in a bicycle wheel. When the bomb explodes, it spreads out, strongly ejecting a large number of pellets on a small surface. Therefore, it can cause many injuries on the body of a person, as in the case of

Mr Duong Van Thuan, 24, a lime factory worker of Vinh Phuc Construction Board, who suffered twenty wounds. Steel pellets from the bomb destroyed many abdominal parts at a time, as in the case of Mr Tran Van Dam, 50, farmer in Thanh Van village, Tam Duong district, who suffered a severe shock and was rushed to the hospital at 18 hours on December 8, 1966. After he partly recovered, an abdominal operation revealed the following injuries:

—Seven large perforations were observed on a 1·50 m. section of large intestine, each perforation separated from the other by about 20 cm. The diameter of each perforation was about 1·5 cm. and its edge was extremely jagged. The victim also suffered a wound deep in the chest. The surgeon had to cut out the section of wounded intestine.

The steel pellets cut a small hole on the skin, but cause a big complicated wound in abdominal parts. It is difficult for the surgeon to make adequate judgement by the way in which the pellets penetrate the body, as in the case of Miss Nguyen Thi Ly, 17, in Vinh Yen town, who was injured by fragmentation bombs at the lower ribs. An abdominal operation revealed: the right side of the liver was marked with a 3 cm. jagged wound. There were two perforations on the stomach, one on the front and the other on the back part. A pellet went through the spinal cord and hit the small intestine, causing a concentration of blood on it.

—The pellets cause infirmities on the human body as in the case of Mrs Ly Thi Hanh, 36, farmer in Thanh Van village, Tam Duong district, injured in the chest and left buttock, making the left arm completely paralysed. The victim was in the second month of pregnancy. The wound caused great pain and seriously threatened the foetus. The victim received medical treatment at the hospital. The second X-ray check revealed another pellet still remaining in the left leg bone. The victim aborted on December 28, 1966.

Almost all deaths happened on the spot, because fragmentation bombs caused wounds in the victims' brain case, chest or many spots on soft parts of the body, creating a state of severe and prolonged shock.

Some deaths happened after operations, as in the case of Tran Van Thanh, 8, a school boy in Vinh Yen town and son of Mr Tran Van Su. The operation was performed at noon on December 9, 1966. There were two perforations on a 1-metre section of small intestine, which was cut out afterwards. The victim died at 820 hours on December 12, 1966, because the wounds were too serious.

Deputy Director of the Vinh Phuc
Provincial Hospital
Dr Nguyen Huu Nghiem

When I finished reading the document, Dr Nguyen introduced three witnesses and put their X-rays on a small viewing machine which had been installed in the conference room of the hostel where we had had breakfast. The first witness was Duong Van Thuan, a twenty-four-year-old furnace worker, who said:

I was coming back from work and was fifteen metres from my house when I heard the planes and the alert. I went to help two friends who were invalids and none of us quite made it. We were caught just outside the shelter by a bomb exploding and I was tossed to the ground. One of my friends, a girl of eighteen named Nguyen Thi Toan, had her left shoulder ripped open and her lung was hanging out. Half of her face was shattered. The stomach of my other friend, Nguyen Khac Sang, twenty-seven, was open and his intestines were torn out. He was dead. I myself was covered with blood and I was taken by others to the hospital. I had twenty-two pellets inside my body. I was operated on twice. The first time, they took fourteen out, then six. The last two eventually worked their way out by themselves; they had been in my thigh.

We looked over his wounds, saw all his pellet marks, then met the next witness. His name was Nguyen Van Le, forty-four, a peasant who was accompanied by the youngest three of his seven children (aged: 18, 15, 12, 8, 6, 3 and 2 months). He said:

I was coming back from the fields, when I heard the alert. My wife, a nurse, rushed out of the house and yelled to me to take the youngest child whom she was holding. I went to the shelter with him and our three-year-old. Our other children were in school, the afternoon session. Then I heard the bombs. A friend rushed up to tell me that my wife had been wounded. She was brought home on a stretcher. She had holes from her stomach to her head. She was dead. Now I am left with six children—my oldest is in the army.

The third witness was Bui Thi Hue, a thirty-two-year-old peasant women who came and sat down at the table, across from me, with one child in her arms and two next to her. She said:

My husband and I were working in the fields when the planes came. Our children were home. After the explosions I rushed home and on my way learned from neighbours that my house had been hit and that my kids had been taken to the hospital. When I got there, I heard my children crying before I saw them. Then I saw my six-year-old girl in convulsions on the table. I asked, 'Why didn't you go to the shelter?' She answered, 'I did, but I fell'. She asked for water. She was suffering a great deal. The doctor signalled to me no water so I told her that if she wanted to live with me she had to be brave and strong and not drink. Her stomach was open. She kept having convulsions. I asked my oldest, a girl of twelve, what had happened. She told me that they were playing when the planes came. They thought they were ours. Then she heard an explosion and ordered her brother and sisters to lie down. Then a bomb hit and she saw blood everywhere. My youngest child, a boy, fifteen months old, was not hit because my eight-year-old was lying on top of him. The girl got a pellet in her head, but survived. The oldest was hit in the behind and back but she's alright. My six-year-old, who suffered so much, well, they tried, but at 5 P.M., she died.

Then we all went walking around the bombed area. It was completely flat and obviously, unequivocally agricultural. Where there was a concentration of houses, they were all typical: mud huts topped by rice-straw roofs. The windows were smashed. Inside, mirrors, pots, pictures, clothes were all pierced by pellets. Among the houses we came across an old man carrying a little girl. His name was Le Van Thuc; he was sixty-one. He was holding his granddaughter, four. He told me that his daughter, the little girl's mother, had been killed by pellets. Then I spotted a little boy working in the fields. I asked him where he had been during the raid. 'Right there,' he pointed to an open field. 'I was behind my buffalo. He got killed.'

We went on, visiting the Tan Phong hospital where surviving victims from the December 8 raid were being treated. I saw one boy who had been hit by a pellet in his forehead, then a little girl who looked like a boy because her hair had been cut. A pellet had grazed the top of her head, opening it up. I could see her brain pulsing through the thin fibre of the healing skin (Photo 21b).

Finally, I returned to our jeep. Judge Vu came over to bid me farewell. I had seen pellets everywhere, in walls, in trees, in telegraph poles—and in scores of kids. I had also seen the area, a peaceful farming spot with less imaginable military targets than the desert of Nevada. Also I had heard everywhere the same complaint: 'They killed my buffalo.' To the farmers this was perhaps the most painful consequence of the raid, for buffaloes are used for ploughing and as beasts of burden. In all, ninety-nine buffaloes had been killed.

Judge Vu shook my hand. 'They want to demoralize us, they want us to tell our Government—enough! *C'est idiot*, they only make us more determined, more united.'

IX

THE SOUTH IN THE NORTH

At 0800 on January 10, 1967, Professor Tsurishima, Lawyer Mata-rosso and I were admitted into an elegant villa, formerly used by the American Consul in Hanoi, for an interview with Nguyen Van Tien, Chief of the Permanent Delegation of the South Viet Nam National Front for Liberation (SVNNFL or, more commonly, NLF). A tall, handsome, white-haired fighter-diplomat, Nguyen was warm, friendly and candid. He was also a good host, insisting that we had some tea and cakes before we got down to business.

When we had finished, he began speaking rapidly but clearly and simply (alternating from French to English) giving us the following over-all picture of how the NLF views events in South Vietnam:

The War of Liberation against the French colonialists began in 1945 in the South. Even then the French received much aid from the United States. After 1954, when Diem was put into power by the United States, and up to 1963, when Diem's successors were appointed outright by the United States, that aid was illegal since it includes aggressive military material which was forbidden by the Geneva Agreements.

The choice of Saigon governments, and their enthronement, was also illegal, though Diem's at least went through a type of assembly. The plebiscite that offered a choice in the South between Bao Dai and Diem was arranged by colours. To vote for Bao Dai a voter had to pick up a red card, for Diem a blue card. The voter then took it into a private room and in secret put it into an envelope. But the envelope was transparent and it had to be put into the urn in front of Diem agents and the security police. Defaced ballots, if they were for Diem, were counted. The same procedure was used for Diem's Assembly. All this we call neo-colonialism because it was manipulated by the United States and the United States was the power behind the scenes. The United States Ambassador had the same role as the Governor under the French.

The plebiscite between North and South was to be held in 1956 but actual aggression in the South by Diem forces began prior to that and United States advisers were already there. By the end of 1965, the United States had 180,000 men; by the end of 1966, 390,000. In every battle after 1965 United States troops were the main forces. In general, we trace three phases in the war in Vietnam: (1) Indirect aggression up to 1961; (2) direct aggression by 'advisers' from 1961 to 1964; and (3) direct outright aggression, but within limits, from 1964 to 1967. We are convinced that there will undoubtedly be a fourth phase, which will begin in 1967.

In 1954, we launched a movement to put into practice the letters of the Geneva Convention. All the chiefs of that movement were jailed by Diem, among them at that time was Nguyen Huu Tho, the head of the NLF. We then launched a movement against terror, against reprisals, against strategic hamlets and the fraudulent elections of Diem. At first, our movement was strictly pacific, but later it was armed. At first it was an isolated movement, operating wherever conditions were the worst, but then we unified it and began to operate in concert. On December 20, 1960, the Front, that is the NLF, was created to coordinate all these movements, with Tho at its head. Many political organizations and religious groups were included, and our only programme was the unification of the country and its independence. The Front began to behave as a legal government; today it is the main government—we say the only government—of South Vietnam. We have representatives in many countries and we have our own press agency. We are active not only in liberation zones but also in zones occupied by the United States. We are a truly representative government.

Between 1954 and 1959, 100,000 unarmed Southern patriots were killed by the repressive forces. From 1960 until 1965, that is to say, once we began our resistance, the armed struggle cost us 70,000 men. From 1954 to 1959, 900 concentration camps were created. After 1959, when our movement for general insurrection was launched, and especially after it was transformed into the NLF in 1960, forcing the population into camps was no longer so easy for the aggressors. Until 1960, one half of the South, in land area, was liberated. Since then, it has grown to four-fifths—80 per cent of the South.

The NLF has a five-point programme which includes independence, democracy (by which we mean liberty), peace, neutrality, and reunification. It was Point Four, neutrality, which, as you can imagine, has been most discussed among us in the Front. Many wanted a socialist commitment, which would not be neutral. But, in order to be truly representative, the Front compromised and decided to stick to neutrality.

I interrupted him at this point to ask him how he envisaged the 'reunification' of a neutral part of the country with a Communist part. His answer:

By keeping each section independent in policy but united in a federation. The body at the top will sit over both regimes. Whether it will be an assembly or council or whatever will be discussed later, that is, after the reunification. But whatever it is, it will not have the power or the right to change the basic commitment or philosophy or either section, North or South. This general policy of ours has been approved by the Government of the North. That is, they have agreed to subordinate their ultimate policy decisions to this body which will sit above North and South. Each section will be independent internally, though of course there will be free travel between them.

During the 1965–66 offensive, the first bayonet contact between the two forces, between the United States and the NLF, took place, and in such contacts the United States came out the worst. Despite the huge American force, the NLF has continued to hold, to consolidate, and even to expand its territory. During the first eleven months of 1966, our forces have killed, wounded or captured 233,000 soldiers, including 100,000 Americans. It is such defeats that have led the United States to launch 'Attleboro' in the winter of 1966. I don't know how much you heard about that battle in the United States, but it was very significant. The United States sent in 30,000 troops and thousands more of the puppet forces. The battle began very badly for the United States and midway in its process the American general in charge of it was relieved of his command. The 196th Brigade, a crack elite American brigade, was thrown into the battle at that point, but it was also routed.

During the first nine months of 1966, in the American-occupied cities of South Vietnam there were three million anti-American demonstrations. Some, of course, were small, with only a few hundred or perhaps just a few dozen participants. And our boycott has been very effective. In the villages throughout the country voting for the constituent assembly that your press talks so much about, the boycott was almost general. At Hue, for example, only 2 per cent of the people voted.

Vietnamese puppet generals have long refused to send troops into the Mekong River Delta. Three times the United States has had to replace them because of their refusals. But now the United States itself is moving into the Mekong. The reason for the puppets' reluctance to go into that area is that it would curtail Saigon's power in the most productive area and that it would commit

137

puppet troops to battle near their homes. Most of our guerrilla fighters, indeed of our forces in general, operate in their own districts. So long as the United States did not enter the Mekong, the area functioned relatively peacefully, and the local people tended to spend most of their time at work. As United States troops enter, however, these peasants become guerrillas.

Until now the puppet troops, theoretically in charge of the Mekong, did not impose their rule and the generals in charge tended to be autonomous. This is one reason also why Ky is in favour of going into the Delta; he wants to impose his will on the generals in the Mekong. So does the United States. As of now, United States forces are present in only twenty-eight out of the forty-two provinces of the South. To have United States troops in all of them would obviously increase the United States position in case of eventual negotiations. This is another reason why the United States is expanding the war. After all, if the Viet Cong are in all forty-two provinces while the United States is in only twenty-eight, negotiations would have to limit themselves to those twenty-eight. The United States is aware of that and is now trying to take in the Mekong.

However, precisely because the area is productive and American troops have not intervened before, a certain nationalist pride on the part of the puppet troops has fortified their desire to keep the United States out. Also, up until now the puppet cadre could pretend to have a kind of personal integrity, since they were 'masters' in the Delta. And, of course, the Viet Cong and these puppets had certain arrangements whereby they left each other alone and everyone could function. With the United States entering the Delta these arrangements are over and the puppets will have to fight. For all these reasons the puppet troops were opposed to the United States entry, so much so that, as I have said, three of their generals have had to be replaced.

Switching subjects, he continued:

Shortly after 1961 the United States allotted $50 million for the creation of strategic hamlets. That money was given directly to local authorities, not to the Government, in order to eliminate inter-mediary thieving. Then, in 1962, strategic hamlets became a national policy. The method was to wipe out all established hamlets; people were ordered to move, their houses were then burned down. If they refused, they were moved by force and all their personal effects were confiscated. This became the practice in the first few months of 1962.

In 'Operation Sunrise', from the end of March to the end of

June 1962, in the southwest, above the Delta, 3,000 houses were burned down, 500 tons of paddy rice were destroyed and 60,000 people were concentrated into hamlets. In one district, the operation, from April 2 to 16, 1962, burned down 209 out of 252 houses, and all the churches and pagodas. By the end of 1962, 8,000 strategic hamlets with 5 million people had been set up.

These strategic hamlets were surrounded by trenches three metres wide, then by bamboo spikes and barbed wire and finally by earth walls. Once inside the walls, there were blockhouses and guard posts and, in between, mines and traps. The guards had two tasks: To keep people out and to keep those in, inside. Inhabitants of a strategic hamlet had to be self-subsistent and so were forced to work in shifts in which families were always divided, as insurance against escape. During a hamlet's construction, the inhabitants had somehow to feed themselves. What they did was to divide up the work so that each dweller, in the first year, gave one to three months of free work to the hamlet. In reality, however, because of resistance by the population the periods varied greatly.

When they did resist they were beaten, tortured and often killed. Inhabitants were also forced to pay, like taxes, for material used to build the strategic hamlets. They needed special cards to leave their area, other cards to go from one house to another, and a list, with photos of each inhabitant, had to be posted on each house. All celebrations or gatherings, even for birthdays, could be held only on permission. Within the camp, houses were organized in groups and within each group all inhabitants were held responsible, so that if one family had contact with us, the whole group was punished by torture or death. In Luong Phu, for example, in a camp of 500 families, 217 people were killed and more than 1,000 were tortured because within those 500 families we had strong support.

There was no such thing as private property in a strategic hamlet. There were no work laws except those imposed by the Government, and taxes are very heavy. All the harvest had to be assembled in a central area and usually only the barest necessities were distributed to each person. Most of the harvest was bought by the Government, forcibly, at 60 per cent of the market value. The officials kept the rest and parcelled out to the people small doses for their daily needs, again as insurance against hoarding or escaping. Most hamlets distribute only three days' worth of food at a time; no hamlet went beyond fifteen days. Night work was not allowed although in the cultivation of rice night work is important. In fishing strategic hamlets, fishermen could not go out according to tides but according to fixed hours.

Fines were levied for everything: if the light in front of the house, which is supposed to burn all night, went out; if a baby cried too loudly; if someone was outside his area at the wrong time, etc., etc. Guards had to be fed by the population, which was also responsible for maintainance and repairs of the hamlet. There were practice alerts all the time, especially at night, when incidents became unavoidable, with people falling into traps.

The NLF has destroyed many of these strategic hamlets. As of now, a little more than 1,000 remain. The new pacification strategy by the United States is basically the same except that it is more brutal and that the hamlets are now called 'New Life Hamlets'. There is a propaganda difference now too: It is the United States which now gives the aid and which distributes the food, not the puppet government. But basically nothing has changed. Besides, United States aid still disappears quickly into the puppet troops' pockets.

When Nguyen finished, we paused for more tea, then various witnesses were ushered in. Three disturbed us greatly, the first by what he showed us, the second by what she said, the third by both. The first was a young (eighteen) peasant named Thai Binh Dan (Photo 24a). He told us that on March 27, 1966, at 5 A.M., a United States plane had circled

over my homeland, Thanh Loi hamlet, Long An province [near Saigon]. Then three F105s and eighteen HU18 helicopters arrived, landing paratroops in three spots. They killed three people, wounded two, plundered the paddy and took one hundred people away to strategic hamlets. They also killed twenty buffaloes. We stayed hiding until they left, then returned to hamlet. But three F105s came back and dropped napalm on our village. One fell close to me and I lost consciousness. Doctors told me later that I was in shock for thirteen days. I drank thousands of glasses of water every day but I could not urinate for five days. After forty-eight days, scars began forming. I stayed in hospital two months more, then I was brought north for additional treatment. People who saw my original burns said my leg was absolutely bare of skin. The pain was fantastic. When bandages were removed, my legs were still bleeding. I am still suffering and cannot hear well. It hurts me to swallow.

The next witness was Tran Thi Van, from Quang Nam province, in the centre of South Vietnam. She was thirty-six years old and had been a resistance fighter against the French near Da Nang. She said:

I came here to be treated in the hospital. After Dien Bien Phu in 1954, I returned to my village to work the land. But Diem forces arrested me to force me to divorce my husband, who had been repatriated north, and marry one of the puppets. I refused. So I was arrested. That was in July 1955. I was questioned about the local women's organization and my activities. I got nothing to eat (my family had to bring me food), but then they let me go. In February 1956, they arrested me again and took me to Phu Ky. They tied me up. The interrogators tortured me, kicked me, hung me by the arms, then dropped me. They warned me to talk or face other tortures. Then they poured soapy water down my throat, little by little so I could not breathe. When my stomach was full, they stood on it so I would vomit. The next day they used an electric prong; they shocked my nipples, ears and toes. The current was low—I could not die—but the pain was unbearable. In the afternoon of the same day, they put bamboo pincers to my fingers repeatedly. Also iron pincers on my thigh. This went on another two days. They made me hang from a plank, if I fell they beat me with rods until I passed out. This lasted twenty days; I was completely naked during the whole time.

Next, security agents told me that they had learned still better ways from American advisers, so I had better talk. They took me out and put me in a hole which came up to my neck. 'You are very stubborn, so I shall bury you alive,' said one, and he started pouring in earth. It was very tight when it got to my chest. And all this time I had nothing to say. One man took a rifle, warned me to talk, then fired near me. After an hour, they pulled me out. Seven days later they brought beer and wine and drank while they beat me. I was tied to a pillar of the house. With their fists they beat me on my chest. Then from 11 A.M. to 1 P.M., naked as I was, I was exposed to the sun. I had to extend my hands with bricks in them. Then they dragged me and beat me in front of the other prisoners, hundreds of them.

For three months I was beaten like this, then sent to a brainwashing school. There were 110 people there, all prisoners from where I had been jailed. These 110 and me, we were forced to describe crimes by Communists and to repent our deeds. If we didn't, we were beaten. Then they released them, all but me. I was taken elsewhere, to Dien Ban prison, then back to Phu Ky for another brainwashing session. I was supposed to confess having been a Communist. After six months I was released.

Two months later I was arrested again by a special group coming from Saigon, calling itself a Pacification Team. With many others, they tied us up and took us to Phu Tho, near Phu Ky. We were divided into small groups (twelve or thirteen) with one agent in each, who reported whether we denounced Communists or not, and if we did not, we were punished by being put on a table and beaten. One man, 'Su', was very seriously beaten, then was covered with alcohol which was lit up and so he was burned from head to belly, while we were forced to watch. They let him lie on a plank for two days until he died.

Then we had a 'remorse session'. For four hours we stood, ten at a time, forced to watch a high-intensity lamp without moving. If we blinked or moved, we were beaten on our legs. Suddenly, three from our group were taken out. We heard shots and then the guards came back and said, 'They didn't repent enough.' They had killed only one, however, because half an hour later two of the three were brought back.

Three months later we were sent to Ky Nhac, a village near to a 'rehabilitation school'. At this point they arrested my mother, took her to a deep pond and kept dunking her head until she lost consciousness. They kept questioning her about Communists and about me. But she said she knew nothing. My father then appealed to provincial authorities but they answered that I had denounced my mother and talked of her Communist activities. Then they arrested my father and brought both my mother and father to where I was. They applied electric rods to them both, asking them to denounce the person who had 'compelled' them to write to the provincial authorities with the obvious intent of overthrowing them. The tortures usually went from 8 to 11 P.M. It was hard on the old. One old man named Hy, sixty, just lay down and died. My father was almost sixty but had been very strong. Still, after months of torture, lack of food, having to sleep on the ground or on jail cement, he was so weakened that when he was released a few months later, he went home and died. My mother was a complete invalid for a few months and then she died too. She could not be helped while she was sick; the neighbours had been forbidden to go to her aid.

I stayed at that 'school' for another six months. Then, twenty days after my release, an agent who claimed to have posed as a Communist vowed that it was I who told him to distribute leaflets, so I was arrested again, with twenty-two other women, this time by the local police, at midnight. At 6 A.M. I was taken to Phu Tho, also in the Phu Ky district, a jail where a man from the Pacification Team, the same one as before, pulled my hair, tied me to a pillar and struck me with an iron ruler on my head. Then a guard took me to a nearby theatre and tied me down to a bench by my hands and feet. They untied me twice a day to go to the toilet, that's all. This lasted four days with nothing to eat and only some water to drink. Then I got soup for the next three days. Finally, I was taken to the Dien Ban district headquarters where they beat me on my head so hard that today my right ear is deaf, the drum is punctured. Next day, they stripped me and used electric wires on my nipples and rubbed my sides with rifle cartridges, scraping the skin. Next day, at 11 A.M., they put a man in the cell next to me. He was already bleeding very badly, but they shoved in a German shepherd dog with him. The dog kept biting him, and I heard his screams for two hours. Then the man died.

The next day I was tied with bamboo and told the dog would come on me next if I didn't talk. I laid down on my stomach and the dog bit me but not hard, just to give me an idea, I guess. Two United States advisers were present when the dog was used. But then I was untied and taken out. Almost every day after that I had to kneel with my arms stretched out holding bricks. One night at about 7 P.M. they told me to talk or be killed. Four men who had been arrested three months before were shown to me; they were very thin, wearing drawers, tied by feet and hands, and they were taken out. I heard some shots. The police then came in smiling and said that the four men had tried to run away and so they had shot them. The chief of police came in and told me that's what I would get.

After seven days I was taken to Thanh Quyet, the headquarters of the Pacification and Administration Group. They kept me in a cell with four men. The room was so narrow we could not move. The four men had only drawers to wear; I had panties and trousers. Next day they tied me up and hung me by my arms. I got the soapy water treatment again. The chief then gave instructions that I be tortured until I talked or died. A United States adviser was present when the chief said this. They tied me to two pillars, stretched out above the ground. They ripped off my trousers and panties. They pressed a piece of hot iron on my sexual organ and the chief himself stuffed it into my vagina. I screamed and then he stuffed a handkerchief into my mouth. After an hour and a half, I passed out.

When I came to they put my pants on me and threw me back with the four men. I stayed in that cell over a month. My vagina wounds got infected, pus came out and the sand of the cell got in the wounds. Then I was given just enough water. to clean my wounds. For food we had two small cups of rice and two cups of water. The guards were sympathetic and tried to pack the rice inside, leaving it loose on top, but the chief tested it and when he found the rice compressed, he punished the chef by not allowing him to eat for one day.

After a month and a half of their torture, I could not move my arms. Then they sent me to brainwashing (indoctrination) school.

143

There I got bandages and after a couple of months, my arms could move normally again, though painfully. I also got a chance to clean out my vaginal wounds. Then I was moved again, this time to Hoi An prison where there were 1,580 prisoners in five houses of one room each (about 15 × 3 metres) and ten small cells for one man or more. In the main rooms no one could stand up. We got almost no food. There was no toilet. I caught dysentery, many others died—147 in all while I was there. We were allowed only one glass of water each day (sometimes only every other day) and we used it both for drinking and washing. If we were being punished we got only one glass in seven days. Our hands were always hand-cuffed. People who were sick in the top bunks simply dropped their stuff on the people below. Beatings and tortures, individually or *en masse*, were usual. I was freed at the end of 1959 after almost two years in this one site.

I went back home and stayed there until 1962, working as a peasant. I was not allowed to move about or leave my village. In 1962, the local troops tried to kill me but the NLF attacked them and kidnapped the worst among the local authorities. I took advantage of this and left with the NLF to go to another town nearby. But I was arrested there after a battle in which four local men were killed by the puppet forces. I was tied up and dumped on top of the four dead men in a truck. We were thrown out in the centre of town. Then I was taken to provincial police headquarters. This was Quang Nam, at Hoi An. The police chief asked me if I knew what a set of torture weapons were. An American adviser, who was present, hit me on my head with a wooden ruler (this was in March 1962). I was dragged to the table of torture. One policeman slapped me, the other kicked me. They tied me up to a bench, lying down. They gave me the soapy treatment again; whipped me everywhere. (During all this time, the American was present, walking back and forth and watching.) From 7 P.M. to 4 A.M. they tortured me, stopping when I lost consciousness and starting again when I came to. From 4 A.M. until 6 A.M. I was kept tied up. At 6.00, I was put into a jeep and taken to Da Nang 'second bureau' and put in a cell just big enough to fit me standing. I remained tied up in that cell for a month, except that I was taken out to be tortured once a day. I couldn't walk after a week. Electric prongs were used; the first days were the worst. Then they took me back to Hoi An, and after fifteen days I was tortured again. The Chief said, 'Elsewhere you didn't talk, here you will.' I was tortured every day, mostly by electric shocks on my nipples. I was kept locked up and handcuffed for four months.

After four months, they took the handcuffs off, calling me

occasionally for interrogation sessions. The first ten days of this period, I received no food, though I got some from the puppet troops and co-prisoners and also medicine. After another five months, I was freed. Meanwhile my niece, Tran Thi Khiem, was captured and was tortured; glass was stuffed into her vagina and she died. But before she died, she admitted that she was me. And since I had used a false name since my third arrest, everyone now thought I was dead. I was finally freed and gained a liberated zone, where I was hospitalized for three months.

The third witness was Hoang Tan Hung, forty-six, a sugar merchant from the hamlet of Tan My, Pho Minh village, Duc Pho district in Quang Ngai province. He told us how on May 10, 1965, at 0700, he was heading toward the provincial capital, with his friends Anh and Son, when two ordinary planes and four jets started strafing and bombing the hamlets of Ba La and Van Tuong, which were four kilometres from where he was going to market:

This area was a puppet-held area, although five days earlier the NLF had won a big battle there. The Americans obviously thought it was now NLF territory, so they bombed it with rockets, explosives and napalm. At the buzz of the planes, we hid in bushes. We heard a big bang and then a huge flame surrounded us. I felt a fantastic heat and ran toward some huts three hundred metres away. But the heat wore me out and I fell. Witnesses ran up to me and saw that I was actually burning and threw earth on my skin, then took me to an infirmary fifteen kilometres away, in the liberated zone.

I was unconscious during the trip and came to only in the hospital. I was told that my body was actually smoking for an hour after I had passed out. I felt as if I was in a furnace and lost consciousness again. I was naked, resting on banana leaves. This lasted for ten days (coming to, passing out). As all my back was burned I could not lie on it. I kept drinking, eating nothing. The pain was tremendous and I had a very high fever. The infirmary could not provide the proper treatment so I had to be moved to a regular hospital. The journey took fifteen days in a hammock. Flies and lice flocked around me and chunks of my burned flesh dropped off. A liquid oozed constantly out of my body. For four months my body stank and I was delirious. I had to be seated because I could not lie down. I could not eat, only take liquids. After four months I became a normal patient; after the fifth month, I was sent home to recuperate in the hospital in my district, which is in a liberated zone. But my home hamlet itself was still not liberated then. I was released from hospital in October 1965, but

I still get very hot, and a yellow liquid still oozes out of my body. I still have to sleep naked and am still a bit too warm today.

Mr Hoang then removed his shirt. His whole back was scarred (Photo 24b). He could not move his head. His left ear had melted into his head and is deaf. His left arm had fused into his body at the top. His back was as hard as a board. The day I talked to him, January 10, 1967, was quite cold and I was wearing a sweater under my jacket, yet he was hot outdoors as well as in. He told us that his body always itches.

He continued:

My friends Anh and Son were also burned, but not as badly. They had to be hospitalized for three months. But they were lucky for, like me, there are thousands. I've seen hundreds myself, in my own village. There used to be 6,500 people in my village living in six hamlets. Now 4,000 are homeless and four hamlets are destroyed. The village was raided because the population rose up against the strategic hamlets in the area.

I asked him if he had ever spent time in such a hamlet. He answered:

Yes, starting in 1961. It was the hamlet of Thanh Lam, in Pho Minh, in the same district and province where I lived in 1965. There were 1,500 people in 450 houses in this strategic hamlet. It was surrounded by a ditch eight metres wide, three metres deep, plus a wall and barbed wire. Inside, the hamlet was divided into twenty squares of houses, all separated by barbed wire. There were mines all around. Each square or section was divided into groups of three houses, guarded by puppet troops. When we were told to move into the hamlet, we were given three days. If we protested, the women were raped, the men beaten, and chickens stolen.

I was a peasant then. I had to start cultivating the land at 6 A.M. and be back by five. Each time we left for work, we had to show a card. To go anywhere but to work we had to have a special permit. If we did not get back to the hamlet by 5 P.M., we were not allowed to come in for the rest of the night and in the morning we were beaten and tortured on the assumption that we had been out helping the Viet Cong. The lights had to be out at 6 P.M. Any movement outside was fired upon. Inside, a special permit was needed to move around, and then only if we held a light in front of us. A family was never allowed to leave the hamlet together. All that I earned was taken away from me in special taxes. People were divided into three groups: dangerous (former resistance fighters); normal workers; families of the puppet troops. The last group could go out quite often; the first, never—except to work under supervision.

I had to be a guard one night out of every two. Whatever medical help there was (a nurse and two aides) was reserved for the third group (puppet families). There was a school, but only families of the puppet troops were allowed to send their children there free. The children of the second group could attend if their parents paid. None of the children of the first group could attend. Payment was not official, but to the masters, to the guards, etc., in other words, bribes. The second group also had to get permission from the chief, which meant more bribes. Occasionally we were grouped either by sections or all together to listen to imaginary victories, to political indoctrination and especially to hear praises of American aid. Shortly after we had moved in, we had an uprising in which three puppets were killed. We took arms and destroyed the hamlet. But we were eventually surrounded by puppet forces and forced to rebuild the hamlet. We revolted again. In fact, there were thirty-eight revolts before we were liberated in 1964. That's when I went to live in Tan My.

Nguyen Van Tien, who had silently sat back listening while these three and other witnesses told us their stories, suddenly spoke up. 'How do you expect us ever to give up?' he asked. 'What you have heard here today happens all the time in the South, everywhere where there are American and puppet troops. Even if a peasant is willing to live under American domination, even if all he cares about is his stomach, he cannot. He sees tortures, murders, massacres all around him all the time. He himself is arbitrarily beaten, taken off his land, forced to be slave labour in a camp.' Then, handing me a folder, he added: 'Look, read this. This happened only a few days ago.' What he handed me was a statement issued by the NLF. It read, in part:

Document No. 12
EXCERPTS FROM THE 'URGENT STATEMENT'
Issued by the Committee of the South Vietnam National Front for Liberation for the central part of Central Vietnam. Mimeographed; December 22, 1966; in English.

The Committee of the South Vietnam National Front for Liberation for the central part of Central Vietnam solemnly and urgently denounces to the people at home and abroad that for more than a month now the United States imperialists, in an attempt to recover from their heavy defeats in the past dry season, and carry out their 'pacification' plan, sent United States marines and Pak Jung Hi [South Korean] mercenaries stationed at Chu Lai to Son Tinh and Binh Son districts, Quang Ngai province, to raid and massacre civilians most savagely, plunder and raze to the ground many villages.

During the raid between November 19 to December 5 against villages west of Son Tinh district, elements of the United States 1st Marine Division and Pak Jung Hi mercenaries of the 'Blue Dragon' Brigade savagely massacred civilians while the people were working peacefully and children studying or playing joyfully in infant classes in the liberated area.

They swarmed up and surrounded one hamlet after another. They arrested the people, forced them into houses, massacred them with gunfire or grenades, and then set fire to these houses. They even killed peasants working in the fields or going on the roads, and children playing or learning at schools. In this way, they massacred more than 100 people in Vinh Loc hamlets, 62 in Phuoc Binh hamlet (An Thuyet village), 57 in Dien Nien hamlet, and nearly 100 in Phuoc Loc and An Tho hamlets. Most of the victims were women, old people, children and peasants. A number of families were completely massacred. More barbarous still, they pushed women, children and old people into shelters, and threw grenades and sprayed poison gas into them. Many of the victims were killed right away with blood oozing from their mouths and their eyes blown out of their sockets. They stripped women to the skin and took turns in raping them to death; among the victims were little girls of 11 or 12 years of age. They also raped many pregnant women and trampled on their belly until the foetus shot out. In Son Tra village, they raped a woman with child, then ripped open her belly, clawed out the foetus and cut it into three parts; then they even cut off the breasts and limbs of the mother. They also thrust sticks into women's genital organs until the victims died to their laughter.

They wrested a number of children from their mothers and cut off their heads and put them in plastic boxes which, they said, would be sent home.

In the first day of the raid from December 5 to 6 against villages east of Binh Son district, they took away a number of civilians and killed many of them. The following morning, when the people were having their breakfast and preparing to go to fields, United States troops and Pak Jung Hi mercenaries came from nearby positions such as Go Trinh, Go Dong, etc., and surrounded Lac Son, Loc Tu, Long Binh and An Phuoc hamlets (Binh Ky village). They arrested 400 civilians, mostly women, old people and children, marched them off in groups of 20 or 30, forced them into houses, then massacred them with grenades. Some of the people survived only to be shot dead at once. Then they pulled out a number of women's and children's corpses, ripped up their belly and took out the livers to eat.

When I had finished reading, Nguyen stood up and said, softly but firmly: 'No matter what happens, the people of Vietnam will continue to fight until they are free of such barbarians.'

X

CONCLUSION

Every Vietnamese is at war—either fighting, working or suffering. He is completely committed and genuinely patriotic. Washington officials may claim that it is tiny North Vietnam which is attacking big America, but the vast majority of Americans don't feel it—and a great proportion does not even agree. In North Vietnam, however, every single man, woman and child knows that it is the American who is the aggressor. He knows it, not through propaganda or brainwashing, but because every day he hears the planes, he sees the bombs and he suffers the raids. There does not exist, I was told, an area that has not been bombed, and many areas, usually the most populated, are said to be hit almost every single day. In some cases, the planes bring not only bombs and rockets but also napalm. And, I was told, about half of all the bombs are the fragmentation type which don't harm machines or buildings, which only rip the bark off trees, but which kill, maim and cause incredible pain to people and animals.

The evidence is overwhelming. My conclusion is simply what I have just described. And what I have just described is what I saw. Some of it was shown to me very carefully. Some I asked to see on short notice or on the spur of the moment. And some I saw strictly by accident. Yet it was all the same—and it was harrowing.

—*New York City*
August 1967

APPENDIX A

EYEWITNESS REPORT ON CAMBODIA

From Hanoi I returned to Phnom Penh, the capital of Cambodia. Between January 15 and January 19, 1967, with other members of my team and those of a new team *en route* to Hanoi, I visited five areas where the Vietnamese war was said to overlap on to Cambodia. The first three were border sites where Cambodians claim that their neutrality is constantly violated. The last two were 'trails', where it is Cambodia which is supposed to be violating its own neutrality.

The first day we journeyed to Svay Rieng and Khet Prey Veng provinces where the Cambodian–South Vietnamese border had been crossed many times by Vietnamese (Saigon) troops, often supported by United States military planes. In the Keo Cheas district I talked to a thirty-year-old border official named Penh Sapath, who told me that he had been wounded on January 9, 1967, at 12.30 P.M., by American planes firing rockets eight hundred metres inside Cambodian territory. At the hospital in Rau I talked to two peasants, Keo Pich, twenty, and Phank Yim, twenty-five, who had been wounded (legs shattered) by a US mine placed by Saigon troops three hundred metres inside Cambodia. At the border town of Prek Neak Loeung, near Kompong Trabek, which we reached by boat, I saw the marks of artillery fire, which occurred, I was told, on November 22, 1966, from 1840 to 2330 hours. One guard, two women and two children were killed, and two guards and three children were wounded. I spoke to one of the wounded guards, Minh Tin, who verified the story. The town, which is separated from Vietnam by a 200-foot-wide river, was clearly marked with towers and flags.

On January 16, 1967, I interviewed a series of Khmer (Cambodian) refugees from South Vietnam in a refugee camp in the Phom Den area, south of Takeo, near the border. One of them, Chau Pen, thirty-five, told me:

I came to Cambodia because of mistreatment by American-Vietnamese forces in my hometown. My house was burned down, my brother and sister were killed at Le Tri, in the district of Tri

151

Tong, eighteen kilometres inside South Vietnam, in the province of Chau Doc. I came here in 1964. Before I came, my village was bombed and I was forced to join a labour brigade which pillaged our own village and confiscated the belongings of all the people there. I was then forced to join the puppet army and saw how anyone suspected of aiding the Viet Cong and anyone who was not exuberantly enthusiastic over the puppet forces and their occupation was immediately suspected of being pro-Viet Cong. Such people were tortured by fish sauce being stuffed down the nostrils. I had been recruited by force and my parents did not even know.

Many of the tortures that I witnessed were also witnessed by American forces. In fact, when I refused to go into the army I myself was tortured and there were American soldiers present. In my case, fish sauce was stuffed down my nostrils, then a soldier stood on my stomach. It was painful but not too bad, more of a punishment than a torture. I saw seven people of my village tortured more seriously, however, and they were tortured in the pagoda of our town. Finally my town was taken over completely and both my brother and sister were shot as Viet Cong suspects. One hundred puppet troops and five American officers began shooting in the town and strafing people as they ran. It was then that I ran and escaped here.

The next refugee I talked to was Chau Sin, thirty-two, a farmer. He said:

I came to Cambodia by escaping at night in 1962 after I had been wounded when American-Vietnamese troops took over my town, Phnom Pi, in Tri Tong district, in the province of Chau Doc, to take us to a strategic hamlet. I saw my village burned down completely and I saw the American-Vietnamese troops shoot people, kick them, torture them, and, in general, treat them like cattle to force them to do their bidding.

Chau Sim, forty, also a peasant, said:

At Pos Tuk, also in Tri Tong district, I was captured in October, 1966, and jailed with four other villagers and with my father as Viet Cong sympathizer-suspects. We were beaten with kicks and sticks before our interrogator. My mother then managed to give the local authorities 10,000 riels for our release and so I was freed and immediately rushed to Cambodia where I arrived on January 8, 1967. When I was beaten, American soldiers were always present, though they did not participate in the beating. My village was completely destroyed, including the pagoda, by artillery fire, and the area around it was sprayed from planes with a red-and-white powder [chemicals].

A peasant woman named Sang, thirty-five, from Pnom Pi, Tri Tong district, said she escaped to Cambodia in 1965 after her village had been completely destroyed by American-Vietnamese forces. She said that in the incident, one day in October 1964, her father and three brothers had been killed. She was out in the fields when the troops arrived, surrounded the village completely so no one could escape and rounded up the men to put them into the Vietnamese army. She explained:

Those who refused were tortured until they gave in or, if they did not, were shot on the spot. When the army seemed satisfied that they had taken as many troops as they needed, they levelled the village, and in the process burned down three pagodas, killing the bonzes within.

Chau Seang, thirty-five, was enrolled in the army by force in 1964 in Cheh Gia province and put into a unit which was ordered to burn down a village which he knew was a Khmer village. He was also told to get information from people by torturing them:

I tried to do as little as possible but I admit that under the threat of my own life I did participate in some of these incidents. A few months later I managed to escape to Cambodia but only after I had finally refused to fire on my people and was tortured for that refusal. One American soldier was present during my torture which included electric rod shocks on my thumbs which, as you can see, are now broken and deformed. Incidentally, when we were ordered to fire on the people, the man who gave the order was an American soldier. My unit, the 11th Battalion, was two-thirds Vietnamese and one-third Khmer.

Chau Pho, thirty-eight, told me that he was in Pnom Pi in 1964 when the village was destroyed by machine-gun fire, the dropping of gasoline, phosphorus and napalm bombs and the strafing of the survivors as they ran out. 'In all,' he said, 'there were seven hundred houses destroyed.'

The camp in which I interviewed these refugees included 1,500 people, of whom 367 were refugees from tortures or mistreatment by American-Vietnamese forces in the provinces bordering Cambodia. All of the 1,500 were Khmer, that is, Cambodians, who at one point or another during the French colonization of Indochina, had gone over into an area now considered South Vietnamese. Most had been repatriated, but not the 367. These had crossed the canal at the frontier by swimming or in small boats. Among them was a bonze called Kan Kang who had seen his pagoda bombed in Tri Tong in 1961 and had come to Cambodia then. The refugee village was two kilometres from the frontier and was under the jurisdiction of the governor of Takeo, whose name was Tum Kim Heng and whom I photographed with the bonze.

On January 17, 1967, I visited the Cambodia-Thailand border in the area near Khemark Phouminville. To get there we went first by plane (a Royal Air Cambodge DC-3), then by jeep, then by boat and finally on foot, reaching at last the four outposts where Thai forces had violated Cambodian neutrality. Those outposts were Cham Yeam, Chhne Ksach, Raivong and Kirivong. At all four sites I saw marks of shells, post-huts burned down and, generally, scorched trees and brush all round. I could see Thai outposts in the background, two kilometres from where we were, and through binoculars I could clearly make out both the Thai flag and, on top of a hill facing it, roughly one kilometre inside Cambodia territory and one kilometre from us, the Cambodian flag.

On January 18, we flew to Stung Treng and from there rode by jeep, first along Route 13 and then along hard trails, to Siem Pang, near the Laotian border. This was the so-called Sihanouk trail, along which Cambodians, according to United States charges, are supposed to be sending war material to the Communist Pathet Lao forces and to the Viet Cong, and along which North Vietnamese supposedly infiltrate into the South. During that day we covered at least two hundred miles of the trail which was navigable by jeep but was broken at Siem Pang by the Ton Le Tong River, across which there were no bridges. The river was deep even though it was the dry season; during the wet season, it must surely overflow. If the Sihanouk trail is used as an infiltration and/or supply route, then it must be of very minor importance. Naturally, there is no way for me to state categorically that North Vietnamese troops do not use this trail; the fact that I did not see any North Vietnamese on it and the fact that the few peasants around to whom I talked said they had never seen any, cannot prove that no Vietnamese or Cambodian ever uses it. But it seemed to me beyond question that the Sihanouk trail has never been a major infiltration route (unless the Cambodian authorities guarding the river are all involved in a conspiracy with the North Vietnamese and help them to build bridges, which they then destroy before the arrival of newsmen).

On January 19, we flew to Labansiek. From there on Route 19, a dirt road, we drove to Andaung Pech where the United States and the South Vietnamese claim is located the headquarters of the 325th North Vietnamese Division. This area is supposedly the centre of the

Ho Chi Minh trail. According to American forces, as reported by UPI on August 5, 1965, the area is crammed with antennae; it is also supposed to have an airport which allows North Vietnamese planes to land and take off at will.

The Ho Chi Minh trail is not navigable by vehicle. It is made up of a series of paths which interconnect. Along these paths are a series of holes which could appear to be individual shelters. These holes are flanked by tall bamboo sticks which could look like antennae. What they are, however, and I photographed them extensively, are holes dug by a Cambodian tribe who search for precious stones. The holes are fifteen feet or more deep and the bamboo sticks are poles used as pulleys to bring the dirt out of the ground. As for the air field, it does, in fact, exist. It was used by the French in the old days to supply their troops stationed nearby. However, it has been abandoned since 1960, when it was last used to evacuate the sick during a malaria epidemic. It is now covered with bush at least five feet tall, making the field absolutely unusuable except for helicopters. (And the United States itself says that the North Vietnamese do not have helicopters.) Furthermore, had the field been used extensively by helicopters at least some of the bush would have been trampled down or cut out, which is not the case.

For two hours I wandered around the town (called Bokeo) near this area. I asked all sorts of people if they had ever seen planes land or take off and/or North Vietnamese troops. No one said yes, all said no. Unless one is prepared to maintain that two hundred different people in a tiny, forsaken town had all been brainwashed to tell the same story in different ways (which would make the Cambodians the greatest propagandists in the world), the charge, that the Ho Chi Minh trail is used as extensively as the United States claims it is, is absolutely groundless. Again, however, there is no way in which I can prove that it has never been used. One can never prove an absolute negative. Still, what I saw made it clear to me that if the Ho Chi Minh trail is used by the North Vietnamese, it serves only to filter foot soldiers in very small quantities.

Bokeo's mayor, Thungdi Nouyim, fifty-two, told me that the area is constantly under surveillance by American reconnaissance planes and that at the beginning the tribe digging for precious stones used to be frightened by these planes and would drop down to the ground when they were buzzed. Now, he said, they are so used to them that they keep right on digging.

APPENDIX B

THE TONKIN GULF INCIDENT—
AND BEYOND

On July 25, 1964, North Vietnam charged that American ships had fired on Vietnamese fishing vessels. (Radio Hanoi, July 25, 1964.)

On July 30, 1964, South Vietnamese patrol boats raided North Vietnamese fishing vessels in the Tonkin Gulf, then, protected by the US destroyer *Maddox*, bombarded the North Vietnamese islands of Hon Me and Hon Ngu. (International Control Commission, July 31; Radio Hanoi, August 1, 1964.)

On July 29, 1964, South Vietnamese Air Force Commander (later General and Premier) Ky revealed that South Vietnamese commandos had been parachuted into North Vietnam. (*Le Monde*, July 29, 1964.)

Such raids had taken place since 1957 and intensively since 1961, especially in the Tonkin area. These commandos usually went in by air but sometimes by sea. (Georges Chaffard, *Le Monde* correspondent in South Vietnam, *Le Monde*, August 7, 1964.)

On August 2, 1964, the official 'Tonkin Gulf Incident' begins. The first statements by Washington and by the American press were that the *Maddox* and *C. Turner Joy* were far out at sea. It turned out differently, however: 'It was testified that they went in at least eleven miles in order to show that we do not recognize a twelve-mile limit, which I believe North Vietnam has asserted.' (Senator Fulbright, *Congressional Record*, August 6, 1964, p. 18407.)

But, the same day, the Pentagon described the incident as 'unwelcome, but not especially serious'. (*New York Times*, August 3, 1964.)

On August 4, 1964, the North Vietnamese 'People's Army High Command' issued a long statement of which the following is part:

This is what happened in the afternoon of August 2. The US imperialists are raising a hue and cry about what they call 'an unprovoked attack by three torpedo boats of North Viet Nam'. They have made such clamours to cover their own acts of provocation and sabotage, their violation of the territorial waters and airspace and their encroachment on the sovereignty and territory of the Democratic Republic of Viet Nam.

It should be pointed out that the above-mentioned activities of the US Navy in North Viet Nam's territorial waters coincided with the activities of US aircraft which, taking off from bases in Thailand and Laos, bombed the Nam Can border post and rocketed Noong De village in Ky Son district, Nghe An province, near the Viet Nam-Laos border on August 1 and 2, 1964.

The High Command of the Viet Nam People's Army strongly denounces to public opinion at home and abroad these provocative activities of the US Government and its henchmen in South Viet Nam and Laos. The Government of the Democratic Republic of Viet Nam regards them as extremely serious violations of the 1954 Geneva Agreements on Viet Nam and the 1962 Geneva Agreements on Laos, and blatant encroachments upon the sovereignty and territory of the Democratic Republic of Viet Nam, which resulted in aggravating the situation in this area.

(DRV Ministry of Foreign Affairs,
Press and Information Department, October 1964; in English.)

On August 5, 1964, claiming another 'unprovoked' attack by North Vietnamese patrol boats on the *Maddox* and *Turner Joy* (of which there were no proof, no photographs, no eyewitness accounts), US bombers, fighters and fighter-bombers attacked North Vietnamese installations, destroying bases, twenty-five PT-boats, fuel depots, etc. (*New York Times* and *Le Monde*, August 6, 1964.)

On August 6, 1964, the North Vietnamese Government issued the following statement (excerpts):

On August 5, 1964, jet planes taking off from the US Seventh Fleet in the Pacific flew in many waves to strafe and bomb a number of places in the Vinh, Ben Thuy area, near the Gianh River mouth and in the close vicinity of Hongay city, causing losses and damages to the local population.

What is extremely serious is that orders for the attack were given to the US Air Force by US President Lyndon Johnson himself.

As is known, the US imperialists are being defeated and bogged down in their war of aggression in South Viet Nam. To extricate themselves from this situation, on the one hand, they are making every effort to step up the war there, and on the other, they are frantically engaging in provocations and sabotage activities against the Democratic Republic of Viet Nam, and threatening to extend the war to the North. At the same time, they are intensifying their intervention in Laos and attempting to jeopardize the independence and neutrality of Cambodia.

(DRV Ministry of Foreign Affairs,
Press and Information Department, October 1964; in English.)

On August 19, 1964, North Vietnam replied to the United Nations, where the United States had lodged a complaint for the DRV's 'unprovoked act of aggression', with the following note (excerpts):

The Government of the Democratic Republic of Viet Nam holds that the 'complaint' lodged by the US Government with the UN Security Council is a slander, an act contrary to the 1954 Geneva Agreements on Viet Nam and should be rejected.

The incidents recently provoked by the US Government in the Bac Bo Gulf (Tonkin Gulf) are part of a pre-arranged scheme. Since late July 1964, the US Government has sent its air and naval craft to intrude repeatedly into the airspace and the territorial waters of the Democratic Republic of Viet Nam. Near the Viet Nam–Laos border, on August 1 and 2, US aircraft bombed and strafed Nam Can and Noong De which are located deeply in Vietnamese territory. Along the coasts, on July 30, US naval craft shelled Hon Me island (Thanh Hoa province) and Hon Ngu island (Nghe An province). In the afternoon of August 2, the US destroyer *Maddox* which had been indulging in provocations along North Vietnamese coasts since the night of July 31, opened fire in Vietnamese territorial waters on patrol boats of the Democratic Republic of Viet Nam, which were thus compelled to take action in self-defence. Immediately after, the United States dispatched new units of the Seventh Fleet into the Bac Bo Gulf. In the night of August 3, US and South Vietnamese war vessels, renewing their provocations, shelled the Ron and Deo Ngang areas (Quang Binh province). Thereafter, Washington circulated the imaginary story about 'second deliberate attack made by an unknown number of North Vietnamese PT boats on the USS *Maddox* and USS *Turner Joy* in the Tonkin Gulf in international waters' in the night of August 4. This was used by President Lyndon Johnson as a pretext to order a raid by aircraft of the Seventh Fleet against many areas of the Democratic Republic of Viet Nam on August 5, causing casualties and losses to the local population. To make up for their defeats and extricate themselves from the quagmire in South Viet Nam, the us ruling circles have, since early 1964, openly stated on many occasions their design 'to carry the war to North Viet Nam'. In the Honolulu Conference held on June 1, 1964, decisions were taken on measures to step up the war of aggression in South Viet Nam and expand it to North Viet Nam. No doubt, the August 5, 1964, act of war against the Democratic Republic of Viet Nam is part of the materialization of the us plan to extend the war to North Viet Nam.

(DRV Ministry of Foreign Affairs,
Press and Information Department, October 1964; in English.)

On September 1, 1964, North Vietnam issued the following statement (excerpts) on the United States position on 12-mile territorial limits:

According to Western news agencies' reports, us Under-Secretary of Defence Cyrus Vance has recently declared that Washington did not recognize the limit of North Viet Nam's territorial waters as twelve miles and recognized a limit of three miles, and us ships had received a formal order not to move inside this three-mile limit. . . .

The question of defining the breadth of the territorial waters is strictly within the sovereignty of each country. The us Government has absolutely no right to decide the breadth of the territorial waters of the Democratic Republic of Viet Nam. The Government of the Democratic Republic of Viet Nam declares that the question of defining the breadth of its territorial waters as twelve miles in accordance with the juridical custom in the country, is within its sovereign rights and in keeping with international juridical custom.

The declaration of the us Under-Secretary of Defence is obviously intended to justify the repeated intrusions into the territorial waters of the Democratic Republic of Viet Nam by the destroyer *Maddox* and other us war vessels since July 31, 1964, and to corroborate in a clumsy manner the imaginary story of a so-called 'attack on us warships in international waters'.

The declaration is also intended to cover up the us Government's dark design to cook up new fabrications about alleged 'attacks against us warships in international waters' as pretexts for increased war acts against the Democratic Republic of Viet Nam.

(DRV Ministry of Foreign Affairs,
Press and Information Department, October 1964; in English.)

On September 4, 1964, North Vietnam's Foreign Minister sent the following message (excerpts) to the participants of the 1954 Geneva Conference:

The US authorities have openly announced the possibility that 'wider action against North Viet Nam might become necessary'; they have ordered US warships to intrude into the territorial waters of the Democratic Republic of Viet Nam (twelve miles), and have even threatened US Air Force action against North Viet Nam. Since August 5, 1964, US air and naval craft have repeatedly carried on their intrusions into the airspace and territorial waters of the Democratic Republic of Viet Nam, and over recent days, the US Seventh Fleet has been placed on a round-the-clock alert.

Thus it suffices for the US Government to repeat such fabrications as the so-called 'Tonkin Gulf incidents' or to stage another provocation to indulge in new aggressive acts against the Democratic Republic of Viet Nam.

It is crystal clear that the US Government is still scheming new military adventures against the Democratic Republic of Viet Nam. The situation in Viet Nam and Indo-China is at present of the utmost gravity.

The Government of the Democratic Republic of Viet Nam has more than once stated its eagerness for peace and its constant desire of respecting and correctly implementing the 1954 Geneva Agreements on Viet Nam, but it is determined to oppose any attempt by the US imperialists and their agents to encroach upon its sovereignty and territory and undermine the peaceful work of the people of North Viet Nam. Any act of provocation and aggression against the Democratic Republic of Viet Nam will surely be thwarted by the strength of the entire Vietnamese people. The US Government will have to bear full responsibility for all consequences arising from its war acts.

The Vietnamese people and the Government of the Democratic Republic of Viet Nam are deeply confident that peace-loving peoples in the world, who have recently voiced opposition to the US war acts against North Viet Nam, will continue to condemn the US manoeuvres to carry the war to North Viet Nam, and to extend strong support to the Vietnamese people's just struggle.

The Government of the Democratic Republic of Viet Nam energetically exposes the US Government's extremely dangerous manoeuvres as mentioned above and earnestly requests the Co-Chairman and the participants of the 1954 Geneva Conference on Indo-China, in accordance with Point 13 of the Final Declaration of the Conference, jointly to study such measures as might prove to be necessary to secure from the US Government an immediate end to all acts of provocation and sabotage against the Democratic Republic of Viet Nam, and to the aggressive war in South Viet Nam as well as the withdrawal of all US troops, military personnel and arms from South Viet Nam, thereby ensuring respect for, and correct implementation of, the 1954 Geneva Agreements on Viet Nam with a view to maintaining and consolidating peace in Indo-China and South-East Asia.

(DRV Ministry of Foreign Affairs, Press and Information Department, October 1964; in English.)

In December 1965, it became clear that the 1964 Tonkin Gulf incident, which eventually led to the continuous bombardment of North Vietnam, followed a series of very serious peace overtures, which the US ignored, then rejected, and which were not made public until the following year. (Bernard Fall, *New York Times*, December 12, 1965.)

In 1966, the link between the US not wanting to negotiate in 1964 and its deliberate escalation of the Vietnam conflict by bombing the North became obvious. Professors Franz Schurmann, Peter Dale Scott and Reginald Zelnik wrote: 'The American air attack on August 5, 1964, on North Vietnam was mounted at a time when there were strong international pressures for negotiations.' (*The Politics of Escalation in Vietnam*, New York: Fawcett, 1966.)

On June 29, 1966, President Johnson ordered raids 'close to the heart of Hanoi and Haiphong' and told his daughter: 'Your father may go down in history as having started World War III.' He added: 'You may not wake up tomorrow.' (*New York Times, Washington Daily News* and *Washington Post*, May 12, 1967.)

It turns out that the very day after Johnson, alone, ignoring the world, the people of the United States, the Constitution, had risked starting World War III, that is on June 30, 1966, he flew out to Omaha and told the people of the United States: 'Peace is more within our reach than at any time in this century.' (*I. F. Stone's Weekly*, May 22, 1967.)

APPENDIX C

GENERAL GIAP'S DOCUMENT

On January 26, 1961, General Vo Nguyen Giap, Commander in Chief of North Vietnam's People's, Army, sent a letter to India's Ambassador M. Gopala Menon, Chairman of the International Commission for Supervision and Control in Vietnam (the ICC), complaining of repeated violations by the South Vietnamese Government and by United States forces of the 1954 Geneva Agreements. He attached to his letter a document in English prepared by the Government of North Vietnam. Nowhere else have North Vietnam's charges against the Diem regime and United States forces been so carefully or eloquently detailed. Excerpts from the document follow:

I

FROM THE CESSATION OF HOSTILITIES TO 1958
Discrimination measures

Immediately after the cessation of hostilities, in the areas under the control of the French Union Forces including the French Expeditionary Corps and the military forces of the Ngo Dinh Diem administration, the authorities ordered their troops to shoot at the crowds of demonstrators from former resistance regions, who were hailing the return of peace: such was the case in Ngan Son, Chi Thanh, Ha Lam, Cho Duoc, Vinh Xuan, Mo Cay, etc. These incidents resulted in hundreds of casualties. After on-the-spot enquiries, the International Commission recorded, in a number of cases, violations of the Geneva Agreements against the South Viet Nam authorities.

After taking over all former VPA resistance regions south of the 17th parallel, and listing former resistance members in every locality, the Ngo Dinh Diem administration put into practice a policy of reprisal and discrimination against individuals and organizations who had participated in the Resistance war.

Former resistance members and their relatives—who were to be classified afterwards as 'illegal' or 'semi-legal citizens'—were compelled to report periodically to the authorities; they were subjected

162

to all kinds of restrictions and prohibitions in their movements, including business movements. In numerous localities such as Khanh Hoa, Go Cong, My Tho, etc., they were issued with red identity cards, as distinguished from white-card holders. In many areas such as Ninh Hoa (Khanh Hoa), the authorities put a red and blue stamp on the soles of the feet of former resistance members at sunset to check on the prints on the following morning.

People who had relatives regrouped to North Viet Nam were forced to cut off all conjugal or paternal relations with them. On December 15, 1954, Le Trung Chi, Chief of Quang Nam province, ordered all the wives of former resistance members, whether the latter were regrouped to the North or still living with their families, to report within three months to the administrative services to make applications for divorce. In implementation of this instruction, 'divorce weeks' were organized by the authorities in numerous localities such as the communes of Duy Trinh (Duy Xuyen district), Dien Ninh (Dien Ban district), Que Xuan (Que Son district), etc. Divorces imposed on the wives of former resistance members were regular occurrences in South Viet Nam. Mothers were also forced to deny their children who had participated in the Resistance war. On December 15, 1954, Mrs Nguyen Giao, at Duy Hung commune (Quang Nam province), was compelled to divorce her husband and to deny her son, both being former resistance members regrouped to the North.

Cases happened when even after his death, the body of a former resistance member was subjected to indignities and shocking violations. The families of Messrs Dao Yen, Ngo Du and Nguyen Huan in Duy Xuyen district, Quang Nam province, were not permitted to wear mourning for them after their murder by the authorities. On account of his participation in the Resistance war the Buddhist monk Che Van Vang in Thanh Phuoc commune, Go Dau Ha district, Tay Ninh province, was refused burial for six days after his death.

Individual arrests

From 1954 to 1955, individual arrests and murders were frequent, and people killed in such circumstances were numbered by the thousand. Some were summoned before the communal council or the district administration, and never came back; others were secretly arrested at night-time, and taken to unrevealed places; others were arrested by the authorities while going to their fields, to market, to fishing ponds or to work in the forests. All were submitted to atrocious tortures before being killed, jailed or sent to concentration camps.

Some typical cases are given hereunder:

The murder of Mr Tran Nguyen:
Messrs Tran Nguyen, Mai, Toai, Tien, Dan and Dieu in Bang Son, Cam Lo district, Quang Tri province, were all former resistance members. On December 22, 1954, Le Dinh Phap, Chief of Cam Lo District, Thai Hanh, a civil official, and Dat, Chief of the district police, ordered Mr Tran Nguyen to be arrested and strangled. Then they had Messrs Mai and Toai arrested and savagely tortured into declaring themselves to be 'members of an assassination committee' of the Government of the Republic of Viet Nam, and author of 'the murder of Mr Tran Nguyen'. On December 14, 1954, the authorities set up a 'military court', which sentenced to death Messrs Mai and Toai; the same sentence was passed against Messrs Tien, Dan and Dieu in their absence.

On the other hand, the South Viet Nam administration lodged a complaint with the International Commission charging the Government of the Democratic Republic of Viet Nam with responsibility for the 'murder' of Mr Tran Nguyen.

On this case, the Commission gave the following finding:
'From the thorough enquiry made into this case by Mobile Team 57, and from the detailed evidence by the Team, the Commission has reached the following conclusions:

'1. The complaint of the French High Command (which then represented the Ngo Dinh Diem administration) that the murder of Tran Nguyen was engineered by an Assassination Committee has been disproved.

'2. The action taken against Mai and Toai, and the sentences passed against Tien, Dan and Dieu in their absence amount to reprisals against former resistance workers and, hence, violation of Article 14 (c).

'3. There is a grave suspicion that the murder of Tran Nguyen was engineered by the authorities with the intention of planting it on the accused.'

On the basis of these conclusions the Commission requested the competent authorities in South Viet Nam to announce the 'innocence' of the five accused persons publicly, and to mete out punishment to those responsible for this affair, in particular, to Le Dinh Phap, Thai Hanh and Dat. (Ref. IC letter No. ICSC ADM III-38 55 139, dated June 17, 1955.)

The case of Mr Vo Luong, buried alive:
Mr Vo Luong, a former resistance member, native of Nhan Phong commune, An Nhon district, Binh Dinh province, was arrested on

October 19, 1954, and savagely tortured by the South Viet Nam authorities in an attempt to force him to declare his activities during the Resistance war. On the night of November 3, he was led by a number of agents of the South Viet Nam administration to a ditch, stabbed, then pushed into the ditch and buried though still alive.

After his torturers had gone, concentrating all his remaining strength, he succeeded in getting out of the ditch (fortunately, it was raining at that time), and made for the nearest village where he was tended; then he was taken on a stretcher to the IC Fixed Team at Qui Nhon.

Dr Vo Van Vinh at Qui Nhon concluded after examination:

'From the character of the wounds, I conclude that the man received many stabbings with a kind of flat, sharp instrument (as shown by the wound on the front part of the left forearm) ending in a sharp angle (traces of stabbings). The location of the wounds also shows that while being injured the man showed his right side and tried to defend himself with his arm (traces of cutting and stabbing).'

After a careful enquiry, on November 9, 1955, the International Commission concluded that 'in this case, there was a violation of Article 14 (c) of the Geneva Agreement'. (Ref. IC letter No. ICSC-FB-55-3-5286, dated November 9, 1955.)

The murder of Mr Tran Tham:

Native of Dai Dien Trung village, Dien Khanh district, Khanh Hoa province, Mr Tran Tham had participated in the Resistance war. Since the restoration of peace, he had resumed his normal activities to support his family. On January 18, 1955, he was arrested by the authorities under the slanderous charges of 'theft of bullocks', taken to the Dai Dien Trung post, subjected to the most savage torture which made him faint several times, and finally he was strangled. After an on-the-spot enquiry by Mobile Team F.16, the International Commission gave the following finding:

'As a result of the investigation, it has been ascertained that on January 18, 1955, Tran Tham was arrested by soldiers from the military post at Dai Dien Trung for alleged theft of bullocks, and was taken to the post. There he was tortured, beaten and throttled, as a result of which he died. It has also been found that Tran Tham was a member of the Resistance movement before the cease-fire.

'The Commission has arrived at the finding that the torture causing the death of Tran Tham constituted a breach of Article 14 (c) of the Geneva Agreement.' (Ref. IC letter No. ICSC-FB-55-2-4569, dated July 20, 1955.)

The murder of Messrs Nguyen Luong and Le Tham:
On October 3, 1954, on orders from the authorities, Major Ho Van Anh led his troops to Dien Ban district, Quang Nam province, to carry out arrests of former resistance members. Mr Le Tham at An Truong commune was shot dead and Mr Nguyen Luong at Thi Nhon commune was stabbed to death.

After an on-the-spot enquiry, the International Commission concluded: 'These murders constitute a violation of Article 14 (c) of the Geneva Agreements.' (Ref. IC letter No. ICSC-ADM-II-50-55-589, dated August 29, 1955.)

The case of Tran Thi Nham alias Ly:
Miss Tran Thi Nham alias Ly, native of Dien Hong village, Dien Ban district, Quang Nam province, was a guerilla fighter during the Resistance war. As she was a former resistance member, and had, on behalf of her village, handed over a petition to the International Commission Team at Da Nang (Tourane), she was arrested on July 28, 1955, by the security service, and subjected to tortures during three consecutive months in the Ky Lam prison. On November 20, she was arrested for the second time, savagely tortured, and again set free over one month later. In March 1956, she was arrested for the third time, and taken to Hoi An where she was subjected to tortures of mediaeval atrocity; knife incision into the flesh, application of red-hot needles to the thighs and nipples, hanging to the ceiling by means of hooks fastened to the feet, tearing out of handfuls of hair. . . . Thinking that she was doomed to die, the authorities gave her back to her family. But with the villagers' assistance, she was brought to the North for medical treatment. When she was admitted to a Hanoi hospital, her body bore over forty wounds which were still bleeding. She has exposed to the International Commission the crimes committed by the South Viet Nam administration. In January 1959, the International Commission sent its representatives to meet her in the hospital, and to hear her expound in detail her case which is still pending.

The case of Professor Nguyen Thi Dieu:
Professor Nguyen Thi Dieu, a daughter of former minister Nguyen Van Hien, and a sister of Doctor Nguyen Thi Vinh, was a member of the Executive Committee of the Nam Bo Women's Union during the Resistance war. After the return of peace, she resumed her normal business as a professor at the Duc Tri girls' school in Saigon. On July 10, 1955, she was arrested and killed most savagely by the authorities. According to the complaint of her eldest brother, Mr Nguyen Van By, an electrical engineer, the autopsy

showed many wounds: 'fractured skull, congestion in the inner ear, bruises on the wrists caused by handcuffs, contusions of the kidneys and bladder caused by kicks'.

Professor Nguyen Thi Dieu was then twenty-nine years old. She had three children and was five months pregnant.

So far, the South Viet Nam administration has persisted in opposing an on-the-spot investigation by the International Commission into this case.

. . .

Some Massacres During the 'Denounce Communists' Campaigns
[The] 'Denounce Communists' campaign resulted in hundreds, sometimes thousands, of victims. Thus the total number of people arrested, wounded, or killed was over 2,000 in the Truong Tan Buu campaign, over 3,000 in the Thoai Ngoc Hau campaign, over 10,000 (including 700 killed) in the Nguyen Hue campaign. . . . A number of campaigns were marked by savage massacres.

Some cases of ferocious persecution are given hereunder:

The general persecution in Duy Xuyen district:
From late 1954 to early 1955, during four consecutive months, the South Viet Nam authorities carried out the 'Phan Chu Trinh campaign' in Duy Xuyen district, Quang Nam province. About 8,000 former resistance members were arrested and subjected to the most savage tortures. On January 21, 1955, in one single day, the agents of the South Viet Nam administration arrested 116 people in Vinh Trinh area, and led forty-seven to the Vinh Trinh dam where they tied their arms and legs with wire, cut their tongues and ears, gouged out their eyes, cut their throats, opened their bellies, poured oil on their heads, and set fire to them. Afterwards they fastened stones to the corpses, and threw them into the river.

The International Commission sent out Mobile Team 103 for investigation into this massacre, but the team 'was not given freedom of movement, documents needed by it were not placed at its disposal and witnesses necessary for holding enquiries were not summoned. This resulted in the Mobile Team being recalled before the fulfilment of its task.' (Ref. IC letter No. IC-FB-3-49-3-154, dated February 6, 1959.)

The destruction of Huong Dien:
Like many other communes of the region, Huong Dien was during the Resistance war a base of the People's Army of Viet Nam in the mountainous area of Quang Tri province.

On July 8, 1955, the South Viet Nam administration sent its

troops to the commune to encircle the Tan Lap hamlet where they burnt down, or destroyed all dwellings and property, and massacred all inhabitants fallen into their hands, irrespective of age. On the following morning, the authorities summoned people allegedly for a 'meeting of Militia men', at Tan Hiep, a neighbouring hamlet; twenty-two persons came, and were foully murdered. On July 14, fifteen women, accompanied by ten children, went to the administration's offices to inquire about their husbands or sons who had not come back from the 'meeting of Militia men'. They were led to the A Che ravine where they were raped, then butchered, disembowelled, beheaded and thrown into the ravine. Before raping the mothers, the soldiers snatched away the children from their hands, stabbed or strangled them to death or struck their heads against the rocks. Their corpses were thrown into the ravine. On July 16, troops came again to Tan Hiep hamlet where three more grown-up persons and thirteen children were massacred, and all houses were burnt down or destroyed. On July 20, the soldiers came to Trai Ca hamlet, but all the inhabitants having fled, they seized all property, and burnt down the thirty houses of the hamlet.

Thus within twelve days, the South Viet Nam administration, putting into action one infantry battalion, razed to the ground the two hamlets of Tan Lap and Tan Hiep, killed 92 persons, including 31 children and 32 women, five of whom were pregnant.

Up to the end of 1955, 2,514,482 persons in North Viet Nam signed 17,422 petitions addressed to the International Commission in protest against the Duy Xuyen and Huong Dien massacres. So far the South Viet Nam administration has persisted in opposing on-the-spot investigations by the Commission on this subject.

The burying alive of 21 persons at Cho Duoc (Quang Nam province): On November 28, 1955, during a wave of 'denunciations of Communists', the authorities savagely tortured twenty-one persons out of hundreds of former resistance members in the communes of Binh Lac, Binh Tuy, Binh Tan, and Thang Trieu (Thang Binh district). Afterwards they put them into a cave, and buried them alive.

On December 1, the relatives and friends of the victims, having discovered the cave, came to unearth the corpses in order to organize funerals. They were encircled on orders from the authorities, and shot at. This resulted in numerous casualties. Great numbers of arrests were made.

The International Commission has decided to carry out an investigation into this case; however, the South Viet Nam authorities have so far refused to agree to such enquiries.

APPENDIX C

The Dai Loc affair:

In 1957, the 'denunciations of Communists' entered an extremely cruel stage, which the South Viet Nam authorities labelled 'the second phase'. In the framework of this great wave of terror, towards the end of 1957, the Quang Nam provincial authorities carried out mass arrests of former resistance members in Dai Loc district (more than 9,000 according to Saigon press reports). The arrested persons were led to so-called 'rooms of denunciation of Communists' which were, in fact, concentration camps, and subjected to tortures of mediaeval savagery. They were taken there high-handedly, leaving their businesses and homes, and threatened with blows and death. Driven into a *cul-de-sac*, thousands of people rose up and armed with sticks, hoes, shovels, etc., fought off the 'teams of denunciations of communists'. Their families sent in thousands of petitions to the provincial authorities, to the 'Government', to the 'National Assembly', and to the press. In spite of the ruling circles' attempts to hide the truth, the persecutions perpetrated in Dai Loc district were revealed by a number of Saigon newspapers.

The various forms of torture

There are 'modern' forms commonly applied in the colonialists' torturing rooms:

— Electric torture;

— 'Punching-ball': The victim is hung head down, and four torturers use his body as a 'punching ball' with kicks and punches;

— Beating the hands with cudgels;

— Pig cage: The victim is forced to lie flat on his belly in an open ditch with just enough place for one person, and overtopped by a cage of barbed wire;

— 'Journey by Dakota': The victim is hung head down with his hands kept in an iron press, and security agents shower him with blows;

— 'Journey by boat': Dirty soapy water mixed with urine and excrement, or small pieces of bone are poured into the mouth of the victim, tied up and compelled to lie on his back on the floor; when the stomach has swelled, a security agent tramples on him with hobnailed boots to make him throw out the water through his mouth, nostrils and anus;

— 'Journey by submarine': Immersion of the victim in cold water for hours;

The forms which were often applied by the cruel despots of the Middles Ages are also resorted to:

— Tearing out handfuls of the victim's hair;

—Kneeling on a board bristling with nails;

—Driving needles into the genital organ;

—Suspension by a hook passed through the hands or feet while the torturers drive needles into the head or belly, or other parts of the victim's body;

—Tearing off pieces of the flesh from the victim's thigh with red-hot pincers, or introducing these tools into his throat;

—Winding around the victim's fingers a bandage soaked with oil (sometimes petrol), and setting it alight;

—Burning the victim's nose and ears with oil (or sometimes petrol) soaked in pieces of cotton;

—Burning various parts of the victim's body by setting fire to bundles of straw or dry grass tied to the body;

—Cutting off the victim's lips, ears, tongue, hands and feet;

—Slashing the victim's stomach.

There are still many other forms depending on particular localities and police agents:

—Nailing the victim to a tree before killing him (case of twenty-three youths at Nhan Hoa Lap and Nhan Ninh communes, Tan An province);

—Trailing the victims to death by a jeep (case of Mr Le Ngo, former chief of a guerilla unit at Phuong Lang Dong village, Hai Lang district, Quang Tri province);

—'The Confession': The victims are obliged to stand balanced on high piles of bricks in a room where the ground bristles with long, sharp steel points, or they have to kneel down on debris of broken glass, the eyes turned towards a lighted lamp placed under a portrait of Ngo Dinh Diem or on a skull. They have to keep such position from 11 P.M. in the evening to 4 A.M. in the following morning. Those who stagger with exhaustion fall on the steel points; at the least movement a shower of blows is rained on them. According to the authorities, this practice is to enable the victims to 'repent' of the 'crime' which they committed in participating in the Resistance war against the French colonialists.

—'The test of strength': The so-called 'die-hard' elements are placed on high platforms and beaten on the head and chest with three-edged iron sticks. Then the torturers holding them by the feet thrust their head against the ground, or grasping them by the hair, they throw them against the wall until their skull and limbs are broken. Relatives and friends of the victims are forced to attend the scene.

—'Exorcising': The victim is put into a jute bag placed on a high stool in a closed room where incense is burnt, and deafening noises of drums and gongs are made as was done formerly in the 'exorcising ceremonies' in Viet Nam. Police agents pierce the victim through the bag with sharp sabres, or set the bag alight after soaking it with petrol. According to them, this form of 'exorcising' is to cast the 'Communist devil' out of the victim.

(The last three forms of torture are applied in Quang Nam concentration camps, especially that of Phu Hoa in Hoa Vang district).

—Running ahead of a jeep: The victim, completely naked, is compelled to run ahead of a jeep along a road fringed with barbed wire on both sides, the least failure would immediately result in the victim being crushed under the vehicle.

With regard to women, there are various forms of torture aimed at terrorizing them or making them barren for ever: thrusting of sticks into the vagina, cutting off of breasts, thrusting of needles into the nipples, burning of the nipples, raping in turns by syphilitic people, putting of snakes into the trousers after tying their legs together. . . .

It can be stated that there is not a single arrested person who has been subjected only once and to only one form of torture. It can also be stated that some have passed through almost every imaginable torture. Subtle tortures are intercalated with violent ones as if the aim is to protract the sufferings of the victim or to demoralize him. Thus, in a variant of the 'journey by boat', 'small pieces of bone are put into the water', and these are to remain in the victim's throat; a variant of the 'journey by Dakota' consists in hanging the victim by five ropes above a trench bristling with long sharp steel points, and slowly cutting the ropes one by one. The suspension by the feet is outdone by plunging the victim's head into a bucket of bran or excrement.

People have been massacred by various means, with those used by feudal despots being resorted to in most cases:

—Shooting;

—Guillotining;

—Shelling and bombing from the air (including napalm bombing);

—Throat-cutting;

—Beheading, disembowelling and extraction of the liver;

—Beheading, with the victim's head being shown through the streets at the end of a stick;

—Beheading and exhibition of the victim's head at the door of the military post;

—Beheading, with the victim's head being used as a target for shooting excercises;

—Cutting up of the victim's body into small pieces;

—Burying alive of the victim. Individual or collective poisoning.

171

Prisons and Concentration Camps

Within the framework of its policy of mass arrests and the promulgation of ordinance No. 6 providing for establishment of concentration camps for the detention of patriots under the pretext of 'national defence' and 'public security', the South Viet Nam administration has, on the other hand, enlarged the system of prisons left by the French colonialists and, on the other hand, set up a whole network of concentration camps in South Viet Nam.

Prisons—At the time of the cessation of hostilities, throughout South Viet Nam there were about fifty prisons located in most cases in big cities and provincial towns.

At present, districts and sometimes even communes have their own prisons. Thus, in a small province like Phu Yen, the figure at one time reached 109 for a population of about 250,000 inhabitants. As there were not enough prisons, the South Viet Nam administration transformed churches, pagodas and schools into jails. In a number of localities, they even used for this purpose underground cellars or former fortifications built during the war. The Nhat Tai and Tuong Giac pagodas . . . , and even the Caodaist Holy See of Tay Ninh, were turned into jails with hundreds of detainees being packed inside.

. . .

The regime of detention is very harsh.

The prisoners are given insufficient food rations.

They are supplied daily with 600 grams of mouldy rice cooked in lime water, and rotten dried fish. They also receive insufficient rations of drinking water and a restricted quantity of water for washing. Medicines are lacking: Sick people are not admitted to any hospital, or are sent there only when their life is doomed. The relatives of the detainees are not allowed to send them a letter or parcel. Ill treatment and savage torture are frequently inflicted. Cases happened when prisoners were executed in the dead of night without reason. Lieutenant-Colonel Nguyen Quoc Hoang, Chief of the Kien Phong province, within a few nights in late June 1960, ordered over fifty detainees in the Cao Lanh jail to be beheaded, their corpses being thrown into the river.

Such a regime has resulted in every detainee catching at least one of the following diseases: beri-beri, heart disease, tuberculosis, dysentery, anaemia. In a prison where about 2,000 prisoners are detained, from 200 to 400, sometimes even 500, people are daily confined to bed owing to sickness while the daily death rate is from one to three.

. . .

Concentration Camps—A number of camps are openly recognized as concentration camps, such as those of Pho Trach, Cho Niu, Dai Loc, etc. But most are camouflaged under various names: 'camps for a just cause' (as was the case in almost all the camps at district level in Trung Bo in 1955), 're-education centre' (as at Thu Duc, Bien Hoa, Phu Loi, Con Dao, etc.). Since 1957, there have existed camps disguised as 'agricultural settlements'.

Up to the end of 1958, the number of 'agricultural settlements' alone reached fifty. In 1960, the figure rose to 126 with more than 200,000 former resistance members being detained there.

In concentration camps, the regime of detention is not less harsh than in prisons. In particular, the political detainees in 'agricultural settlements' are required to work very hard at least for twelve hours, sometimes even for eighteen hours, a day. Their task is to build military bases, strategic roads, and military storehouses.

Here are some characteristic features of concentration camps in South Viet Nam:

'*The Con Son (Poulo Condore) political re-education centre*', established on an island several hundred kilometres away from the mainland, is used on a permanent basis for the detention of about 4,000 prisoners.

As regards food, the lack of vegetables there is such that the political detainees are obliged to eat herbs; shortage of water has resulted in their being compelled in a number a cases to quench their thirst with their own urine. The children who have followed their mothers, or who were born in the camp, are deprived not only of water for washing, but even of food; their mothers and many other detainees have to feed them out of their meagre daily rations of rice. In camp No. 1, chains of 1·5 or 3, or even 10 kilograms, are attached to the political detainee's feet. Those who are 'punished' are put into dark underground cells. Those who are still strong enough have to dive into the sea in search of coral, or to climb up rocky mountains in search of nests of salangane.

The daily average death rate is from two to three; in particular, in September 1957, it amounted to twenty. In addition, there were daily from four to five hundred people seriously sick. As a result of this regime, from December 1956 to 1959, more than 3,000 former resistance members were executed or died from starvation, torture or sickness. In December 1959, 200 political detainees were massacred at one time.

'*The Hoa Vang re-education camp*' is a small camp in Quang Nam province. Established in April 1960, it is used for the detention of about 300 former resistance members, sent there on account of their being 'illegal' or 'semi-legal' citizens, or arrested during mopping-up operations carried out by the regular army. Like others, the Hoa Vang camp is fenced in by barbed wire and surrounded by watch towers, but its distinctive feature is the existence of a kind of 'no-man's land' labelled 'forbidden area': whoever enters there, for any reason whatever, is immediately shot dead or at least arrested.

It is in this camp that the prisoners are commonly subjected to the most atrocious and subtle tortures described above: 'confession', 'test of strength', 'exorcising'.

The death rate here is very high. In the first two months alone after the establishment of the camp, more than thirty deaths were recorded.

The network of 're-education centres' and 'concentration camps' in general is developing. For instance, in the 1961 budget, the appropriations for 're-education camps' amount to 190,000,000 South Viet Nam piastres, thus showing an increase of 72,299,000 as compared with 1960; this increase alone is greater than the whole appropriations for the Ministry of the Economy, which account for only 66,216,000 piastres.

Hindrance to, and Sabotage of, the Investigations by the International Commission for Supervision and Control

Since the International Commission assumed the responsibility of supervising and controlling the implementation of the Geneva Agreements concerning Viet Nam, it has instituted, in terms of Article 37 of the Agreement on the Cessation of Hostilities in Viet Nam, the practice of investigations both documentary and on the spot to bring violations to light. But since that very day, whenever the Commission decided to carry out investigations into any case in South Viet Nam, the authorities there always tried by every means to hamper and sabotage the enquiries. They refused to produce witnesses and documents required by the Commission, imposed restrictions on the investigation teams' movements, committed violent actions against the VPA liaison officers, and even the Commission's teams, threatened the witnesses, and took reprisals against them. They went so far as to stage investigations by false teams with a view to finding out which witnesses would speak against them, and what they would say; by doing so, they aimed at persecuting such witnesses before the arrival of the true team of the Commission. Besides, they attempted to annul the validity of Article 14 (c) of the Geneva Agreement concerning Viet Nam by limiting it within the 300-day period; such interpretation was a brazen distortion of the Geneva Agreements, and was rejected by the International Commission.

Nothing is more illustrative than to let the International Commission point out the South Viet Nam authorities' manœuvres to restrict and hinder its activities in this field.

—With regard to the investigation by Mobile Team 24 into the reprisals against Mr Tran Het at Ky Lam commune, Dien Ban district, Quang Nam province, the Commission concluded that:

'1. French liaison officer expressed inability to produce witnesses.

2. Chief of province refused to give guarantee that no reprisals would be taken against witnesses. Some local authorities refused to give evidence.

3. Security of VPA liaison officers threatened. Demonstration against team and VPA liaison officers.

Withdrawn by the Comission due to lack of co-operation of local authorities and lack of security arrangement for the team and VPA liaison officers without completing all of its tasks.'

(Ref. Fourth Interim Report of the International Commission in Viet Nam to the Co-Chairmen of the Geneva Conference, appendix V, paragraph 33.)

—With regard to the investigation by Mobile Team 26 into the burying alive of Mr Vo Luong (Binh Dinh province) the Commission gave the following finding:

'Due to lack of security arrangements, team stayed in Nha Trang and went daily to the scene of the incident. There were demonstrations against the team and the presence of VPA liaison officers.'

(Ref. Fourth Interim Report, appendix V, paragraph 35.)

—With regard to the investigation by Mobile Team 57 into acts of reprisals perpetrated in Quang Tri, the Commission recorded the following:

'Not enough security arrangements on first day of investigation. An angry crowd surrounded the team but the team managed to get away.'

(Ref. Fourth Interim Report, appendix V, paragraph 37.)

—With regard to the investigation by Mobile Team 61 in Tam Ky (Quang Nam province), the Commission recorded that:

'From the date the Commission asked for concurrence to the date the team was recalled, there was a total delay of ninety-seven days. Team unable to make any investigation.'

(Ref. Fourth Interim Report, appendix V, paragraph 38.)

—With regard to the investigation by Mobile Team F. 29 (Cap St Jacques) into arrests and reprisals denounced by the inhabitants of Hien Hoa, the Commission recorded that:

'A number of witnesses prevented by soldiers from appearing before the team.'

(Ref. Fourth Interim Report, appendix V, paragraph 25, heading: 'Mobile elements of fixed team'.)

The International Commission has been meeting with ever-increasing difficulties in the supervision and control of the implementation of Article 14 (c) in South Viet Nam:

'In the Sixth Interim Report, the Commission had informed the Co-Chairmen of its difficulties in the supervision of the implementation by the parties of the provisions of Article 14 (c). Those difficulties have persisted and increased as the Commission has not received the necessary assistance and cooperation from the Government of the Republic of Viet Nam and has, therefore, not been able to supervise the implementation of Article 14 (c) in accordance with the Geneva Agreement.'

(Ref. IC letter No. IC-ADM-VI-DI-57 dated April 11, 1957, to the Co-Chairmen of the Geneva Conference.)

'The difficulties with regard to supervision and control of the execution of Article 14 (c) in the Republic of Viet Nam, mentioned in the Sixth Interim Report, have persisted and increased.'

(Ref. Seventh Interim Report of the International Commission to the Co-Chairmen of the Geneva Conference, chapter III, paragraph 19.)

'During the period under report there was no change in the stand of the Government of the Republic of Viet Nam with regard to Article 14 (c), as mentioned in the Seventh Interim Report.'

(Ref. Eighth Interim Report of the International Commission to the Co-Chairmen of the Geneva Conference, chapter III, paragraph 14.)

'During the period under report there was no change in the stand of the Government of the Republic of Viet Nam with regard to Article 14 (c) as reported to the Co-Chairmen separately, and as mentioned in paragraph 19 of the Seventh Interim Report.'

(Ref. Ninth Interim Report of the International Commission to the Co-Chairmen of the Geneva Conference, chapter III, paragraph 11.)[1]

Despite such restrictions and hindrances by the South Viet Nam administration, after investigations into a small number of cases, the International Commission recorded that in forty-two cases (involving 2,749 persons arrested, wounded, or murdered) the

[1] Fourth Interim Report covering the period from April 11 1955, to Aug. 10, 1955. Sixth Interim Report covering the period from December 11, 1955, to July 31, 1956. Seventh Interim Report covering the period from August 1, 1956, to April 30, 1957. Eighth Interim Report covering the period from May 1, 1957, to April 30, 1958. Ninth Interim Report covering the period from May 1, 1958, to January 31, 1959.

South Viet Nam administration had taken reprisals against former resistance members, thereby seriously violating Article 14 (c) of the Geneva Agreement.

Such a situation has only increased the South Viet Nam administration's apprehension about the International Commission's investigations; that is why, since mid-1956, it has not allowed any team of the Commission to investigate into cases of terror and reprisal in South Viet Nam. At present, the following teams, the despatch of which has been decided by the Commission, are still unable to go to South Viet Nam to carry out their missions:

—Mobile Team 90: murder of one, arrest of twenty-three and detention of fourteen former resistance members, in Huong Tra district, Thua Thien province.

—Mobile Team 93: massacre at Huong Dien (Huong Hoa district), reprisals against former resistance members at Huong Hoa district, and massacre at A Luoi (Phong Dien district) resulting in thirty-one adults and two children killed. All these localities belong to Quang Tri province.

—Mobile Team 105: enquiries into a number of concentration camps in Thua Thien province (Dai Loc, Pho Trach, Cho Niu, Con ong Cai, Dong Hy and Trach Hoa).

—Mobile Team 117: burying alive of twenty-one former resistance members at Cho Duoc, reprisals against forty-four persons in Tan Luu and An Tra villages, murder of six former resistance members in Trang Binh districts. All these localities belong to Quang Nam province.

—Mobile Team 121: arrest and detention of eight former resistance members in the prisons of Cap St Jacques and Xuyen Moc (Baria province).

—Mobile Team 122: arrest of three former resistance members in Saigon.

—Mobile Team 123: murder of Professor Nguyen Thi Dieu.

—Mobile Team 87: cases of reprisals in the Demilitarized Zone.

—Mobile Team 85: arrest and torturing of seventy-nine former resistance members in Hong Ngu district, Chau Doc province.

—Mobile Team 104: massacre of three families of former resistance members at Gia Rai (Bac Lieu province).

A number of teams were withdrawn without completing their enquiries owing to difficulties encountered in South Viet Nam: Mobile Teams 24, 61; in particular Mobile Team 103 had to give give up its enquiries on the massacre in Duy Xuyen, Quang Nam province.

In spite of all attempts to hinder the enquiries by the International Commission, and to annul the validity of Article 14 (c) with a view to evading its binding force, the South Viet Nam authorities have been strongly condemned by public opinion and, so far, the validity of Article 14 (c) continues to be recognized. Therefore they raised the question of so-called 'subversive activities' and repeatedly tried to bring pressure to bear on the International Commission so that the latter recognized this question as attracting the Geneva Agreements (although there is no relevant provision in the Geneva Agreements). By so doing, they aim at interpreting reprisals against former resistance members as 'punitive measures' against 'subversive activities', thus using the question of 'subversive activities' to annul the validity of Article 14 (c), and at the same time to slander the authorities of the Democratic Republic of Viet Nam.

II
FROM 1959 TILL NOW

In spite of the ferocity of the 'denounce Communists' campaigns, and all manœuvres to evade the binding force of Article 14 (c) of the Geneva Agreement, the South Viet Nam administration has suffered a bitter failure in its anti-communist policy: the indignation of the broad masses of the people has been mounting, the Ngo Dinh Diem regime has clearly appeared as a fascist dictatorial regime while the US imperialists' policy of intervention and war in South Viet Nam has been laid bare.

At a conference held on March 27, 1958, by the 'Party of Labour' which is the party of South Viet Nam ruling circles, Ngo Dinh Nhu, adviser to the administration, was compelled to recognize this failure, and exhorted his agents to intensify terror and repression; he went so far as to make this impudent declaration: 'It does not matter whether the people love or hate us.'

The events in Iraq increased the fears of the South Viet Nam ruling circles, and they committed a frantic act: the food-poisoning of 6,000 political detainees in the Phu Loi concentration camp on December 1, 1958. This mass food-poisoning had been carefully prepared with a belt of troops posted around the camp to repress any opposition from the victims, and to prevent the local population from coming to their rescue. That very night, over 1,000 persons died instantly under the effect of the poison. The survivors who climbed up to roofs to cry for help were shot dead. Fire was also ordered to be opened on those who remained in the buildings and urged for assistance. To remove all evidence, the authorities ordered the buildings to be set alight after pouring petrol on them. The survivors succeeded in extinguishing the fire. Later on, a curfew was proclaimed in the surrounding region, the bodies were removed and thrown into the sea, all traces were thus wiped out.

At the same time, the survivors were removed to other prisons and concentration camps, and replaced with new detainees brought in from other jails with a view to making any investigation impossible.

Prior to this, the Vietnamese people had been ceaselessly protesting against the policy of terror and reprisal, and the Ngo Dinh Diem dictatorial regime. Progressive opinion the world over had also repeatedly condemned this policy. But never has the movement of protest at home and abroad against the US–Diem clique spread to such extent as after the Phu Loi massacre.

This political failure dealt a heavy blow to the Ngo Dinh Diem regime. However, the Ngo Dinh Diem ruling clique stubbornly persisted in its bloody dictatorial policy. It advocated an even more ferocious repression to suppress any opposition and any popular aspirations for peace and national unity.

. . .

Some typical operations of reprisal

Since December 1958, more than 15,000 soldiers of the regular army and equivalent forces of militiamen and civil guards have been carrying out an operation of reprisal in West Nam Bo, under the orders of Colonel Nguyen Van Y, commander of the 5th military region and the supervision of Nguyen Van Vang, 'delegate of the Government' in the region, and many American military advisers, including General S. Williams, chief of MAAG, and Lieutenant-Colonel John H. Chamberts.

The centre of the operation was Ca Mau, Can Tho and Ba Xuyen provinces.

In Ca Mau, over three regiments and one battalion of commandos, scattered into small groups, lay in ambush at the edges of forests, and along roads, or encircled villages and hamlets. Whoever fell into their hands was arrested, tortured, then killed. The corpses were cut into pieces. Women were raped in turns, subjected to electric tortures, or to the thrusting of a stick into their vagina, etc. Sheep-dogs were used in man-hunting, and all people caught were bitten to death. A number of women were raped in the presence of their husbands who were afterwards shot dead before their eyes. At night, mass executions took place, the victims' heads were cut off, their skulls broken and their corpses thrown into rivers. According to still incomplete data, from February 14 to April 15, 1959, alone, ninety-two former resistance members were killed, twenty-eight seriously wounded, and more than 1,000 jailed in Ca Mau area. In addition, considerable damage was caused to houses and crops. . . .

During several days in succession, from October 10 to 15, 1960, the South Viet Nam authorities launched in this region repeated air raids involving dozens of military planes; even napalm bombs were dropped on places such as Trai Day, Sao Luoi, Cai Cam, Tan Quan, Cong Nghiep, Tan Hung Tay (Cai Nuoc district). This resulted in hundreds of casualties and many houses burnt down.

At Long My (Can Tho province), three battalions of the regular army, together with militia and civil guard forces, carried out an operation in twelve communes with a view to herding 11,895 families of former resistance members into the Vi Thanh-Hoa Luu concentration camp. They divided this area into many squares, each including from 100 to 200 families, and raided them one after the other. In May 1959 alone, over 900 mopping-up operations and commando raids involving forces upwards of one group were recorded. In the three communes of Vinh Thuan Dong, Vinh Xuong and Long Binh alone, 115 people were killed within six days in late May 1959. The victims were subjected to the most savage torture before being killed; their corpses were cut into pieces, and their heads planted on banana stems set floating adrift along rivers. In some places, by way of intimidation, people were guillotined by scores, in presence of hundreds, sometimes of thousands of onlookers.

The cruel agents of the administration cut down all trees, burnt down or destroyed all houses, and razed to the ground eighty-six hamlets. Churches, temples and pagodas were desecrated.

On Long Phu island (Soc Trang province), 200 South Viet Nam soldiers rushed into the An Thanh Nhi commune, shooting indiscriminately at the people. More than 200 persons took refuge, and locked themselves up in a local militia post. But the assailants broke through the fence, tied them up, tortured them most savagely, and raped all the women, including a ten-year-old girl. Within an hour or more, they killed ten persons, raped six women to death and seriously wounded about 200 people. Many houses were burnt down, considerable numbers of oxen, pigs, and fowls taken away or killed. In face of such acts, Father Le Huu Phuoc from Rach Trang church approached the officers commanding the operation, but received only the following reply: 'We are acting on President Ngo's order. Approach him, if you like.'

The Saigon special military court dragging along with it the guillotine, followed close on the military forces' heels. It held many sittings in the provinces of Can Tho, Ca Mau, Tra Vinh and My Tho, and passed numerous sentences of death or hard labour under law 10-59. The death sentences were immediately acted upon on the spot.

APPENDIX C

According to still incomplete data, from the beginning of 1959 to the end of 1960, the reprisals launched in West Nam Bo resulted in tremendous losses:

3,848 killed;

5,622 seriously wounded;

16,539 arrested;

24,000 herded into concentration camps;

13,000 tons of paddy and other foodstuffs plundered or burnt down;

10,000 houses, big and small, burnt down;

20,134 head of cattle taken away or killed.

The operation is still going on.

In Quang Ngai province, the operation of reprisal launched under the command of Lieutenant-Colonel Bui Huu Nhon, commander of the 3rd military region, involved the 2nd infantry division together with militia, civil guard, commando and security forces, in total over 10,000 men. Launched at the beginning in the districts of Ba To, Minh Long, Son Ha, Tu Nghia, Mo Duc, Duc Pho and Nghia Hanh, it was extended later on to the district of Tra Bong. The districts of Son Ha, Ba To and Tra Bong in particular, were the scenes of dozens of raids.

It is to be pointed out that in this operation the most savage methods of torture and massacre were resorted to:

Mrs Gi Vit (Son Ha district), having resisted the attempts to force divorce on her, was tortured into infirmity. Mrs Truong Thi Lang, though pregnant, was subjected to 'a journey by Dakota', then hammered into abortion. Mr Vo Van Hu alias Vinh (Son Ha district) was shot dead after his eyes had been gouged out; his corpse was thrown out on a rock. Mr Dinh Het (Ba To district) was forced to drink poison. Mr Dinh Ca Ty (Ba To district) had his tibia broken. Mrs De's corpse (Tra Bong district) was burnt to ashes. Mr Hoa, an old man of over sixty (Son Ha district) was burnt alive. Mr Vo (Tra Bong district) had his head cut off and exhibited in front of the administrative buildings. Mr Nhan's head (Tra Bong district) was used as a target for shooting exercises until it was broken into pieces.

. . .

APPENDIX D

FEBRUARY 1965

Date	Time	Names of establishments raided
7		Hospital of Quang Binh province (1st time)
8		Infirmary-Maternity house of provincial capital of Ho Xa, Vinh Linh (1st time)
11		Hospital of Quang Binh province (2nd time)
20		Infirmary-Maternity house of Vinh Thai village, Vinh Linh (1st time)
20		Infirmary-Maternity house of Vinh Kim village, Vinh Linh (1st time)
		Monthly total of raids: 5

MARCH

3		Hospital of Huong Son district, Ha Tinh (1st time)
19		Health station of Thanh Chuong district, Nghe An (1st time)
19		Pharmacy of Thanh Chuong district (1st time)
21		Infirmary-Maternity house of Quang Phuc village, Quang Binh (1st time)
22		Infirmary-Maternity house of Huong Lap village, Vinh Linh (1st time)
26		Infirmary-Maternity house of Huong Lap district (2nd time)
26		Infirmary-Maternity house of Canh Duong village, Quang Binh (1st time)
31		Hospital of Huong Khe district, Ha Tinh (1st time)
		Monthly total of raids: 8

APRIL

4		Consultation room and Health station of Dong Hoi provincial capital (1st time)

* See Chapter VI, Document 5.

182

Date	Time	Names of establishments raided
4		Infirmary-Maternity house of Phu Bai, Dong Hoi (1st time)
6		Hospital of Huong Khe (2nd time)
13		Infirmary-Maternity house of Hai Trach village, Quang Binh (1st time)
14		Infirmary-Maternity house of Duc Trach village, Quang Binh (1st time)
23		Infirmary-Maternity house of Dai Trach village, Quang Binh (1st time)
28		Infirmary-Maternity house of Thanh Trach district, Quang Binh (1st time)

Monthly total of raids: 7

MAY

4		Vinh Linh medical service and hospital (1st time)
16		Pharmacy of Cam Xuyen district, Ha Tinh (1st time)
23		Hospital of Nghia Dan district, Nghe An (1st time)
23		Hospital of Duc Tho district, Ha Tinh (1st time)
23		Infirmary-Maternity house of Vinh Long village, Vinh Linh (1st time)
27		Huong Khe hospital (3rd time)
28		Huong Khe hospital (4th time)

Monthly total of raids: 7

JUNE

3		Huong Khe hospital (5th time)
4		Tuberculosis hospital, Nghe An (1st time)
10		Duc Tho hospital (2nd time)
10		Nghi Loc pharmacy (1st time)
10		Vinh pharmacy (1st time)
10		Câu Giat pharmacy (1st time)
10		Pharmacy of Nghê An province (1st time)
11		Huong Khê hospital (6th time)
12		Quynh Lâp leper sanatorium (1st time)
13		Quynh Lâp leper sanatorium (2nd time)
14	7 A.M.	Quynh Lâp leper sanatorium (3rd time)
14	2 P.M.	Quynh Lâp leper sanatorium (4th time)
14		Hospital of Quang Trach district, Quang Binh (1st time)
14		Ba Don sanatorium, Quang Binh (1st time)
15	4.10 A.M.	Quynh Lâp leper sanatorium (5th time)

Date	Time	Names of establishments raided
15	6.30 A.M.	Quynh Lâp leper sanatorium (6th time)
15	1.50 P.M.	Quynh Lâp leper sanatorium (7th time)
16		Old-aged rest-home of Nga ba Môi, Thanh Hoa (1st time)
16	7 A.M.	Quynh Lâp leper sanatorium (8th time)
16	1 P.M.	Quynh Lâp leper sanatorium (9th time)
16	12 P.M.	Quynh Lâp leper sanatorium (10th time)
17	9 A.M.	Quynh Lâp leper sanatorium (11th time)
17	2 P.M.	Quynh Lâp leper sanatorium (12th time)
18		Huong Khê hospital (7th time)
18		Hospital of Son La province (1st time)
21		Quynh Lâp leper sanatorium (13th time)
26		Hospital of Viêt Trung state farm, Quang Binh (1st time)
27		Hospital of Hà Trung district, Thanh Hoa (1st time)

Monthly total of raids: 28

JULY

1	Hospital of Tuyên Hoa district, Quang Binh (1st time)
8	T.B. hospital of Thanh Hoa province (1st time)
9 10 11 10	{ (Hospital, medical service and other special medical stations of Yên Bai province [5 times in 3 days]) Quynh Lâp leper sanatorium (14th time)
11	Cua Lo sanatorium of Nghê An province (1st time)
14	T.B. hospital of Thanh Hoa province (2nd time)
20	Hospital of Ky Son district, Nghê An (1st time)
24	Hospital of Quang Binh province (3rd time)
25	Hospital of Tuong Duong district, Nghê An (1st time)
25	Hospital of Con Cuông district, Nghê An (1st time)
25	Hospital of Nghê An province (1st time)
25	Quynh Lâp leper sanatorium (15th time)
27	Hospital of Quang Binh province (4th time)
28	Hospital of Dô Luàng district, Nghâ An (1st time)
29	Hospital of Nam Dinh province (1st time)
30	Hospital of Hà Tinh province (1st time)
31	Quynh Lâp leper sanatorium (16th time)

Monthly total of raids: 19

APPENDIX D

Date	Time	Names of establishments raided
		AUGUST
1		Hospital of Ha Tinh province (2nd time)
3		Quynh Lâp leper sanatorium (17th time)
4		Quynh Lâp leper sanatorium (18th time)
7		Quynh Lâp leper sanatorium (19th time)
7		Medico-maternity station of Son Giang village, Ha Tinh (1st time)
12		Hospital of Thach Hà district (1st time)
13		Hospital of Huong Khê district (8th time)
13		Hospital of Ha Tinh province (3rd time)
14		Hospital of Vinh city (Polish equipped) (1st time)
14		Quynh Lâp leper sanatorium (20th time)
15		Hospital of Ky Anh district, Ha Tinh (1st time)
16	1.30 P.M.	Hospital of Ky Anh district (2nd time)
16	3.15 P.M.	Hospital of Ky Anh district (3rd time)
16	5 P.M.	Hospital of Ky Anh district (4th time)
16	9 P.M.	Hospital of Ky Anh district (5th time)
17		Quynh Lâp leper sanatorium (21st time)
17		Medico-maternity station of Huong Lôc district, Hà Tinh (1st time)
20		Quynh Lâp leper sanatorium (22nd time)
21		Tuberculosis hospital of Thanh Hoa province (3rd time)
22		Quynh Lâp leper sanatorium (23rd time)
25		Quynh Lâp leper sanatorium (24th time)
27		Duc Tho hospital (3rd time)
29		Quynh Lâp leper sanatorium (25th time)
		Monthly total of raids: 23
		SEPTEMBER
5		Quynh Lâp leper sanatorium (26th time)
6		Hospital of Quang Binh province (5th time)
10		Hospital of Ha Tinh province (4th time)
11		Hospital of Quang Binh province (6th time)
19		Hospital of Quang Binh province (7th time)
22		Hospital of Tinh Gia district, Thanh Hoa (1st time)
23		Hospital of Quang Binh province (8th time)
24		Hospital of Quang Binh province (9th time)
24		Hospital of Ha Tinh province (5th time)
25		Phu Ly hospital, Nam Ha province (1st time)
27		Medical station of Câm Nhuong village, Hà Tinh (1st time)
		Monthly total of raids: 11

Date	Time	Names of establishments raided

OCTOBER

Date		Names of establishments raided
5		Hospital of Ha Tinh province (6th time)
6		Tuberculosis hospital of Ha Tinh province (1st time)
8		Quynh Lâp leper sanatorium (27th time)
8		Hospital of Ha Tinh province (7th time)
9		Hospital of Quang Binh province (10th time)
10		Hospital of Ha Tinh province (8th time)
10		Ha Tinh tuberculosis hospital (2nd time)
11		Quynh Lâp leper sanatorium (28th time)
12		Health station of Vien Thanh village, Nghê An province (1st time)
13		Hospital of Ha Tinh province (9th time)
14		Hospital of Quang Binh province (11th time)

Monthly total of raids: 11

NOVEMBER

Date		Names of establishments raided
3		Health station of Xuân Truong village, Ha Tinh (1st time)
5		Health station of Xuân Hoi village, Ha Tinh (1st time)
11		Ha Tinh hospital (10th time)
11		Ha Tinh tuberculosis hospital (3rd time)
18		Ha Tinh hospital (11th time)
19		Ha Tinh hospital (12th time)
22		Hospital of Phu Tho province (1st time)

Monthly total of raids: 7

DECEMBER

Date		Names of establishments raided
2		Hospital of Nghia Trung district, Nam Hà (1st time)
6		Uôong Bi hospital (1st time)
16		Health station of Hoang Que village (1st time)

Monthly total of raids: 3

1965: 129 bombing and strafing raids

FEBRUARY 1966

Date		Names of establishments raided
1		Health station of Vinh Tan village (1st time)
3		Quynh Lâp leper sanatorium (29th time)
5		Hospital of Nga Son district, Thanh Hoa (1st time)
12		Hospital of Quynh Lâp district, Nghê An (1st time)
15		Assistant doctors' school of Nghê An (1st time)

Monthly total of raids: 5

Date	*Time*	*Names of establishments raided*

MARCH

5		Quynh Lâp leper sanatorium (30th time)
14		Health station of Ky Ninh village Ha Tinh (1st time)
16		Health station of Hung Hoa, Nghê An (1st time)
20		Quynh Lâp leper sanatorium (31st time)
20		Health station of Nghi Hai village, Nghê An (1st time)
21		Health station of Huong Thuy village, Hà Tinh (1st time)
28		Huong Lâp hospital, Vinh Linh (1st time)
29		Huong Lâp hospital (2nd time)
		Monthly total of raids: 8

APRIL

5		Quynh Lâp leper sanatorium (32nd time)
13		Duc Tho hospital (4th time)
16		Health station of Dien Thanh village, Nghê An (1st time)
19		Health station of Dong Xa village, Cam Pha (1st time)
20		Hospital of Ha Tinh province (13th time)
21		Quynh Lâp leper sanatorium (33rd time)
24		Quynh Lâp leper sanatorium (34th time)
24		Health station of Dien Van village, Nghê An (1st time)
27		Health station of Dien My village, Nghê An (1st time)
29		Health station of Liên Thanh village, Nghê An (1st time)
29		Hospital of Hà Tu coal mine (1st time)
		Monthly total of raids: 11

MAY

6	8.30 A.M.	Quynh Lâp leper sanatorium (35th time)
6	12 A.M.	Quynh Lâp leper sanatorium (36th time)
8		Hospital of Hà Tu (2nd time)
10		Hospital of Hà Tinh province (14th time)
11		Hospital of Hà Tu (3rd time)
12		Hospital of Hà Tinh province (15th time)
14		Hospital of Hà Tinh province (16th time)
21		Hospital of Hà Tinh province (17th time)

Date	Time	Names of establishments raided
22		Hospital of Hà Tu (4th time)
26		Hospital of Phat Diêm district, Ninh Binh (1st time)
29		Hospital of Hà Tu (5th time)

Monthly total of raids: 11

JUNE

Date	Time	Names of establishments raided
1		Provincial hospital, station for the protection of mothers and children and assistant-doctors' school of Thanh Hoa province (1st time)
12		Quynh Lâp leper sanatorium (37th time)
13		Health station of Huong Linh village, Ha Tinh (1st time)
19		Quynh Lâp leper sanatorium (38th time)
22		Hospital of Bac Thai province (1st time)
24		Quynh Lâp leper sanatorium (39th time)

Monthly total of raids: 6

1. *Total*: 80 establishments raided

1965	129 raids
First half of 1966	41 raids

From February 7, 1965, to June 30, 1966 170 raids

2. *Peak months in bombing raids:*

June 1965	28 times
July 1965	19 times
August 1965	23 times

3. *Peak days in bombing raids:*
   (a) *May 23, 1965:*
       —Hospital of Duc Tho district (Ha Tinh)
       —Hospital of Nghia Dan district (Nghê An)
       —Medical station of Vinh Long village
   (b) *June 16, 1965:*
       —Old aged rest-house of Nga ba Môi (Thanh Hoa)
       —The 8th attack on Quynh Lâp leper sanatorium (7 hours)
       —The 9th attack on Quynh Lâp leper sanatorium (13 hours)
       —The 10th attack on Quynh Lâp leper sanatorium (24 hours)
   (c) *July 9, 10 and 11, 1965:*
       —Medical service of Yen Bai province
       —Hospital of Yên Bai province
       —Anti-epidemic station of Yên Bai province

—Anti-tuberculosis station of Yên Bai province
—Station for the protection of mothers' and children's health
of Yên Bai province
—Medical workers' training school of Yên Bai province

(d) *July 25, 1965:*
—Hospital of Tuong Duong district (Nghê An)
—Hospital of Con Cuông district (Nghê An)
—Hospital of Nghê An province
—Quynh Lâp leper sanatorium (15th time)

4. *Repeated attacks in one day, on one establishment:*
June 15, 1965:   4.10 A.M. ⎫
                 6.30 A.M. ⎬ Quynh Lâp leper sanatorium
                 1.50 P.M. ⎭
August 15, 1965: Hospital of Ky Anh district (Ha Tinh)
August 16, 1965: 1.30 A.M. ⎫
                 3.15 A.M. ⎪ Hospital of Ky Anh district
                 5.00 A.M. ⎬ (Ha Tinh)
                 9.00 P.M. ⎭

5. *Kinds of establishments bombed and strafed:*
—Province hospitals   12 (3,610 beds)
—Specialized hospitals   7 (3,950 beds)
—District hospitals   22 (1,150 beds)
—Village Infirmary-maternity houses   29 (362 beds)
—Other medical establishments   10
                                        ——
                          Total   80 (9,072 hospital beds)

6. *Medical establishments repeatedly raided:*
—Hospital of Quang Binh province: 11 times
           February 7, 1965   September 19, 1965
           February 11, 1965   September 23, 1965
           July 24, 1965   September 24, 1965
           July 27, 1965   October 9, 1965
           September 6, 1965   October 14, 1965
           September 11, 1965
—Hospital of Ha Tinh province: 17 times
           July 30, 1965   November 11, 1965
           August 1, 1965   November 18, 1965
           August 13, 1965   November 19, 1965
           September 10, 1965   April 20, 1966
           September 24, 1965   May 10, 1966
           October 5, 1965   May 12, 1966

October 8, 1965   May 14, 1966
October 10, 1965   May 21, 1966
October 13, 1965

—Hospital of Huong Khê district (Ha Tinh province): 8 times
March 31, 1965   June 3, 1965
April 6, 1965   June 11, 1965
May 27, 1965   June 18, 1965
May 28, 1965   August 13, 1965

—Quynh Lâp leper sanatorium: 39 times
June 12, 1965   August 17, 1965
June 13, 1965   August 20, 1965
7 A.M. June 14, 1965   August 22, 1965
2 P.M. June 14, 1965   August 25, 1965
4.10 A.M. June 15, 1965   August 29, 1965
6.30 A.M. June 15, 1965   September 5, 1965
1.50 P.M. June 15, 1965   October 8, 1965
7 A.M. June 16, 1965   October 11, 1965
1 P.M. June 16, 1965   February 3, 1966
12 P.M. June 16, 1965   March 5, 1966
9 A.M. June 17, 1965   March 20, 1966
2 P.M. June 17, 1965   April 5, 1966
June 21, 1965   April 21, 1966
July 10, 1965   April 24, 1966
July 25, 1965   8.30 A.M. May 6, 1966
July 31, 1965   12 A.M. May 6, 1966
August 3, 1965   June 12, 1966
August 4, 1965   June 19, 1966
August 7, 1965   June 24, 1966
August 14, 1965

APPENDIX E

BREAKDOWN OF UNITED STATES RAIDS ON SCHOOLS (DOCUMENT IN ENGLISH)*

List of Provinces and Schools Bombed and Strafed from August 5, 1964, until the End of September, 1966

Province	Total number of schools bombed and strafed	Primary schools	Elementary schools	Primary and elementary schools	Secondary schools	Vocational schools	Complementary education schools	Infant schools	Other schools
1 Vinh Linh	16	11	2	1	1		1		
2 Quang Binh	46	17	20	3	2	2	1	1	
3 Ha Tinh	74	30	30	5	4	2		1	2
4 Nghe An	62	18	15	3	4	7		15	
5 Thanh Hoa	41	13	23	4				1	
6 Nam Ha	9	3	3		2			1	
7 Ninh Binh	2	1				1			
8 Thai Binh	5	3	2						
9 Hung Yen	1	1							
10 Ha Tay	1		1						
11 Tuyen Quang	3	1	2						
12 Phu Tho	10	3	2	3	1		1		
13 Nghia Lo	1				1				
14 Son La	12	4	2		2	2	1	1	
15 Yen Bai	11	4	2		1	2	1	1	
Total	294	109	104	19	18	16	5	21	2

* See Chapter VII, Document 8.

INDEX

INDEX